THE TRANSFORMING POWER OF REVIVAL

Harold Caballeros
&
Mell Winger,
Editors

All Scripture quotations, unless otherwise indicated, are taken from the *Authorized King James Version.*
Other versions used are:
*AMP. N.T.*Scripture quotations are taken from the *Amplified New Testament*, copyright 1954, 1958, 1987 by The Lockman Foundation. Used by permission.
*NIV*Scripture quotations are taken from the *Holy Bible, New International Version, NIV*. Copyright 1973, 1978, 1984 by International Bible Society.
Used by permission of Zondervan Publishing House. All rights reserved.
New American Standard Bible, 1960, 1962, 1963, 1968, 1971, 1972, 1973, 1975, 1977 by The Lockman Foundation. Used by permission.
New King James Version, 1979, 1980, 1982 by Thomas Nelson, Inc. Publishers. Used by permission. All rights reserved.

Cover design by Freddy Murphy

The transforming Power of revival.
Harold Caballeros & Mell Winger.
Editors.

Published by,
Editorial Peniel
Boedo 25
Tel: (01) 981-6034
E-mail: penielar@peniel.com.ar
Buenos Aires Argentina
order additional copies to:
Peniel Productions.
Phone: 718-788-2482
Fax: 718-788-7760
E-Mail: penielusa@juno.com

I.S.B.N. N: 987-9038-24-X
Catalog Number: 316.034

Edition N°:1, Year 1998

Printed in Colombia
Impreso en Colombia

Dedicated to:

Cecilia Caballeros and Paula Winger,
our precious wives,
who have encouraged us to
pursue our dreams of seeing
the transforming power of revival

TABLE OF CONTENTS

TABLE OF CONTENTS

Acknowledgments

We would like to express our heartfelt gratitude to the people who were instrumental in making this book a reality.

First, we thank our editorial assistants, Paula Winger, Marialyse Bianchi, and Lucrecia Ortiz Tejada, whose long hours and thoroughness were critical to meeting our deadlines.

We also extend our appreciation to our team of translators, whose help has been invaluable: Karla María Labbé Fernández de Noriega, Mayling Mansilla de Monzón, Cynthia Calderon Mansilla, Ilse Chambers, Asuncion Arimany, Ximena Herrera, María de los Angeles Herrera de Hernández, Francisco Bianchi, Claudia Benítez de Soto, Consuelo de la Campa de Benítez, Allyson Cannard, Edgar Núñez, Marialyse Bianchi, Lucrecia Ortiz Tejada, Carlos Hernández, and Boris Martínez.

We also would like to thank Oscar Benítez, the Coordinator for the World Congress, for his tireless work on the Congress and his wise counsel.

We certainly are very grateful as well to our publisher and friend, Omar Daldi, of Editorial Peniel.

Preface

Keeping with the purpose of the World Congress on Intercession, Spiritual Warfare and Evangelism, which took place in the city of Guatemala, we prepared our hearts to develop this book with the objective of planting a seed of faith and hope in the nations of the earth. We believe that we will see the fulfillment of the prophetic word that we received concerning this Congress:

And in this mountain shall the Lord of hosts make unto all people a feast... ***And he will destroy in this mountain the face of the covering cast over all people, and the veil that is spread over all nations*** *(Isa. 25:6-7).*

We asked all the authors to write a chapter in which they would share the desire of their hearts for the Body of Christ, their contribution to the move of God in the nations. Each one of them responded to us in an immediate and selfless way. The book was designed with two purposes in mind. The first: to be a contribution to each delegate at the World Congress. The second: to be a tool that could bless those who were unable to attend this marvelous event, but who have in their hearts a burning desire to see a change in their cities and nations. God willing, may this be an instrument of inspiration and blessing for each of these readers.

In some cases, the chapter was written especially for this book. In other cases, the authors utilized material they had previously written. Nevertheless, in all cases, each chapter was edited and adapted to flow within the prophetic framework God outlined for us in the World Congress.

We want to express our gratitude to each of the contributors and especially to Bill Greig III and Kyle Duncan of Regal Books for their advice and gracious help.

Mell Winger
Harold Caballeros
Guatemala, October, 1998

Introduction by Harold Caballeros

I like gardening very much, and it never ceases to amaze me what I call, the mysterious power of the seed. It impresses me how an insignificant, small seed, placed in watered soil, can give birth to a tree or a plant, and provide us with flowers or fruits of beautiful colors and delicious flavors.

For me, it continues to be one of the greatest mysteries, and I would even call it a miracle. The satisfaction we receive from seeing a plant grow from a seed we have planted, is something incomparable.

My wife, Cecilia, and I were having lunch one day at an Indian restaurant with Dr. T.L. Osborn. He made a comment, one of those comments loaded with wisdom and anointing, which really impacted me: The written seed, printed, is the most important of all. If you write a book, he continued, that book will go to unsuspected places, and will bless people time after time. The devil fights writing in a special way, because he knows the power of the printed seed.

The joining of these two concepts of seeds has given birth to the book you now have in your hands. I believe in the law of sowing and reaping. Dr. Osborn drew my attention to the system of blessing from God through the medium of the written word. We live in a very special season of the Holy Spirit. This generation is beginning to see the glory of the movement of God like never before. Reports on revival are great, and they come from all continents of the earth. Without a doubt, these are exciting days!

Nevertheless, even if it is correct to rejoice with everything He is doing, and submerge in the river of God, it is also critical for us to recognize the times of God and to act responsibly, optimizing the means He has given us to fulfill the tasks we have ahead.

Let us not forget we have a commission to perform. God calls us the light of the world and the salt of the earth and this certainly includes many obligations.

I have had the privilege of meeting and sharing the pulpit with some of the greatest ministers that you can imagine. I have seen how God uses them and I have been blessed by all of them. I have found Christ in each one, and the favor of God on my life has allowed me to become friends and have fellowship with them. This is why I ventured to ask them to write a chapter for this book. I contacted them and said, Give me your best seed for the nations of this earth, and this is what they wrote in response.

The book you are about to read contains the best seeds of outstanding ministers that God is using in these times throughout the world. If you wish to serve the Lord, or have the desire to impact your nation for Christ, take this document for what it is, a vision from God to transform our present conditionwith prophetic strategies for the 21st century. Read it time and again and allow God to give you dreams and visions that will help you to forge a better future for your country, to the glory of our Lord Jesus Christ.

Harold Caballeros
October 1998

CHAPTER

PROPHETIC PATHWAYS

Harold Caballeros

Harold Caballeros is the pastor of El Shaddai Church in Guatemala City, Guatemala. El Shaddai's ministry emphasizes discipleship, Christian education and communicating the Gospel through mass media. A lawyer by profession, Rev. Caballeros was called by God to the ministry. His desire to see revival shake the nations has taken him from solely a local church ministry to an international prophetic ministry. He has preached the Gospel in more than 45 nations in all the inhabited continents. The Holy Spirit is enabling him to bring together a ministry network reaching into many nations. This network's focus is church planting, with a special call to Spain and Portugal. What began as a local church has birthed an international apostolic ministry.

The 90s have been identified as the decade of prayer and spiritual warfare. Undoubtedly, God has emphasized these topics in His Church. Many of us have been privileged to participate in the worldwide movement of prayer that the Holy Spirit has initiated in every inhabited continent of the world. During the last eight years we have experienced great victories, but there have also been times when we have wept and suffered.

We have learned a lot, and personally I feel that this movement has reached its maturity. I feel that the moment has come for us to compare notes, draw conclusions and define strategies based on what we have learned. It is also time to let the Holy Spirit take us by the hand and project us into the future.

I personally, together with the church I lead, have walked through a series of circumstances that have shaped my way of thinking in relation to intercession, spiritual warfare and evangelism. I have traveled a path in which the Holy Spirit has challenged me several times in a continuous process of training and applying what we've learned. These challenges and the fruits of constantly seeking His face have been engraved in our ministry and have become teachings that the Lord has allowed me to share throughout the world.

The chronological process of what we have lived has shaped the order in which the World Congress on Intercession, Spiritual Warfare and Evangelism was designed and also the flow of this book. I would like to remind you that this is my point of view, as a local pastor. Let me lead you along this path which we embarked upon almost ten years ago.

Spiritual Mapping

It was 1990 when El Shaddai Church dedicated our new property to the Lord and everything seemed like a celebration. I never imagined that a small earth mound on the back of the property would unchain a series of events that would profoundly impact our ministry. Due to a legal problem related to the land leveling, we discovered that this mound was not just a bunch of dirt-it was a national monument. We were completely amazed to find out that this monument is "The Grand Snake Mound of the Valley of Guatemala."

When we researched this, our surprise was even greater. The measurements of this "monument," built by hand over 200 years before Christ, were 30 meters wide, 15 meters high and 21 kilometers long. Can you imagine a handmade snake of that size?

Why would someone want to build such a monument? Trying to find the answer to this question, we became acquainted with the god worshipped by the first inhabitants of what we know today as the valley of Guatemala. His name was Quetzalcoatl, the feathered snake. Our research yielded unexpected results. Our country had been offered and dedicated to this principality. What we discovered after this was even more revealing: this god's features were reflected in all of our society. This is how we discovered the principle stated by the apostle Paul in chapter one of the book of Romans: We can perceive the invisible through the visible things.

We began to see that the physical, natural realm was a reflection of the invisible spiritual powers that had originated what is seen. Little by little, we became aware that the root of all the problems that plagued our country coincided exactly with the "pacts" made between the early inhabitants (the stewards) of this land and the "powers" they worshipped.

Immediately we began a prayer thrust called "Jesus is Lord of Guatemala." Our mission: to enlist an army of intercessors that would pray an hour a day for Guatemala. Our goal: to redeem our nation in order to give it to Jesus Christ.

About that time, the Lord caused our paths to cross with a brother who became very special to us. His name was George Otis, Jr., and he coined the term "spiritual mapping." Now we had a name for a discipline that was just starting to develop.

God guided us to divide our research efforts into three areas: spirit, body and soul (1 Thess. 5:23). Part of our work is documented in chapter 5 of the book *Breaking Strongholds in Your City.* [1]

The most important conclusion we arrived at was the understanding that the powers, that by definition are disembodied spirits, cannot subdue men to slavery directly. They must use the power that comes from the soul.

Also we learned that a principality or power (Eph. 6:12) that has certain features works by generating strongholds, arguments or arrogance. In other words, it exercises its power through concepts, ideas or ideologies (2 Cor. 10:4-5) to shape the prevalent way of thinking in a community. I like to call this the "culture of the social conglomerate." It is precisely the way of thinking that drags people into slavery.

In different places, the commanding strongholds may consist of a mentality of sickness, or immorality or defeatism and these strongholds will correspond to the ruling spirits in that place. Generally, we will see that the features of the spirits are reflected in those mental strongholds. That is how the powers hold the people captive and stop the advance of the Gospel.

Someone once asked me, "What is the use of spiritual mapping?" I answered, "to know the reality of what we encounter." Spiritual mapping is equivalent to the intelligence or espionage in war. How can we succeed in defeating what we don't recognize? Jeremiah 1:10 commands us to demolish, tear out, destroy and overthrow in order to build and plant. How are we going to

accomplish this if we don't know what we are dealing with?
We systematized our work, and I could say that we reached a level of proficiency. However, we always understood that spiritual mapping is just a tool to provide us with spiritual intelligence. Spiritual mapping is for the intercessor what an X-ray is for a doctor. It is a means to diagnose the spiritual reality that affects our communities.

Spiritual Warfare

What we learned through spiritual mapping gave us the necessary information to pray effectively for our nation. We understood what the real needs were, the origins of the different problems, and above all, the elements of darkness that were keeping people in the slavery of unbelief (2 Cor. 4:4).
The intercession thrust, "Jesus is Lord of Guatemala," experienced great blessing. The whole nation was shaken by God's answers to the saints' prayers. We experienced huge changes in different areas of the society. We had great blessings politically, socially, and even economically. God's mercy allowed us to enter the area of prophetic intercession-the marriage of the ministries of the priesthood and the prophetic. We became deeply involved in prayer, fasting and intercession for the nation.
Everything seemed to be all right until I had a conversation with a church member whom I appreciate very much. He asked me, "Have you seen that this certain church is growing?" I said, "Yes, I've heard it is growing." He asked again, "Have you heard that this other church is also growing?" I agreed again, but I probably wasn't prepared for the next question. "How is it that we pray and pray yet we do not grow?" he asked. I must tell you that the question really hit its mark. This is what I call the little reminders or challenges of the Holy Spirit.
Immediately I was on a quest for an answer. We were certainly praying, and every battle seemed crowned with victory, but the local church itself wasn't growing like every pastor would wish. What was going on?
The answer was not delayed, and it literally became one of the truths most frequently mentioned by those who teach about this topic: Spiritual warfare is not an end in itself; it is just a tool for effective evangelism.
Personally I don't believe that spiritual warfare deals only with binding and loosing. Of course, everything has its place, but spiritual warfare is definitely much more than that.
I have come to understand that spiritual warfare is fought on three battlefronts:
1. War in the air. The battle that takes place during prayer is against dominions. This can include prayer, fasting and intercession. But it can also

include carrying out prophetic acts, indentificational repentance, etc.
2. War in the souls and minds of men. This is specifically the destruction of strongholds. Here, the arguments, concepts and haughtiness that have risen up against the knowledge of God are disarmed.
3. War in men's hearts. Here it is necessary to emphasize concepts that are vital for Christ's body, such as unity and holiness.
We have designed a very efficient system of fighting the battle simultaneously on these three fronts. In every service held in the church, we assign a different group for each battlefront. The intercessors and I agree in prayer before the service and they are in charge of binding Satan's powers and loosing God's anointing over the congregation that listens in the sanctuary and by radio. While they keep these spirits tied in the heavenlies, I am in charge of preaching, bringing down the strongholds in people's minds, using as a weapon the sword of the Spirit, the Word of God. A third team made up of ministers gets ready to gather the harvest, minister salvation, deliverance, and prayer for any other need in those who respond to God's Word by coming to the altar. I have personally noticed the great support in having the intercessors pray while I preach.
Finally, I would like to underscore the concept that spiritual warfare is not something that we do only for a period of time. Rather, spiritual warfare is a way of life. We are immersed in a conflict that will last until Christ has abolished every dominion, every authority, and every power (1 Cor. 15:23-28).

Evangelism

Most believers understand that the reason we are still "in the world" is to evangelize those who do not yet know Christ. We are not here to reach a greater level of salvation or sanctification, because the salvation that the blood of Jesus Christ already gained for us cannot be improved upon. What, then, is the purpose of our existence in this earth? It is what we commonly call the Great Commission (Matt. 28:19).
What I had not understood was the need for joining the concepts of spiritual warfare and evangelism within the context of the local church.
Suddenly we began to have a considerable number of conversions. The prayer marches, fasting periods and intercession had subjugated the powers of darkness. The strong man was bound and defeated, and we started to reap the reward. Many people found Christ in every meeting. Apparently we had hit the target. Yet something was still missing. Many of these new believers did not return to church after their conversion. We were trying different methods, but it still seemed that something was lacking.

Discipleship-Assimilation of New Believers

Again, we started seeking the guidance of the Holy Spirit in order to organize the local church for growth. The plan was to integrate the concepts we had recently learned in spiritual warfare, prayer and intercession together with evangelism through the existing structure of family (cell) groups in the church. I was discovering the same principles that made Yoido Full Gospel Church in Seoul, Korea, the largest church in the world under the leadership of Dr. David Yonggi Cho.

The results of combining these concepts were amazing. Soon our family groups became evangelistic groups that applied the principles of spiritual warfare in order to become effective soulwinners. Since we had not been applying the principle of assimilating new believers, the family groups became the ideal method for us to accomplish the Great Commission locally. God did not call us to make believers; He called us to make disciples. Having a great number of conversions is not enough. It is necessary for new Christians to learn to walk the path of discipleship.

We now had the vehicle to evangelize people, disciple them, and make them evangelists. Fantastic!

We had a celebration to commemorate the achievements of the year that had just ended. When we saw the graphics projected on the screen, I could not contain my emotions any longer. The growth graphic clearly showed an increase in new converts every time spiritual warfare activities took place. On one occasion, in just one Saturday, more than 800 people were saved and most of them became church members. Our concepts evolved to the point that we no longer just talked of the number of salvations but rather the number of new people assimilated into the church. It soon was 100 a week, then 120, 140, even 235 a week! It seemed like now we finally had all the elements together. But…the Holy Spirit brought another challenge.

Discipleship through Christian Education

Few things impress us as much as the sovereign acts of God. Apparently He takes advantage of every circumstance in our life to break through and bring growth and expansion to our minds.

I had a very big problem due to the construction of the church building. Once again the conflict originated in connection with the "The Grand Snake Mound of the Valley of Guatemala." However, this time it was a serious legal problem that almost took me to jail. While waiting for a legal audience with the judge in charge of the case, I stayed secluded in my house for four days. It was a time of great pressure, but probably one of the greater opportunities

for blessing in my life.
The Lord surprised me once again. "So, you want to take this nation for the Gospel," He asked me. After making sure that this is the vision of my life, He added, "I will reveal to you the most powerful weapon for the possession of the nation-Christian education."
We had had a Christian school for ten years. But I must admit that the vision was never in me. My wife and sister-in-law carried the vision throughout these years, but I had not received the revelation.
God's next two arguments were impressive. The first was clarifying the mistake of the Christian Church which consists of "going for yesterday's generation and not for the future one." We invest in all kinds of plans for adults, yet we pay very little attention to children.
Secondly, God reminded me of an experience I had long ago when I traveled to the United Kingdom.
After preaching in Nottingham, I was able to visit Wales. I had a strong desire to visit the Biblical Institute of Wales. I was motivated by two very important reasons. The first was due to the great impact the book Rees Howells, Intercessor had upon me. The second was an interest in visiting the city where the Welsh revival started at the beginning of this century.
Once again, I found myself unprepared for the revelation that the Lord wanted to give me. Rev. Samuel Howells' assistant met me at the train station, and while he was driving me to the Institute, I could see the incredible Welsh churches. I greatly appreciated their marvelous architecture. However, I was surprised to see that some of them had been turned into restaurants, others were for sale, and some had even become Muslim mosques. To my surprise, I was informed that only one percent of the inhabitants of Wales is Christian. It was tragic to see what had happened in this place which once witnessed God's power in such a way that, in just six months, half a million people were converted. My conclusion was the phrase we have all heard, "God doesn't have grandchildren."
If we do not invest in affecting the next generation, if we do not educate children in God's Word, then every time a generational cycle starts we have to evangelize again the children of those who were believers. This makes it very difficult to "make disciples in all nations."
I would like to ask you a very simple question. Which is easier: to demolish, ruin and destroy strongholds and arguments in people's minds or to have the mind of an infant that has not been contaminated and is ready to receive the planting of the Word of God? The answer is obvious.
Without Christian education, every revival is condemned to live for only one generation.

Community Transformation

I was invited by Brother George Otis, Jr. to preach in a congress he organized in Seattle in November, 1997. The pressure that was on me the day I arrived at the congress was great. I have a strong ability to communicate whatever I believe in. But if I, myself, am not persuaded, I find it impossible to proclaim something as if were the truth. I owe it to my natural father, who sowed in me of a series of principles I am not able to betray.

Precisely because of those principles, I approached George immediately and told him: "I need to talk to you before the congress starts. I am having enormous difficulty with many things being called spiritual warfare today. When the Bible talks of spiritual victories, the results are evident and measurable. I am concerned about spiritual warfare testimonies that lack a genuine application." The entire movement is in danger if we don't find a way to link what we do to clear, concrete and provable results.

George understood my restlessness. I think he appreciated my sincerity and, with his characteristic kindness, he took a paper out of his briefcase and told me, "You are the first one I will show this document to. I am working on a concept that is born out of the same concern you have just expressed to me. I have called it 'community transformation,' and it is a way to measure the impact our prayers have in our community."

I felt a tremendous relief. It was the answer to my restlessness. We would now have a way of giving prophetic guidance to those interested in praying, interceding for and "taking" their cities for Christ. We now had a scale to measure the results. You will find a detailed exposition of this subject in Spiritual Mapping Research Questions, by George Otis, Jr.2

Spiritual warfare is only one aspect, a piece of the gears in God's machinery to bless the earth and its inhabitants. The revival, a result of the saints' pleas3, is another part of this machinery. Christian education is a way of assuring that the revival will affect future generations. The reformation and restoration of a community are ways of measuring the impact of revival.

Spiritual awakenings in the past, such as the Reformation in the 16th century and great revivals such as the one in Wales, confirm our belief that transformation is a possible, real, and tangible result of God's move, and, judging by our society's condition, it is desperately necessary.

Revival and Social Impact

If we are talking about a continuous process, we would have to say that our prayers, if guided by the Holy Spirit, will be answered by God. As in Daniel's case in Daniel chapters 9 and 10, the answer will bring a move of the Holy

Spirit. This is what we call a revival or awakening. If this revival we deeply desire is produced, we would have the right to hope for a lasting impact and effect-a transformation.

History shows us that revivals are agents of great change in every level of society. Time and time again God has moved, the resulting revival produced reform, and this reform has brought restoration.

Revivals have brought a new awakening that, in many instances, have produced true revolutions in the areas of evangelism, Christian education and social ministry. Great universities, hospitals and church buildings are today's witness of the Holy Spirit's movement in previous times.

But the most important factor that catches my attention is to verify that during a revival, the Gospel permeates society and it's way of thinking. In other words, the enemy's strongholds, and the powers in the air that produced them, are both brought down by the power of God. While the heavens are open, the way of thinking changes, lining up with the Word of God. The words of Thomas Jefferson, writer of the Declaration of Independence, greatly impressed me. He recognized that his way of thinking was a product of the society of that time, in other words, Christianity and a biblical mindset.

I am absolutely persuaded that real revival is one that produces a social effect, a transformation.

I will not use this space to talk to you about Almolonga's transformation, because Mell Winger has dedicated a complete chapter in this book to that subject. But I would like to say that, in this particular case, the process that took place started because of discipleship and prayer, just as in Acts 19. Then it was followed by a consistent practice of deliverance ministry. Through spiritual warfare the demonic powers were broken, and the empire of the territorial spirits was dethroned. This open heaven brought a great freedom for evangelism. The resulting revival transformed the life and the culture (the people's way of thinking). They changed their habits and abandoned their ungodly traditions. This transformation even went so far as to affect the natural elements, making Almolonga the most fertile land in the whole country. Certainly, this is a marvelous example from God, a laboratory that allows us to testify that "there is nothing impossible for God."

I have told you about the path that we have had to walk in this decade and what has served as a foundation to prepare the agenda for the World Congress. We have followed the same agenda in this volume.

God's great challenge is before us. Do you want a holy transformation in your nation? I pray to God that this sequence allows us to have a Congress that makes a differences, opens a path to the future, and releases to us the prophetic strategies for which every one of us is praying.

CHAPTER 2

IT'S WORTH IT TO PAY THE PRICE!

Omar Cabrera

Together with his wife, Marfa, Rev. Cabrera pastors Vision de Futuro, the world's fourth largest church. With its headquarters in Santa Fe, Argentina, this centrifugal church reaches out to more than 100 cities and towns throughout the country. Rev. Cabrera is an author and international conference speaker.

On a Personal Note...

I admire Rev. Omar Cabrera very much. I have always thought he is one of the best, if not the best, preacher in Latin America. He is an evangelist, pastor, teacher, and pioneer in the work in Argentina, and a role model worthy of imitation. Rev. Cabrera and his wife, Marfa, have walked a path in the areas of spiritual warfare, evangelism, and most recently, mass media communication. Their children, Omar Hugo, Perla Doris, Claudio and Natascha follow in their parents' footsteps in such an anointed way that I can assure you that Argentina will continually be blessed by their ministry.

Omar's contribution in this chapter is fundamental. It is about the fruit of four decades in the ministry. When I read it I immediately felt the presence of the Holy Spirit and my heart burst into spontaneous praise and worship to God.

Harold Caballeros

The multitude had gathered in great expectation, many having come long distances, holding onto the hope that God would manifest Himself in their lives. Others were there because they needed the spiritual nourishment of the Word of God. Many had come simply because they had been invited and perhaps were curious to see if God truly could meet their needs.

Coming into this atmosphere, I was suddenly electrified by a tremendous spiritual power. One could physically feel the presence of God, and I sensed an unusually heavy anointing.

It was moving to see a multitude hungry not for bread, but for the power of God. The attitude of their open hearts reminded me of a baby opening his mouth to be fed by his mother.

That night, as we have seen so many times because of the mercy of the Lord, God's power was unleashed in miracles and wonders. The healing power of God came over many bodies; people of all ages were liberated by this divine virtue. I was especially touched to see the youth give themselves to the Lord while experiencing the manifestation of His power.

Of course, when we reflect on anointed times like this in the cities where we minister, we give thanks to God for the multitudes, the miracles, and the outpouring of the Holy Spirit, but we must always remember that He is interested in each of us individually in a very special way.

The Lord's fundamental desire is that we draw near to Him. He wants us to be ever mindful that, as we come close to Him, He is able to use us, giving us His grace to develop a genuine ministry in the Church that is His body.

In 40 years of ministry the Holy Spirit has taught me that we must go at His speed without striving, knowing that in all things God gives the true growth. It is not achieved by our abilities or personal methods. Just like a seed, no amount of desire or effort on our part will speed it along; it needs time to grow.

Things happen similarly in the spiritual world. There is timing that God has determined that we must respect. For this reason, the Bible says, "But when the time had fully come, God sent his Son..." (Gal. 4:4, NIV).

Over the years we have continually seen the faithfulness of God. When we faithfully respond to Him, His faithfulness is fully manifest. The Lord is consistently the initiator in our relationship with Him. He shows His love, His sacrifice, and puts in us His desire for us to be used in His work. Nevertheless, there comes a moment when we must be pushed a little further inside. He wants to bring us to the point of desiring to live in sincere consecration to Him.

The Road to Consecration

How can we arrive at true consecration? One of the ways is prayer. A servant of the Lord faithfully sets time aside daily to seek God. Many start by reading the Bible or by meditating on a certain verse of Scripture, which helps prepare their hearts to come into the presence of the Lord.

Part of the success we've experienced in the ministry that God has given to us is due to the fact that I dedicated many days shut in, praying and seeking God. I would say that we were born into the ministry, the fruit and direct result of fasting and prayer. This has been my practice to consecrate myself more to the Lord.

At other times consecration comes through an act of sincere repentance. When the Word and the power of the Holy Spirit have touched the most intimate fibers of our being and we repent of those things that we have been doing in rebellion against His perfect will, we have come to a place of greater consecration to God. This was the case with David in the marvelous chapter, Psalm 51, where he asks God to give him an upright heart and cleanse him profoundly of his errors and sins.

When we study the lives of the men of God in Scripture, we see that consecration was also linked to fasting. Moses was fasting when he came face to face with God (Ex. 34:28). Daniel accompanied his prayer with fasting that moved the foundations of the powerful Babylonian empire (Dan. 10:3). The Lord fasted while He was taken by the Spirit to the desert. To His disciples, He said, "When you fast..." (Matt. 6:17). He implied that it should be a part of daily life when walking in communion with Him. He didn't say, "If you fast," as if it were an option. When we enter into fasting, we experience a sharpening of our senses to be able to hear the Lord. Fasting can help lead us into a more passionate consecration.

At other times, we have experienced that pain has taken us one more step forward in consecration toward God. I would like to make it clear that I do not preach, nor do I believe, the doctrine of human suffering as a means of reaching redemption or sanctification. But we cannot deny that, as disciples of Christ, we will pass through the baptism of suffering as He did. Sometimes the Lord takes us down paths of persecution that deeply hurt. Other times He may let us suffer as a learning experience in warfare, i.e., to expose the enemy's attacks and to see how Satan is out to rob the beauty God has created.

At times like this, we must consider that God has plans and purposes that we do not understand. "His thoughts are higher than our thoughts, and His ways higher than our ways" (Isa. 55:8). Never should we question God. When the Lord allows us to hurt, not only physically but also emotionally and spiritually, it is that we may use this crisis to consecrate ourselves to Him.

No one likes to suffer, but everything that comes through opposition, persecution, and discrimination takes us not only toward unity, but also toward consecrating ourselves more fully to the Lord. When we think of the New Testament disciples who, after being beaten, praised God, we see that their suffering unified them in such a way that they prayed with such consecration that the place where they were shook, and they were filled with the power of the Holy Spirit (Acts 4:31).

Complete Consecration

The complete consecration comes when we add one ingredient that we are missing, and that is "an iron resolution not to give up." Some people seem to be consecrated to God, and it is pitiful that at times it is only a pretense to help them climb up positions or status inside the Church. At any cost, they want to have a place in "the work." For example, one woman said that she would not stop, come what may, until she saw her husband on the platform. But when difficulties came along, she decided to give it all up. There are people who seem to have everything together, but are not willing to experience persecution or to receive correction for their misconduct or wrong attitudes. The saddest part is that some of these people are pastors and when the first adversity comes they use the simplest excuse to give up and leave everything. They were never true pastors, but only hirelings, as the Lord mentions in John 10:12-13.

Those who are genuinely consecrated are willing to fight against all odds, keeping watch over the flock of the Lord, humble and willing to go forward because of a love for God and souls. A truly consecrated person is unwilling to relent, but responds to those fighting against him with love and mercy. In addition, a truly consecrated person even forsakes all things in order that the power of God may be manifest in the midst of contradictions and oppositions.

The Price to Pay

"If anyone comes to me, and does not hate his own father and mother, wife and children, and brothers and sisters, yes, and even his own life, he cannot be My disciple" (Luke 14:26, NASB).

When the Lord uses the term "hate," it doesn't mean that we should despise our loved ones. I am convinced that the family is most beautiful gift God has given to us. But this word "hate" is from a Hebrew word used in the Jewish culture, meaning "not to put in first place, or to give more credit to," in this case, especially referring to fathers, mothers, sisters, brothers, or possessions, even though these form a vital part of our lives.

If because of family, friends, or profession we postpone the call of God, we are making a mistake because we must recognize that when we accept Christ we place our lives under His lordship and authority.

We often see Jesus being followed by multitudes, displaying His divine saving and healing power, freeing the demonic strongholds and even resurrecting the dead. The Gospel of John says that the multitudes "followed him because of the signs he did in the sick" (John 6:2). Many of them only followed Him for the blessings that He imparted to them and their family members. This is not necessarily bad, because the love of the Father wants to express itself to us even though we are not as grateful as we should be.

By the grace of God, we have had the blessing of experiencing prosperity in various areas of the ministry. We have been blessed spiritually and economically, which allows us to make significant investments into the work of the Lord. We rely on different methods to spread God's Word. Doors that were once closed are now opening two at a time. All of this success can deceive us; it can make us think that we have risen so high that we will never fall. Nevertheless, this is exactly when we should be most consecrated to the Lord. In this vulnerable state the enemy desires that our accomplishments lull us to sleep so that he can send a surprise attack and lead us into error.

The only way we can continue standing against all the dangers that harass ministries today is by completely consecrating ourselves to the Lord. If we are going to be His disciples, if we are willing to take His message to the world, there has to be in us a complete renunciation of our own lives, and we must live solely and only for Him.

One day when I was a young seminary student I visited a small church in Buenos Aires. There a visiting pastor took us through the entire Bible in one sermon! His message didn't make very much sense and I couldn't concentrate. He didn't know how to preach and yet the Holy Spirit used him. The only thing I remember about this message was that suddenly he said with a very potent voice, "Those that God calls who do not multiply their talents will go to hell." Although the theology of that statement is dubious, it really led me into a glorious experience.

These words "They will go to hell" echoed in my mind again and again. I felt perturbed, but I knew that in my inner being, in the depths of my heart, God had spoken to me. That same night there was an all-night prayer meeting planned. Every student searched for a place to kneel down and pray. When it was almost three in the morning, I was entering into some type of trance. It was as though I was outside my body. I found myself in front of a scene that appeared to be Calvary. It was all so real to me. I was in the midst of a great

storm with lightning and thunder. I heard agonizing screams of desperation. I felt that the earth trembled under my feet and there I contemplated Christ, crucified, lifted up between heaven and earth, in the midst of this darkness.
Suddenly, I heard a voice say, "This is the price of your salvation." I felt remorseful, and I realized that everything that I could give up to follow Him was nothing in comparison to His suffering on the cross. For one brief instant, while I compared my sacrifice to His sacrifice, something happened inside my mind and heart. I resolutely decided that what my parents, friends, or people from my church might think, or what my future might hold, would no longer be of concern to me. My will had come to a point where it broke before the presence of the Crucified, and I was willing to make a complete renunciation of all and solely serve Christ Jesus, my Lord.

For Those who Want to Serve the Lord

Very few times have I shared this experience, but thinking of hundreds of brothers and sisters the world over who desire to serve the Lord, I want to express very clearly what I have learned in my walk with Christ.
Jesus cannot have disciples who melt like sugar when a few water drops fall on it. He cannot have followers that, when the fire of the trial comes, wilt like herbs that can't resist the heat of the sun. Christ cannot trust the riches of His glory to people who flee or give up without a fight when the wolf comes. He cannot give the power of the Gospel to people who have a weak or unstable character.
Because of this, to effectively serve the Lord, we must be completely consecrated to Him, renouncing everything that comes between God and us. A complete change of life has been required of His servants. Every habit that is dear to us and that seems to enrich our personality, we are to leave to one side. This change of life should be without ambitions or selfish desires and without affections that tie us to the world and to the flesh.
We have to get to the point where we can say, "I am completely dominated by God."
This consecration is never complete; it is ongoing. By the measure of grace that God gives, enabling us more and more, we must continue this process of consecration. The Lord is telling us, "To go further and deeper you must consecrate yourself more; you must look for My face in daily communion."
How I thank the Father for your life, knowing that you have read this chapter and are ready to consecrate yourself eternally to the service of the Lord. Let's agree together in this prayer of consecration:
Eternal God, we consecrate ourselves to You in this hour. Touch us with fire from the altar, we beg of You. We give ourselves up to You so that you may bless us. We want

to see Your glory, and have Your fresh anointing. Accept us; we want to only do Your holy and perfect will. Help us to be faithful in all we do. Reveal Yourself to our hearts; we want to know You more.

We recognize that You are the only One worthy of all glory, forever and ever. Amen.

CHAPTER 3

THE PURPOSE OF THE ANOINTING

Carlos Annacondia

According to C. Peter Wagner, Carlos Annacondia, a businessman turned evangelist, is perhaps "the most effective evangelist in modern history." In the last 12 years, Rev. Annacondia has led over 3 million people in making public decisions for Christ. His massive evangelistic campaigns, featuring healing ministries and overt confrontation with the demonic, have drawn worldwide attention.

Rev. Annacondia lives with his wife, Maria, and their nine children near Buenos Aires, Argentina, where he operates a nuts and bolts factory.

On a Personal Note...

The evangelist Carlos Annacondia blesses us not with just one, but two, chapters. The Purpose of the Anointing and Vision to Reach the World both blessed me from the very first moment I read them. My heart was so touched by the Holy Spirit's presence, I immediately started hearing His voice. I believe He will speak to you the same as He did to me.

What can I say of evangelist Carlos Annacondia that hasn't been said before? Let me tell you an anecdote that will show you the caliber of this man of God. Some months ago I had the opportunity to be in one of his crusades in the city of Quilmes in Argentina. Carlos had invited me to preach to the pastors and spend a few days with them. During those days, the marriage of his son, Angel, to Cecilia took place. The wedding was going to be right in the middle of the crusade, which lasted several weeks. I asked myself, as others did, "What will Carlos do the day of the wedding?" Anyone would have thought that Carlos would choose a preacher to fill in for him that night, but that was not what happened. He went to the wedding, but when the reception began, he left and went to the crusade! That is the love this evangelist has for lost souls.

In a time when many want to receive a ministry similar to the one Carlos has, his life and example remind us that we all have our own altar-a place to encounter God.

Harold Caballeros

We are living in difficult times, where needs have multiplied and the pain in people is uncontainable. Like never before, there is a hunger and thirst for God all over the earth. Those who have traveled to other countries have witnessed it. Men are raising their eyes to heaven, searching for an answer in God. The Gospel of Jesus Christ cannot be preached with persuasive words of human wisdom, but with the Holy Spirit's demonstration of power, so that the faith of those who believe is not based on human wisdom but on the Holy Spirit's power (I Cor. 2:7).

The Bible has been clear that the power we need to make a difference in the world is the anointing. For Isaiah wrote, "...the yoke shall be destroyed because of the anointing" (Isa. 10:22, KJV).

There is a new trend in the world. I would say that the Church has rediscovered something that has always been there: it is called the anointing.

What is the Anointing?

The anointing is God's provision for His Church to be powerfully equipped to impact the skeptical and incredulous world. People, in general, realize they need supernatural help. Men know that society does not have the answer to their needs. So they look for help in the supernatural. This explains the recent growth in occultism and New Age religions.

Some time ago, God gave me a message; He told me that He is very concerned because people are dying without knowing Him and are lost because we are not obeying His command to go into all the world and preach the Gospel (Matt. 28:19-20).

As the Church, God has given us a great challenge. He is concerned and has poured out His Spirit to equip us, so that we can do the work that He has entrusted to us.

How do we Receive the Anointing?

The disposition of our heart is very important in receiving the anointing. The heart must be willing to seek God. He is the rewarder of those who seek Him (Heb. 11:6). There are many who are not willing to pay this price.

You don't receive the anointing by going here and there, looking for it. Some discouraged brothers told me, "We went to Toronto, to Pensacola, to England. We've done spiritual warfare. Nevertheless, everything is the same. Where is the failure? We want to see our city bow at the feet of Jesus Christ."

They asked me, "What is the secret of receiving the anointing?" I told them, "There is simply no secret. God has not changed." John 7:37 says: "...Jesus stood and said in a loud voice, 'If anyone is thirsty, let him come to me and drink'" (NIV). Jesus is the source of power. We must humble ourselves and seek Him. He is not a famous pastor, nor a powerful preacher; He is Jesus. Nothing has changed.

Scripture tells us the price that God demands for receiving an anointing that remains. God has instituted simple spiritual laws. His Word was written so that anyone could understand it. Leviticus 6:12 says: "The fire on the altar must be kept burning; it must not go out. Every morning the priest is to add firewood and arrange the burnt offering on the fire and burn the fat of the fellowship offering on it" (NIV).

In the Old Testament, the priest had the responsibility to keep the fire of the altar burning. The Word says: "the fire will burn constantly." If the priest had that responsibility, how much more do we, as kings and priests, need to keep the fire of the anointing burning in our hearts.

However, we are always in a hurry. We do the work but we forget the Lord of the work. We should not leave the altar; there is wood to be added to the fire each morning so that the anointing is flowing through us to produce fruit. God anoints us for the same purpose that He anointed Jesus. Acts 10:38 tells us that He was anointed with the Holy Spirit and power to do good and heal the oppressed. The anointing comes upon the Church to do good, preach and heal all those oppressed by the devil. The purpose of the anointing is not to fall down; that is just a manifestation. May we all laugh in the Spirit, may we all fall down and prophesy. But even more so may we preach with a passion for lost souls, who are without God and without hope.

Christ died for this purpose: souls. Therefore, the fire of God should be in our hearts. The Lord said that revival starts in the servants' hearts and finishes in the hearts of the servants. When there is passion for the souls, there is revival. When passion for the souls is gone, revival is over.

Revival is over when the altar's fire is put out. Jesus says, "...If anyone is thirsty, let him come to me and drink.... Streams of living water will flow from within him" (John 7:37-38, NIV). We should preach a gospel with results. The purpose of the anointing is to do good and heal those oppressed by the devil. Sometimes we pay so much attention to church buildings and other vain things that we neglect the most important thing: that Jesus died. Let us not lose the little time we have left to win the world for Him. I know and listen to the pain in people; we must not stop. God equipped us with the anointing of the Spirit with one purpose: souls. The Master prepared the disciples to win souls. The pastor disciples his church to win souls. The evangelist preaches to win souls. The prophet brings the Word of God so that the church is organized with one purpose: souls. The apostle sows and plants churches for the souls. Christ died on the cross for souls.

If you do not use the anointing that God gave you, it will disappear. In 2 Kings 4:1-6 the Word speaks of the widow's oil. The oil symbolizes the Holy Spirit. This woman had only one jar and the prophet said: "Look for more jars." The number of jars determined the amount of oil. We are those jars full of oil. The anointing is in us. And for what purpose? To stay within our four walls? To say, "We have to win the world for Christ," and yet never go out? The world is lost, and God grieves to watch millions die without Him.

Not long ago, when I finished a campaign, the pastor asked me to say the closing words. I stood behind the pulpit and started thanking God for the souls saved. Suddenly I stopped. God was speaking to my heart, "Look at the walls. Tell the people the walls are tired of hearing the Gospel. Each brick could have a master's degree in theology by now. It is time to take the pulpits out into the streets and to the parks, because that is where the people that need God are." We all thought that God was happy for the 10,000 souls saved, but He was saying: "In this city, there are 250,000 more who do not know Me." We must not stop preaching. There is little time left for so many people. Today is the day that multitudes die without God.

We are those jars that fill the empty ones. When we preach, we are filling the empty jars. When we pray for the sick, we give them the oil we have. When we testify or cast out demons, we giving what God gave us. And the more we give, the more we receive. The oil flows when we give. When we keep this fresh oil to ourselves, the same thing happens to us that happened to the widow: when the jars were full, she said to her son: "Get me more jars." He said, "There are no more jars" and the oil ceased. When we don't give what we have, the oil stops. That is why the altar is left empty and does not have fire, because the oil has stopped flowing.

This is our responsibility as priests. We cannot allow the fire in the altar to be extinguished because we are busy.

God gave us the anointing for one purpose: to bless. There are many empty jars that need what we have, and there is an altar that is waiting for us. There is wood to be put into the fire.

At the altar we will understand many things that today we do not understand when we are reasoning in the natural. God cannot speak to us if we do not enter into His presence. God cannot purify us if we are not at the altar.

Once a brother told me, "When I rush out of the house and do not have a time with God, do not pray or place my problems at the feet of Jesus, my burdens are dumped on the first one to cross my path. I get angry. Everything bothers me. I become irritated for no reason." Do you know why? Because he did not burn off the dross at the altar.

In Matthew 25, the Lord speaks of the "foolish virgins." They were waiting for the bridegroom and, because he was late, they went to sleep. Suddenly, the bridegroom came and they quickly got up to prepare their lamps. Five of them had oil, but the other five did not; their lamps had gone out. There was no more oil, which symbolized the anointing. They were unwise. The Lord came and took the ones that had their lamps full.

By no means must we lose what God has given us. In order to maintain the anointing, we must give out and we must seek God at the altar. There we will find the fire and the anointing. We give and we receive. When we stop giving, we lose the anointing; when we lose the anointing, we no longer wish to go to the altar, or to reach out to the hurting, or to pray, or to read the Bible. However, when the fire is burning, things are different: there is passion for souls and there is blessing from God.

How is your passion for souls? Have you worked hard for God and let the fire at the altar go out in the process?

The Word warns us: "Above all else, guard your heart, for it is the wellspring of life" (Prov. 4:23, NIV). We cannot say: "I am going to look for the anointing." If there is not a willing heart, forget it. If the fire has been put out, go back to the altar. Pour out your heart with tears. God is not going to turn away a contrite and humble heart. Let us stop being lazy and stop waiting for someone to help us.

The Word says, "Seek the Lord while he may be found" (Isa. 55:6, NIV). God wants to anoint us. If the fire has gone out, rekindle it. If the anointing is gone, let us seek God and do what He says. It is time to turn off the television and tune in to God. (Ten years ago, I took the TV set out of my house because I love my family and I love myself. Maybe that seems fanatical, but I am weak; if I have a TV, I will turn it on.) It is time to consecrate ourselves and give Him everything. It is time to humble ourselves.

Do you know the wonders He can do with a consecrated person? How long has it been since you cried for a lost soul? How long has it been since you poured out tears for the suffering? "Those who sow in tears, will reap with songs of joy" (Ps. 126:5, NIV).

I feel the voice of God telling me: "to the altar, Carlos, run to the altar, I am waiting for you. The fire is waiting, bring a lot of wood for I am going to purify you, I am going to talk to you. I am going to give you the method to win your city for Christ."

Let us sanctify ourselves to God. If we consecrate our life to Him, the anointing will grow and the devil will be afraid. Let us start defeating the demonic hosts and we will be able to see the souls being rescued for Christ. There has never been so much pain in the world as there is today. Thank God for the Church's past accomplishments, but the coming years will be better still. It depends on us-we have to keep the fire burning at the altar.

I have a wood-burning stove at home. At night, I fill it with logs and by morning, there are only ashes. There are no more flames. But if I stir the ashes, I always find a small coal. I look for small branches and put them near it until they light up. Then, I place small logs that light up when I blow on them. When the small logs are burning, I place an even bigger log on top and, in half an hour, I have a raging fire again.

Maybe ashes are covering the altar of your heart, but underneath there is a small coal that is still burning. The passion did not die; it is just asleep. The passion for God and the lost is still there.

When I hear the painful cries of people begging for help, I am glad because I know God is going to meet their needs. But I feel sad when people are distant and indifferent. I hurt when the Church is busy with other things while souls are lost. Jesus left the 99 to go look for the lost one (Luke 15:4).

I just want to say that God is brokenhearted. There are people dying without Jesus. There are people being violated, dying in accidents, and being murdered. Youngsters are ruining their lives with drugs. There is no time to lose. He has given us the tools we need to reach the world.

Nowadays, there are hundreds of Christian conventions but not many evangelistic crusades. This is not revival. Conventions are good, but campaigns are even better because we go out to win souls. What good is it if we go to conventions, but do not go out to win souls? What good is it if we do spiritual warfare, if we do not go out and preach the Gospel?

Perhaps I speak as an evangelist. Nonetheless, Jesus taught us the way. He went out to the streets. He taught in the synagogues and won souls and healed the sick in the streets. I believe each one of us has a responsibility. Let us ask God to forgive us so that we may experience again that first love that we should never have left (Rev. 2:4). What am I good for, if I do not win lost souls?

Let us cry out to Him: "Lord, give me passion lest I die!"

CHAPTER 4

VISION TO REACH THE WORLD

Carlos Annacondia

The time has come to leave the banquet, to stand up as the Church and go back to the streets. There is a world that is waiting, desperately searching for a supernatural answer. There is thirst and hunger to hear the Word.

Recently, I went back to Mar del Plata, a beautiful tourism city in Argentina. When I arrived at the hotel, they told me it was a privilege to have me there and offered their personnel at my service. When I went into my room, I reflected back to

September 1984 when I came to this city for a crusade. This time, the woman in charge of the hotel received me very differently. Back in 1984, with tears the receptionist asked me to tell her about Jesus. "I need Jesus," she cried.
I knew something was about to happen. That woman was the first convert of the 83,000 decisions for the kingdom of God. What a big difference! In 1984, the church had dared to defy the devil and stand in the middle of the city and preach the Gospel in the streets. Satan started to step back. Today we can see the outcome of the big harvests that God has given us. In those days, the churches were small; today there are big churches. We are enjoying the harvest, but the Lord Jesus is sad.
Not long ago, I had a vision of a big oasis full of exotic plants, palm trees, flowers and gardens. The Church of the Lord was there, lying on the beach, talking and enjoying refreshments. This place was beautifully shaded and fresh. But then, I found myself at the end of the oasis, where there was a high fence separating it from a desert. What a contrast! There was no shade, no palm trees, refreshments, or food. What I saw was a multitude of men and women, some lying on the ground with their eyes open and their hands raised up, their tongues swollen due to thirst. They were looking at the Church, crying, "Help us!" But the fence kept us from reaching them. We were the ones who had erected this fence.
It is very nice to be comfortable; God's blessing is beautiful. He pours out the anointing so that the church is full, we speak in tongues, we enjoy God's food. The sick are healed, the joy of God is poured out, we clap our hands and sing. But out there is a world that is dying while we comfortably enjoy ourselves. I was struck by the difference in Mar del Plata. The hotel's receptionist recognized me. "Mr. Annacondia", she said, "Call us if you need anything." In contrast, in 1984, a woman who did not know me approached me crying, wanting to know about Jesus. I profoundly believe that soon the Lord will raise up the Church again. God is going to raise up people with a burden for lost souls, men and women who will be willing to leave the shade, go around the fence to go out to the desert, and give what they have received.
What you have received by grace, give in grace. "Anyone, then, who knows the good he ought to do and does not do it, sins" (Jas. 4:17, NIV). Not long ago, God said to me, "I have a lot of children but few disciples." We are very comfortable in the "oasis;" we sing and applaud. Notwithstanding, the Lord taught us the parable of the 99. The shepherd left the 99 to look for the lost one and came back joyously. Jesus said that there was more joy in the kingdom of the heaven for the repentant sinner than for 99 righteous that do not repent (Luke 15:7).
I remember when I was in Tartagal Salta, a northern city in Argentina, almost at the border with Bolivia. A woman with cancer came from Tucuman, a city

more than 300 kilometers away. She could not stand up and her family did not know if she would go back home alive. She was not a believer but her relatives were. They brought this woman before me and said: "Pastor, she is dying. We brought her from Tucuman." I simply told them: "Here is Jesus of Nazareth, who came to do good and heal those oppressed by the devil." We prayed for her and the next day she came back, jumping and full of joy. God had torn out the cancer and had healed her! This is the purpose for God's anointing: to do good!

How can we win the suffering world? With persuasive words full of human wisdom or with the Holy Spirit and demonstrations of power? Needless to say, this woman's family came back every night. More people from Tucuman also came because God had worked a miracle.

When I was first converted, people would tell me about Tommy Hicks' campaigns. I used to say, "That's history." Every time I go to Mar del Plata, I am reminded of the year 1984. But that is already history. God wants TODAY! Let us not live in the past; let us look ahead with expectation to what God will do in the earth.

Yesterday's blessings are old. We cannot sleep on our triumphs; we cannot live on memories. God wants men and women who will raise banners and go ahead. This is no time to be sitting down, to treasure our blessings as keepsakes.

How many souls have we baptized in the last few months? How many have assembled in the church? I read a Christian newspaper, and in the last few months, I counted nearly 400 seminars, congresses, conventions, etc. and only two evangelistic campaigns. What is happening? Do we no longer have compassion? Why don't we go out into the streets? During 1985-1986 there was not a street in Buenos Aires that was not having a campaign. We have done a good work and won thousands. We have seen the crippled walk, lepers healed and the dead raised. But this is history; there is a world that is dead and there is a God that is burdened for these lost ones. We cannot continue living in the past. Let's put our feet on the ground and go into the streets with the Gospel.

In 1984 in the city of La Plata, the principle city in the Buenos Aires province, there were four or five churches; today there are 100. These first four or five were on the street. Now God wants to see the 100 in the street. Wake up, Church! Who is willing to respond to the call of the suffering? We have the anointing and we can do it; God is expecting us to do it

Perhaps you will say, "Brother, you did this because you paid the price." What price? One day I got down on my knees and said to the Lord: "I waited for 35 years for someone to speak to me about You." I did not live in the desert or in the mountains; I lived in the Buenos Aires (a city of 13 million inhabitants) and a foreigner came and spoke to me about Jesus. I met Jesus and one day I said: "Lord, I do not want others to suffer the way I did. Let me talk to them about You." God answered, "I am giving you what you asked for, but are you willing to pay the price?" And I said: "What price?" The price is that often you will have to leave your family, spending nights away from home, unable to sleep, letting people look for you from all over, without any rest. This is the price; the rest is free.

God gave the Holy Spirit to men by grace and not by works. All we have to do is decide that we want to make a difference and God will equip us. All we need to have is a burden for the lost. Look at the needs of the whole nation. People are truly lost! It's because the Church has not taken the responsibility to do the job.

Not long ago, I was in Sweden, where there was a great revival 40 years ago. God directed me to minister to some youths who were asking for souls. We prayed for them and they received the anointing. Recently, I spoke with some missionaries there and they told me that these youths were revolutionizing the place! God can revolutionize your city if you can believe. God wants to use you. Church, be encouraged!

Love the Lost Souls

One day I was crossing the street when a taxi driver stopped me and said: "Brother Carlos, thank you." I did not recognize him, but he continued, "In the year 1986, in the Buenos Aires campaign, I was there. I was a drug addict but I accepted Jesus and was set free from drugs and now I am serving God." There is no better music to my ears or no better movie for my eyes, than to hear and see the lives transformed by Jesus. I am inviting you to be a part of this gift from heaven.

Maybe many of you would say, "I do not know how to preach." Neither do I. I simply try to say what is in my heart. One day in Bolivia, I preached the Gospel and there was a Hindu that did not understand Spanish. But he felt the presence of the true God accepted Jesus with tears. He did not even know the name of the God that was there; he did not understand a word I preached, but he accepted Christ. All through the night, he saw a figure in front of him, saying: "You have done the right thing, you have accepted the true God."

Later I ran into him in the United States. Out of the midst of a sea of turbaned heads, someone suddenly came up and embraced me, saying: "You are my father." I told him: "I have never been to India." He explained how, in Bolivia, he had received Jesus without understanding what I was saying. He continued, "Now I preach, I have a radio program, and I am a pastor. God uses me in miracles and I am going to India to preach to my people. Thousands will accept Jesus."

You do not have to be a great preacher, all you have to do is open your mouth and God will fill it. Ask God to use you; consecrate your life to Him. Do not be content to stay as you are- go back to your first love, to your first works. Don't worry about professionalism. Don't look to other people for what God has for you; He is the fountain and source.

Men with willing hearts will shake nations. God can do it now in your life. He can anoint you from head to toe. His fire will give you love for the lost and power to preach. You will never be the same!

CHAPTER 5

INTERCESSION AND RECONCILIATION

René Peñalba

Rev. René Peñalba pastors Living Love Church in Tegucigalpa, Honduras. The church was founded in 1974 and today is a growing, dynamic congregation of about 4,000 members.

Rev. Peñalba's love for the work of the Lord and strong dedication have led him into a season of extraordinary self-study and research. His academic pursuits have been in various disciplines.

During the period of 1983 through 1991, he was the president of the international

church network called "Living Love." Presently, he is the national coordinator of the Spiritual Warfare Network in Honduras, president of the Fellowship of Evangelicals in Honduras, and vice president of the Fellowship of Evangelicals of Central America in Honduras (CEDECA). He is a member of the National Forum on Convergence (FONAC) under the direction of the president of Honduras. In addition, he is a founding member of an organization that aids children and families, led by the first lady of Honduras. He is the author of several books, including The Mind a Battlefield, Problems in Daily Living, Superior Leadership, and Incorporating Growth Groups in an Established Church. In 1997 he received his doctorate in divinity from the Asian Seminary of Christian Ministries, headquartered in Manila, Philippines.
He and his wife have two children.

On a Personal Note...
"Intercession and Reconciliation" is a chapter that undoubtedly will minister to each reader in a very special way. It seems as if the Holy Spirit has put in the pen of our Central and South American authors a word specifically for the prayer warriors.
I am in complete agreement with René as to the need of a preparation time to allow the Holy Spirit to cleanse us before going into the battle. We have been witnesses of painful casualties in the past and we need sincere documented warnings such as this one, to avoid problems in the future.
René is part of the group which helped us initiate the Spiritual Warfare Network, when our territory was limited to Central America. We have worked together since the first meeting.
The church Amor Viviente ("Living Love"), which René pastors, hosted the Iberoamerican Consultation in 1997 and we were witnesses then of the precious ministry God has given him.
A beautiful friendship, respect, and Christian fellowship has grown between us.

Harold Caballeros

"All this is from God,
who reconciled us to himself through Christ
and gave us the ministry
of reconciliation."
(2 Cor. 5:18, NIV)

Since intercession and spiritual warfare are our concern and our burden, let us be careful not to carry it out in only a mechanical way. Let us seek to know exactly and perfectly God's strategies, His promises and His authority, as well as the obstacles and hindrances we can face.

This chapter will call our attention to one of these obstacles in order that we might maximize our power and effectiveness in intercession and spiritual warfare. This obstacle is a lack of reconciliation.

INTERCESSION AND RECONCILIATION: BIBLICAL EVIDENCES OF THEIR INTERRELATIONSHIP

Reviewing what the Scripture says about prayer, it is clear that our prayers can be greatly hindered. In 1 Peter 3:7 we read, "Husbands...be considerate as you live with your wives, and treat them with respect...so that nothing will hinder your prayers" (NIV).

It is evident that the context of this warning is the marriage relationship. Nonetheless, the application of these exhortations goes beyond the context of marriage and extends to different types of interpersonal relationships. It is crucial to create awareness among God's people that, very frequently, we erroneously focus our attention only on whatever is related to "spiritual authority," "God's promises," "warfare strategies" and the like, forgetting that attitudes can be either facilitators or obstacles for spiritual authority, God's promises and warfare strategies to work.

Ephesians chapter 2 teaches us the tremendous work of reconciliation between Jews and Gentiles that God, through Christ, accomplished:

"Remember that at that time you were separate from Christ, excluded from citizenship in Israel and foreigners to the covenants of the promise...But now in Christ Jesus you who once were far away have been brought near through the blood of Christ. For he himself is our peace, who has made the two one and has destroyed the barrier, the dividing wall of hostility...His purpose was to create in himself one new man out of the two, thus making peace, and in this one body to reconcile both of them to God through the cross, by which he put to death their hostility..." (Eph. 2:12-16, NIV).

Note that Paul places emphasis on three extraordinary actions of Jesus Christ:

1. He tore down the wall of separation and division.
2. In his body He reconciled both parties.
3. Through the cross, He put to death hostility.

Surely, this has a direct application that goes beyond the Jew-Gentile relationship level to the relationship between human beings in general. This results in the wonderful possibility of no longer being "foreigners or aliens, but fellow citizens with God's people and members of God's family (Eph. 2:19, NIV).

Let us think for a moment: What would happen if, instead of living in what Christ has done for our reconciliation, we dedicated ourselves to going back and reconstructing walls and barriers in our relationships? Paul says, "If I rebuild what I destroyed, I prove that I am a lawbreaker" (Gal. 2:18, NIV). Each time we rebuild what God has already destroyed for our own good, we make ourselves enemies of His will and transgressors of His plan. How, then, can our intercession and spiritual warfare make any impact if we resist God's plan by maintaining attitudes of unforgiveness and bitterness? "For if you forgive men when they sin against you, your heavenly Father will also forgive you. But if you do not forgive men their sins, your Father will not forgive your sins" (Matt. 6:14-15, NIV).

Intercession is intimately linked with forgiveness of nations and their individual and collective sins, including generational sins (such as idolatry) whose effects continue to the third and fourth generation. But, let us ask ourselves, how can we ask God to grant His forgiveness to individuals, families and societies, when we, the intercessors, are in urgent need of forgiving one another and reconciling with each other?

Not only is the effectiveness of intercession closely connected with our heart of reconciliation, but even the impact of evangelism can be diminished by an unforgiving attitude in believers. "If you forgive anyone his sins, they are forgiven; if you do not forgive them, they are not forgiven" (John 20:23, NIV). Without getting into theological arguments, it is clear that even if God is the only one that can forgive sins, Christ's disciples and the Church have the power and authority to "tie or untie." That is to say, we have the power to confirm or stop what God has potentially already done, in favor of the people.

Jesus Christ said: "I tell you the truth, whatever you bind on earth will be bound in heaven, and whatever you loose on earth will be loosed in heaven. Again, I tell you that if two of you on earth agree about anything that you ask for, it will be done for you by my Father in heaven" (Matt. 18:18-19, NIV). This passage is related to John 20:23. It clearly says that our actions and attitudes have direct and immediate repercussions in the celestial and spiritual sphere. To bind and loose, in heaven as it is in the earth, starts with

our attitudes, especially concerning the agreement that is required for reconciliation.
Matthew 18 speaks of coming into agreement. This agreement begins with our attitudes. If our attitude is not harmonious, reconciliatory, and forgiving, the immediate and direct result is an absence of power for us to bind and loose in the Name of Jesus!
This leads to the conclusion that without agreement evidenced by a reconciliatory attitude there is a lack of spiritual power available for the people of God. We can raise our voice "in the Name of Jesus" but nothing will happen if we are not reconciled to each other.

A KEY PASSAGE ON RECONCILIATION

In Matthew 5:23-24, Jesus gives an interesting discourse concerning reconciliation: "Therefore, if you are offering your gift at the altar and there remember that your brother has something against you, leave your gift there in front of the altar. First go and be reconciled to your brother; then come and offer your gift" (NIV).
From this passage, we discover three crucial insights for our spiritual life: First, the need for self-reflection. Second, reconciliation is a priority. Third, the degenerative process in the absence of reconciliation.

The Necessity of Self-Reflection

"...and there you remember..." (v. 23). Self-reflection is the ability to go back and retrace our steps, analyzing how we have conducted our life and relationships.
The phrase "there you remember" is reminiscent of the parable of the prodigal son in which a young man asks his father to give him the inheritance to which he was entitled. Once he received it, he departed for a far away place to live a disorderly life in the company of people with low morals.
"When he came to his senses, he said, 'How many of my father's hired men have food to spare, and here I am starving to death!" (Luke 15:17, NIV).
"Coming back to your senses" is equivalent to the phrase "and there you remember." These have the same meaning and importance. Both make reference to the ability and need for self-reflection, which is no less than the disposition to see inside yourself, the way you really are, with all the virtues and imperfections!
The future of the prodigal son depended on verse 17. What if the young man had not meditated on and evaluated his conduct in a critical manner? He would have prevented the possibility of a happy homecoming and

reconciliation with his father.
What concerns us, as the people of God, is that there will be no possibility of a wonderful life in the house of our Father. We will neither experience the joy of His promises accomplished in us, nor the power flowing in and through us, unless we have a self-reflective attitude, placing our attitudes and conduct on the balance scale.
When we resist "remembering" something that is necessary to face, we deceive ourselves. James made this very clear when he wrote, "Do not merely listen to the word, and so deceive yourselves. Do what it says" (Jas 1:22, NIV).
Avoiding to face the reality of what we are, besides leading us into self-deceit, also hinders transformations in our life. As a result, we move away from the wonderful power of the Word of God operating in our favor.
Nonetheless, how do we acquire the capacity to discern ourselves? How do we achieve the capacity for self-reflection?
Obviously, we are not capable; we need the help of the Holy Spirit. Jesus promised, "When he [the Holy Spirit] comes, he will convict the world of guilt in regard to sin and righteousness and judgment" (John 16:8, NIV). Thank God, Christ Himself made the provision to prevent the loss of our conscience! This suggests that there is no excuse.
It is the Holy Spirit who prompts in us this process of " there you remember" and "coming to our senses." His help leads us toward reconciliation and consequently, to the power of God for a victorious life and effective intercession.

The Priority if Reconciliation

Matthew 5 continues to instruct us to, "...leave your gift there in front of the altar. First go and be reconciled to your brother..." (v. 24, NIV).
The second insight from Matthew 5 is that reconciliation is a priority. What do I mean by saying this? Reconciliation must take a truly prominent place in our lives and relations. If we pay attention to the context of the scripture, we will notice that the situation describes an in-depth spiritual exercise: bringing an offering to God. In essence, this means that reconciliation has a predominant place, even above devotion and spiritual exercise. We should not hide our broken relationships behind the facade of spirituality and religiosity.
The Latin root of the word reconcile is reconciliare "to turn to friendship or bring together again." It is "the one that had been separated, being restored to communion or company." It is quite reasonable to join this definition with the words that Jesus Christ said, "Any kingdom divided against itself will be

ruined, and a house divided against itself will fall" (Luke 11:17, NIV). Division in spirit, relations and communion are the result of the lack of reconciliation. Does this not describe many in the body of Christ? If this is the case, how can we engage in effective intercession and spiritual warfare in this condition? Further still, how can our efforts to help reconcile the lost to God through evangelism be effective, while we are in need of reconciliation ourselves?

The Apostle James said, "Submit yourselves, then, to God. Resist the devil, and he will flee from you. Come near to God and he will come near to you. Wash your hands, you sinners, and purify your hearts, you doubleminded" (Jas. 4:7-8, NIV).

I want to make a brief reference to these verses, to give amplification to what we have been saying. We notice that the fight against the evil spiritual forces is related to four decisions or determinations:

Surrender to God's authority.

Draw near to God.

Cleanse sinful conduct.

Purify the doubleminded spirit which originates in the heart.

Specifically, I want to emphasis the word "doubleminded." This is the same word that is used in James 1:8, where it says: "... a doubleminded man [is] unstable in all he does." The word translated as "doubleminded"in both passages, literally means: "of split loyalty."

What is the significance of all this? The split loyalty is precisely what provokes ruptures, divisions, resentments and separations in human relations. Divided loyalty prevents a reconciled attitude between many members of the body of Christ and prevents us from authoritatively resisting the devil and his fleeing from us.

Do you see the connection? We must proceed to repair all fragmented loyalties and all doubleminded spirits that have brought pain and broken relations among God's people. Otherwise, it is not possible to conduct powerful warfare prayer over the forces of the enemy!

The Degenerative Process in the Absence of Reconciliation

The third insight found in Matthew chapter 5 is the quick digression relationships take when conflict remains unresolved. We read, "Settle matters quickly with your adversary who is taking you to court. Do it while you are still with him on the way, or he may hand you over to the judge, and the judge may hand you over to the officer, and you may be thrown into prison"(Matt. 5:25, NIV).

Notice that "with your brother" is the first manner of reference to the conflicted relationship in Matthew 5:23ff. Immediately in the next reference, "brother" is no longer used; the word becomes "adversary." If we follow the sequence, we shall notice that afterwards the word "adversary" is no longer used, but "judge" is. After this word, we find the word "police," and finally, "jail."

What does this constant change of words mean? It is the evidence of the degenerative process that relations in conflict suffer when they are left to take their course.

To leave relations without reconciliation is dangerous, indeed, contrary to the popular saying that "time heals all wounds." I believe that in some cases, the passing of time actually makes things worse!

The unresolved conflicts in relations tend to produce a state of oppression, jail and slavery. In my role as a pastor and counselor, I have seen many relationships degenerate to the point of "not leaving there, until the last debt is paid."

Let us not assume that this only applies to relations at the individual level; it also applies in the collective level so that it is possible to experience oppression and slavery in a family, a culture and even a whole nation. This brings me to the conclusion that, most probably, there are nations and cultures trapped in some kind of jail due to unresolved conflict. Could there also be churches and even denominations in oppression due to the same cause?

I hope the study of this passage will convince us sufficiently to examine with the best possible conscience, not only how we are using the spiritual warfare strategies, but also how we are regarding reconciliation in our attitudes and relations.

FOUR TREMENDOUS IMPEDIMENTS TO RECONCILIATORY INTERCESSION

A person undergoing difficulties and conflicts regarding his own self worth, most assuredly will have problems perceiving others and the complexities in his relationships. The four destructive attitudes of imbalanced self-esteem, resentment, envy, and bitterness, whether applied to the life of a servant of God or a church, can contaminate our prayers and intercession.

Imbalanced Self-Esteem

A typical case of this problem is seen in King Saul, who deprived himself of a healthy and edifying relationship with David. Consequently, instead of being an instrument of God in David's life, he turns into his fierce adversary.

"When the men were returning home...the women came out from all the towns of Israel to meet King Saul...As they danced, they sang: 'Saul has slain his thousands, and David his tens of thousands.' Saul was very angry...'They have credited David with tens of thousands,' he thought, 'but me with only thousands...' And from that time on Saul kept a jealous eye on David" (I Samuel 18:5-9, NIV).

The biblical writer makes the remark that David "behaved prudently." This means that the conflict did not have anything to do with David; he didn't originate it, but it was caused by Saul's internal condition.

The truth is that when a person is insecure in himself, he will have difficulties in his ministry and, consequently, with those surrounding him. One of the resulting problems is to suspect that others are stealing what belongs to him, whether ministry, the affections of those around him, or opportunities.

Let us ask ourselves: How could a person in this condition raise a powerful intercessory prayer before God? It can hardly be done since the power of God is neutralized by this internal conflict. Perhaps for this reason, Paul emphatically expressed: "...Do not think of yourself more highly than you ought, but rather think of yourself with sober judgment in accordance with the measure of faith God has given you" (Rom. 12:3, NIV).

Though Paul refers to not having a higher self-concept than we should have, his exhortation could also include the other extreme: having a very low concept of oneself. For our balance as believers, we need to see ourselves "with prudence" and "with faith." Whatever does not correspond to this comes from an internal conflict in our soul.

Going back to Saul's situation, we see that the people had joyously assembled not to David, but to Saul, their king. It happens that when a person has low self-esteem, he is never satisfied. That is to say, this person never has enough respect, admiration and appreciation and is always complaining about not receiving enough from the people surrounding him.

There are many that lift up fervent intercession and spiritual warfare prayers, but they are without power and do not achieve their expected results because their eyes are full of resentment, due to their low self-esteem. Sadly, they blame others for what is happening to them.

Resentments

"...The older son...called one of the servants and asked him what was going on. 'Your brother has come,' he replied, 'and your father has killed the fattened calf...' The older brother became angry and refused to go in...He answered his father, 'Look! All these years I have been slaving for you and never disobeyed your orders. Yet you never gave me even a young goat so I could celebrate with my friends. But when this son of yours who has squandered your property with prostitutes comes home, you kill the fattened calf for him!' 'My son,' the father said, 'you are always with me, and everything I have is yours. But we had to celebrate and be glad, because this brother of yours was dead and is alive again...'" (Luke 15:25-32,NIV).

This is a classic case of someone who, due to resentments, stops perceiving his resources, gifts, position and opportunities in the Kingdom.

The resentments, just as in the last example, often originate when the person wrongly believes that others have taken the place or the position that belongs to him. This leads us into resentment, which in turn prevents us from enjoying our call and vocation in God.

In such a condition, we will not be able to direct our intercessory prayer for the benefit of others. I am saying this, because the older son in our story could not intercede for nor rejoice in the deliverance of his brother. His discernment was blocked; he could not see himself as an instrument for his brother's welfare who once was "dead and had resurrected; had been lost and now has been found."

Contrary to adopting an intercessory attitude, this young man was trapped in self-pity, negative feelings, and false perceptions regarding the way his father had treated him. His complaint reveals his heart, when he says: "Look! All these years I have been slaving for you ...Yet you never gave me..." Obviously, he had an erroneous perception since the biblical writer indicated in the previous verse that the father "had divided his property between them" (v.12).

Notice, resentments blur our perspective and lead us to perceive life, relations and opportunities in a negative way. This prevents us from being sensitive intercessors in someone else's favor and turns us into victims of unhealthy self-pity.

Envy

"For the kingdom of heaven is like a landowner who went out early in the morning to hire men to work in his vineyard. He agreed to pay them a denarius for the day and sent them into his vineyard...About the eleventh hour he went out and found still others standing around...He said to them, 'You also go and work in my vineyard'...the owner of the vineyard said to the foreman, 'Call the workers and pay them their wages'...The workers who were hired about the eleventh hour came and received a denarius. So when those came who were hired first, they expected to receive more. But each of them also received a denarius. When they received it, they began to grumble against the landowner. 'These men who were hired last worked only one hour,' they said, 'and you have made them equal to us who have borne the burden of the work...'"(Matt. 20:1-12, NIV).

Envy is always arguing this way. It claims that others do not deserve what they possess or have accomplished. Envy is always convinced that it has done more work and has more merit than others have; it is also displeased with what others obtain.

Again, as stated previously, let us ask ourselves: How can anyone in such a condition release powerful intercession in favor of those who walk in darkness? Impossible! For one simple reason: envy cauterizes our conscience and prevents us from seeing or feeling others' needs because we are preoccupied with claiming our own rights.

A church that has fallen into envy's net lacks the discernment and power necessary to become an instrument of God in spiritual warfare and intercessory prayer.

Bitterness

"See to it that no one misses the grace of God and that no bitter root grows up to cause trouble and defile many" (Heb. 12:14, NIV).

In this verse, we see Esau as someone from whom roots of bitterness sprang up. Where does this condition come from? What are its effects?

Esau's root of bitterness was a product of:

1. A deep feeling of failure when he sold his birthright for a plate of food.

2. Feelings of resentment and hatred against his brother, or perhaps against his mother also, for deceiving him.

Roots of bitterness are dangerous because their effects are completely harmful, not only for the bitter person, but also for those around them. A root of bitterness:

1. Causes us to miss the grace of God. Few experiences could be so dramatic and destructive as being separated from God's grace.

2. Causes trouble. This is an obstacle and stumbling block in our life, call, or relationships.

3. Defiles (contaminates) many. A contaminant is a toxic element, poisonous and dangerous. This describes the effect of the root of bitterness!

In view of the above, how can we be instruments of God for intercession and effective spiritual warfare while we are trapped and entangled in roots of bitterness? The answer is obvious!

Success in this battle depends on our liberation from those "inward enemies" which are as dangerous as the enemies in the "celestial regions." Therefore, let us examine ourselves, not to feel guilty, not to back away from the fight, but to be better prepared and, hence, to have absolute victory in the power of the Lord.

HOW DO WE REACH A RECONCILIATORY INTERCESSION?

Now, to conclude this study on the vital relationship that exists between intercession and reconciliation, let us explore five steps to walking in reconciliatory intercession.

Step 1. Repent from ecclesiastical sins.

Ecclesiastical sins are the ones that are committed in the body of Christ, against the body of Christ. The Bible says: When you sin against your brothers in this way and wound their weak conscience, you sin against Christ" (1 Cor. 8:12, NIV). We must admit that we have sinned against Christ and against ourselves. How? you might ask. We have sinned with our criticism, denial, murmuring, jealousy, fighting, and uncovering of "our brother's nakedness." Practicing these types of sin has brought great oppression and illness to the body of Christ. We have also diluted God's anointing by our behavior. This must change in order for the power of God to be poured out in all the earth and in order for us to be able to see great revival, which, like fire, will spread to the last corner of the planet.
Let us understand: It is in our hands to "bind and loose" the blessing and the power of God. If we want it to flow freely, let us proceed by dealing with ourselves. The Apostle Peter well said that "you also, like living stones, are being built into a spiritual house to be a holy priesthood, offering spiritual sacrifices acceptable to God through Jesus Christ" (1 Peter 2:5, NIV). As previously stated, we must deal with ourselves in such a way because "...it is time for judgment to begin with the family of God; and if it begins with us, what will the outcome be for those who do not obey the gospel of God?" (1 Pet. 4:17, NIV).
Also, in the book of Acts there is an important warning: "Repent, then, and turn to God, so that your sins may be wiped out, that times of refreshing may come from the Lord" (Acts 3:19, NIV). What the people of God need in many countries is a time of refreshing, and it comes when we repent and turn to the Lord in total openness. This, no doubt, will result in tremendous power from God flowing in and through us, having as God's seal, miracles and wonders that will testify all around the world.

Step 2. Search for Forgiveness to run through the Body.

Speaking of results in unity and in healthy relationship among God's people, the psalmist said, "How good and pleasant it is when brothers live together in unity! It is like precious oil poured on the head running down on the beard, running down on Aaron's beard...For there the Lord bestows his blessing, even life forevermore" (Ps. 133, NIV). Yes, God blesses His people in a great way when healing occurs in relationships. Nonetheless, in order to receive significant healing, forgiveness is a must.

Wherever human beings are present, conflicts in relations are soon found. The biblical provision for problems among human beings is forgiveness.

Of course, believers know a lot about forgiveness. That is not the problem; but most of what we know, we try to apply to non-believers and to those we try to win for the Lord… forgetting that there are many passages in the Holy Scriptures oriented to the sons of God, regarding our need of forgiveness (see Matthew 18:21-25). It is evident that the application of this passage is in the context of our relationships as sons of God.

As we notice in this passage, the verdict is quite strong. The word for the one punishing those who do not forgive has been translated "executioner." A better translation might be "anguisher." This word indicates the level of oppression that can overcome God's people when they refuse to allow forgiveness to permeate their relationships.

If we want to experience true peace and blessing and also be God's instruments to do His work, we have to practice forgiveness and make it known in the body of Christ.

It would be a good practice in every city and in every nation, if the leaders of God's people would meet together to experience fraternal encounters with mercy, repentance and forgiveness. This would be a way to release the power of God to visit us and loose us from spiritual bondages that have held us so long, incapacitating us from doing the work of the Lord in our countries, with the power and vigor God wants us to exert.

Step 3. Pray in favor of others.

United prayer is one of the most refreshing and wonderful experiences that is happening among God's people all around the world. I do not doubt that we have prayed, but our prayer has been largely according to the interest of our congregational or denominational circle.

What is happening in many countries now is that the pastors are meeting to pray one for another, forgiving one another and repenting to one another. The result is simply wonderful: The power of God is being poured out in churches and ministries that were once dry and empty. As a result, thousands of souls are coming to those churches, finding salvation and new life!

United prayer has a common factor: a sense of need and belonging that is filling pastors who once were characterized by isolation, self-sufficiency and indifference for the rest of the Body. This has brought a change in attitude; many pastors, leaders and churches are meeting and praying with a renewed fervency, repenting from that for which Paul criticized the Corinthians when he told them: "The eye cannot say to the hand, 'I do not need you.' And the

head cannot say to the feet, 'I do not need you!'" (1 Cor. 12:21, NIV).
It is really beautiful to see this sense of need arise again in the body, with the resulting action of leaving those attitudes that have sickened and harmed the Church of Jesus Christ. This is accomplished by returning to the wonderful experience of united prayer!

Step 4. Affirming the Vision of the Church being One Body

Now, there are fewer pastors and churches that have separated themselves from the rest. There are less "island" pastors and churches because the movement of the Spirit of God is uprooting many away from this condition. We are starting to understand that, "Now the body is not made up of one part but of many...in fact God has arranged the parts in the body, every one of them, just as he wanted them to be...As it is, there are many parts, but one body" (1 Cor. 12:14-20, NIV).
Affirming the vision of the Church being one body is bringing health in the Church of the Lord; denying this vision, or attacking it, makes you become an instrument of evil, a virulent agent for the body of Christ. Fortunately, there are many pastors, leaders and churches that are leaving the old attitude and bad habit of isolation. Now they are dedicating themselves to construct and affirm the vision that Christ's body is one.

Step 5. Discovering the Blessing of Diversity

For generations, diversity has been the reason of disagreement and discouragement for the people of God. Nonetheless, the "re-reading" of the Bible, inspired by the Holy Spirit, is bringing revelation and meaning to texts that have always been there, but our understanding was once obscured.
Speaking of diversity, the Apostle Paul taught the following: "There are different kinds of gifts, but the same Spirit. There are different kinds of service, but the same Lord. There are different kinds of working, but the same God works all of them in all men. Now to each one the manifestation of the Spirit is given for the common good" (1 Cor. 12:4-7, NIV).
The Greek word that is translated as "diversity," is the word diáiresis. This word, in turn, is related to the word diairéo, which basically means, "distribute." Diáiresis appears in verse 11 of this same chapter, when he says, "All these are the work of one and the same Spirit, and he gives them to each one, just as he determines." This same word is also used in the Prodigal Son parable, when it says, "He divided his property between them" (Luke 15:12, NIV).
We notice the diversity of gifts, operations and ministries in the body of

Christ is not the product of a mistake, nor does it manifest imperfection, but on the contrary, it is evidence of the richness and mercy of God, who has "distributed" among us "His property," obviously for our blessing and wellbeing!
Let us rejoice, then, in diversity. Regarding this, let us not forget to always do the following simple actions: 1. Understand diversity. 2. Take advantage of it. 3. Promote it.

Breaking the Actual Curses in the History of God's People

There has been antagonism in many cities and nations in churches and even denominations, wherein people have allowed their differences to become real curses that hinder the advancement of the Church of the Lord.
You may ask yourself, how can this be possible? I will tell you that the Bible says, "An offended brother is more unyielding than a fortified city, and disputes are like the barred gates of a citadel" (Prov. 18:19, NIV). A castle with strong locks is what, according to this passage, characterizes blocked relationships and someone's oppression. This means that a close relationship can turn into bondage, and a solution to the conflict will be very difficult. I am convinced that there are offended brothers and many "locked" relationships, the products of destructive words and actions, which are operating as curses among the people of God.
We must look for healing and liberation from these conditions in order for the work of the Lord to continue powerfully. Let us not forget that the Scripture is clear,
"...An undeserved curse does not come to rest" (Prov. 26:2, NIV). In some cases, we are the cause… by our attitudes and conduct.

CHAPTER 6

ESSENTIAL FACTORS IN SPIRITUAL WARFARE

Emeka Nwankpa

Emeka Nwankpa from Aba, Nigeria, is a former lawyer trained for the ministry by British missionary S.G. Elton. Rev. Nwankpa has a calling to teach intercession and spiritual warfare and has ministered in many nations on four continents over the last 20 years.

He is a member of the Advisory Board of the International Fellowship of Intercessors and the Advisory Board of the International Christian Chamber of Commerce, Nigeria. Rev. Nwankpa is also

the coordinator of Intercessors for Africa, on the Board of Trustees of the International Third World Christian Leaders Association and the coordinator of the United Prayer Track-Africa Region under the AD2000 banner.
Rev. Nwankpa is married to Bade and they have three teenage children.

On a Personal Note...

I am a person who rejoices in God's great variety. I have learned to find Jesus in every race and in every continent. What a blessing for us to have the ministry of Rev. Emeka Nwankpa. The elements of guidance we find in the chapter "Essential Factors in Spiritual Warfare" belong to the class of proven strategies. These are not theories; they are realities learned from the field.

For those of us who have had the opportunity to minister in Nigeria and other regions in Africa, it has been very special to experience the refreshing anointing of the Holy Spirit. The African churches exhibit a very interesting combination of giftings. On the one hand, they express a daring strength, and on the other hand a depth of spiritual knowledge. It is obvious for those who have been with the African Church that their knowledge of spiritual realities is more abundant than in the western cultures.

Without a doubt the reader will find in the following chapter recommendations that answer the command found in Proverbs, "...By wise counsel wage war" (Prov. 20:18).

Harold Caballeros

In spiritual warfare there are certain factors that ensure victory. A careful study of some of the physical battles that were fought in the Old Testament provides us with the knowledge of many of these essential factors.

One insight we receive from the Old Testament is that God wanted His people, and still wants His people, to learn war (spiritual warfare). This is so crucial to understand because, contrary to popular belief, our inheritance has to be fought for. It is clearly stated that God left some enemies to test the sons of Israel who had not experienced the wars of Canaan and to make sure they learned war. "Now these are the nations which the LORD left, that He might test Israel by them, that is, all who had not known any of the wars in Canaan (this was only so that the generations of the children of Israel might be taught to know war, at least those who had not formerly known it)" (Judges 3:1-2, NKJV).

Pastors and ministers of God must teach God's people to know war. Salvation is free; similarly the children of Israel did not contribute any effort to be brought out of Egypt. But after they came out of the wilderness and crossed Jordan, they had to fight for every inch of their inheritance. These were hard, long campaigns to obtain their inheritance. Eventually when Joshua came to the end of his ministry the Israelites had fought 31 kings in all. God did not want them to face war in their state of inexperience. At the same time He did not want them to go back to the house of bondage. He therefore led them through the training period in the wilderness to prepare them for the wars of Canaan. This training strengthened them to be able to take their inheritance. Likewise the Church must learn spiritual warfare to be able to fulfill God's plan for it on earth. Spiritual warfare has to be learned and practiced. There is no alternative way to deal with principalities and powers and all the forces of darkness.

As the Spirit of God moves in nations such as South Korea, Argentina, China, the Philippines and Nigeria, believers are discovering that God wants the Church to learn spiritual warfare systematically and confront the powers of darkness in a strategic manner in order to take cities, break the grip of the strong man over nations and redeem the land. The Spirit of God is revealing the Scriptures afresh in an applicative manner to be used in prophetic prayer and prophetic action, which are critical facets of spiritual warfare.

One of the physical battles in the Old Testament from which we can gain insights into warfare is found in Judges chapter 5. From this powerful passage, known as the Song of Deborah, we see five essential factors in victorious spiritual warfare.

When God Marches with us His People

"Lord, when You went out from Seir, when You marched from the field of Edom, the earth trembled and the heavens poured..." (Judges 5:4, NKJV).

In the song of Deborah (following the victory that God gave her and the army of Israel against Sisera who commanded 900 chariots of iron) we see the prophetic insight into the secrets of the outcome. It is essential that God's presence go with us into spiritual warfare. Leaders of congregations or prayer groups must ensure that all necessary steps and precautions are taken to have God's presence. If the Holy Spirit is not going before, then please do not undertake spiritual warfare. We glean from Deborah's song that one of the most powerful reasons for their astounding victory was that God marched with them.

The Old Testament also illustrates the dangers of engaging in warfare apart from the leading of God's presence. When the sons of Eli, Hophni and Phinehas, presumptuously carried the ark of God into battle the army of Israel shouted so loud that the earth shook and fear gripped the Philistines, yet the presence of God was not with them. Because of their flagrant sins of adultery and the depths of their wickedness, God had put a curse on their father, Eli, and his family (I Sam. 2:27-36). This included Phinehas, his wife, and Hophni. Hophni and Phinehas died in that battle against the Philistines; the ark of the Lord was captured. The news of these events caused Eli to fall backwards and die. Tragically, the wife of Phinehas died in childbirth on the same day.

Another example is when the people of Israel refused to go into the promised land at Kadesh Barnea. God was angry-and showed it-prompting Moses to intercede. Moses told the children of Israel what God had said and they mourned greatly. The next morning they rose up and on their own wanted to go into battle without the presence of God among them (Num. 14:40-45, NKJV). From this account we learn that when a family or church fellowship has been rocked by sin or scandal, it is best to wait on the Lord in repentance and intercession until there is certainty that God's presence is there among the people before embarking on spiritual warfare.

When God marches with His people, supernatural things happen. As He led Israel with the pillar of cloud by day and the pillar of fire by night in the wilderness no one could successfully attack them. Moses understood this when he said: "If Your presence does not go with us, do not bring us up from here" (Ex. 33:15, NKJV).

When Leaders Lead

"When leaders lead in Israel, when the people willingly offer themselves, bless the Lord!" (Judges 5:2, NKJV).

One key factor in warfare is the quality of leadership. Ordinary human military organizations around the world place a great premium on training good and responsible officers to lead the troops. In the Israeli army the officers have a reputation of leading from the front to inspire the men. Similarly in spiritual warfare, it is of the utmost necessity that leaders-anointed, knowledgeable leaders-actually lead in times of prayer warfare. This is because spiritual warfare is a dynamic exercise. It can ebb and flow. A sensitive leader can discern in the Spirit which way things are going and give the people necessary direction to follow. This is applicable whether it is a prayer meeting, a prayer project, or a prayer journey. It has to be said, of course, that the leaders must yield themselves to the Holy Spirit and must lead accordingly.

In many cases, the quality of a spiritual warfare exercise largely depends on the type of leadership exercised in the meeting. During a prayer conference in Asaba some years ago I was leading a session of prayer. We were praying about certain matters that affected our nation of Nigeria at the time. In the course of the prayers a prophecy in other tongues came forth. There was silence. As we waited, a woman rudely broke the silence with a staccato interpretation which I discerned was not of the Lord. I immediately switched off the microphone and motioned to some young men to quietly take the woman out of the meeting because she refused polite indications to stop. Just after this mild drama the real interpretation flowed from a very reliable channel. It was a strong and clear word for the conference that helped give direction for prayer in the nation. It became clear that the enemy quite often likes to jump into the breach just before the real thing comes along. Just before Isaac was born, the devil arranged for an Ishmael. And just prior to David appearing on the scene, the enemy moved the people to ask for a king. They were given Saul. This Satanic strategy has to be borne in mind during spiritual warfare meetings.

In fact, it takes seasoned and experienced leadership to discern, judge and handle a prophecy in the course of a meeting, as not all the utterances may be from the Lord. Furthermore, after a strong message, especially in a prayer conference or in a church meeting, it requires discerning leadership to steer the prayer time in such a direction as to fully cover all the major points of the message so that no word falls to the ground.

So much prophecy is left to trail off in meetings that one wonders whether the Church still appreciates prophecy. Or even worse, in some circles every prophecy attracts applause and so with every message preached. This makes it difficult, if not impossible, for any rebuke from the Lord to be taken and the proper spiritual response to messages is not carried out. In such settings strategic spiritual warfare can never really get off the ground because the Holy Spirit and the Word of God are treated lightly. Preachers entertain to light or tumultuous applause as the fancy takes the congregation. Leadership in such places needs to seek the Lord in repentance.

When People Offer Themselves Willingly

"When leaders lead in Israel, when the people willingly offer themselves, bless the Lord!" (Judges 5:2, NKJV).

In normal military experience conscripts and stragglers are not always dependable soldiers because they fight against their will, are less amenable to discipline, and are prone either to mutiny or desert whenever they have the opportunity. Volunteers are normally more reliable because they have willingly offered themselves to serve in the military. David's army was entirely made up of volunteers though they were men in distress, in debt and discontented with the events then taking place in Israel (1 Sam. 22:2). But they eventually became an unbeatable fighting machine. King David and his men never lost a battle.

Gideon's army of 300 drastically pruned from the original 32,000 volunteers was men who could obey orders strictly. They succeeded in their mission. Unwilling soldiers murmur, grumble and are not willing to take risks.

These same principles apply even more strictly in spiritual warfare. An unwilling prayer partner is more than a hindrance because of the spiritual law that states: "Can two walk together, unless they are agreed?" (Amos 3:3, NKJV). In spiritual warfare there must first be a willing mind. This was why Gideon was instructed by God to tell the volunteers these words: "Now therefore, proclaim in the hearing of the people, saying, 'Whoever is fearful and afraid, let him turn and depart at once from Mount Gilead" (Judges 7:3, NKJV).

God applies this principle firmly in choosing men who would carry out certain special assignments. Peter, while on the rooftop in Joppa, was hungry for natural food, so God took the opportunity to offer him food from heaven. A sheet containing all kinds of four-footed beasts of the earth, creeping things and birds of the air was let down in front of him. A voice came to him: "Rise, Peter; kill and eat" (Acts 10:13, NKJV). Peter said, "Not so, Lord! For I have never eaten anything common or unclean" (Acts 10:14, NKJV). The voice spoke to him again: "What God has cleansed you must not call common" (v. 15, NKJV). This was done three times and the sheet was taken up into heaven again.

Peter failed a vital test. He lectured God on his dietary preference rather than obeying the command given him. Thus, he proved that he could not handle the commission to the Gentiles because he was too ethnocentric. God had to find Saul (Paul) who would later say: "For though I am free from all men, I have made myself a servant to all, that I might win the more; and to the Jews I became as a Jew, that I might win Jews; to those who are under the law, as under the law.... to those who are without law, as without law (not being without law toward God, but under law toward Christ), that I might win those who are without law; to the weak I became as weak, that I might win the weak. I have become all things to all men, that I might by all means save some" (1 Cor. 9:19-22, NKJV). Paul eventually received more revelation than Peter. Later Peter wrote that Paul's revelations were hard to understand. We must be willing soldiers in the Lord's Army.

When Rulers Offer Themselves with the People

"My heart is with the rulers of Israel who offered themselves willingly with the people. Bless the Lord!" (Judges 5:9, NKJV).

The combination of good leaders and volunteers who are willing to offer themselves in warfare is certainly a great asset. An army can have good soldiers, but without willing leaders the morale would not be particularly high. In the battle to deliver Israel in Judges chapter 4, Barak willingly placed himself under Deborah's leadership and went with the army to fight Sisera. The other tribal leaders did so as well. The victory that resulted in this setting began a change in the fortunes of Israel after many years of subjugation and humiliation by their enemies. Likewise David's mighty men (his leaders) and the rest of the army were a combination that recorded some unequalled exploits in their day. Leaders need to offer themselves willingly for spiritual warfare because they provide a necessary ingredient that no other person can contribute. When leaders are willing to participate in the rigors of spiritual warfare with the rest of the congregation, it is always encouraging to everybody.

Causing the Elements and Heavenly Bodies to Affect Earthly Matters

"They fought from the heavens; the stars from their courses fought against Sisera" (Judges 5:20, NKJV).

On at least three occasions in the Old Testament, leaders speaking by faith interfered with movement of the heavenly bodies to affect the events of their day. In Joshua 10, the warrior leader spoke to the sun and moon to stand still in the heavens so that he could proceed in a battle against the Amorite kings (Josh. 10:12-13, NKJV). This powerful development caused the sun and moon to stand still for about a day and affected the outcome of the battle to the detriment of Israel's enemies. In the book of Isaiah when King Hezekiah faced imminent death and was told to set his house in order, he turned his face toward the wall and cried bitterly and repentantly unto God. The Lord sent Isaiah back to tell him that 15 years were to be added to his life. The Lord also promised that He would deliver Hezekiah and the city of Jerusalem from the hand of the king of Assyria. The prophet finished his message to the king with this assurance: "And this is the sign to you from the Lord, that the Lord will do this thing which He has spoken: 'Behold, I will bring the shadow on the sundial, which has gone down with the sun on the sundial of Ahaz, ten degrees backward.' So the sun returned ten degrees on the dial by which it had gone down" (Isa. 38:7-8, NKJV).

This interference with the solar system encouraged a despondent Hezekiah and also balanced out the remaining part of the day that was affected in the miracle in the book of Joshua. The full day of 24 hours had now been cut off from the calendar of time. The third time heavenly bodies affected earthly events was, of course, Deborah's reference. Her prophetic praying caused the stars to fight against Sisera and his army. Another Old Testament example of someone's faith altering nature is described in the book of James. Here we are challenged to realize that Elijah, who prayed and locked up heaven so that it did not rain for three and half years in Israel, was a man of like passion as ourselves (James 5:17-18). In spiritual warfare we must understand that if it becomes necessary to resist or overcome enemy motivated forces, by prophesying into the elements, we need to do so boldly.

Entering a Strong City in the Spirit

Cities differ from each other in certain respects. They may be financial centers, industrial centers, occult centers, political centers or strategic in other ways. As you read the history of a city, or consider its contribution to the present, its importance or notoriety may become quite clear. However, in military consideration you look at a city from a slightly different perspective. If you were a defender of Babylon in the days of Nebuchadnezzar, for instance, you would be confident that its walls and the 20-year supply of food would beat any siege. If you were an invader you would want to devise a strategy to conquer the city depending on the resources available to you. The Bible reveals God's strategies for capturing strong cities, and through careful study we can learn certain principles that apply in dealing with our cities today, always keeping in mind that our warfare is not against persons or physical structures, but against principalities and powers.

God is spirit. That which is born of the spirit is spirit. We have to deal with spiritual forces in spiritual warfare. Moreover we are seated (strategically) in the heavenly places together with Christ, not in a physical sense but in a spiritual sense. It therefore is not difficult to understand the concept of entering a city in the spirit. We need to assiduously plead with the Holy Spirit to bring us into a city in the spirit. We may live in a city in the physical sense for many years, knowing only physical facts and statistics without seeing into the spiritual realm. But when we are led into that realm by the Holy Spirit, we see infinitely more and even occasionally we can see things and situations through the eyes of God. A good example is the vision which God granted Demos Shakarian, which led him to found the FGBMFI (Full Gospel Businessmen's Fellowship International). He saw men and women all over the world, lifeless, sad and dejected, but soon after, lifting up their hands, alive and rejoicing.

God took Ezekiel in the spirit a number of times to show him certain things. In chapter eight of the book of Ezekiel we read what God showed him in the city of Jerusalem, (Eze. 8:3-16). God took him in the spirit and showed him the various sins that the inhabitants of Jerusalem were committing in various hidden spots of the city. Ezekiel was shown the image of jealousy that made God angry. He was shown, through a hole in the wall of another part of the city, a room where 70 elders were engaged in worshipping idols portrayed on a wall. He was also shown women weeping for Tammuz, the Babylonian god, at the door of the gate of the Lord's house. Finally he was shown a group of 25 men at the door of the temple of the Lord, between the porch and the altar, who had their backs turned toward the temple and their faces toward the east, worshipping the sun. After all these visions God then began judgment upon the city (Eze. 9:1-11).

As intercessors seek the Lord concerning a city or nation, God can give a vision or revelation that brings a clear understanding of what the situation is in the spirit realm. Unless and until God brings us into the city in the spirit it is not possible to bind the strong man over the city. Testimonies of people who have had this experience invariably show that more often than not it has occurred during or after a fast in which they were waiting on the Lord for that specific purpose. As the Lord brings us into the city in the spirit, we see and perceive more clearly the problems we deal with and the position of the enemy.

God Deals with Impossible Odds in Warfare

This principle of entering a city in the spirit is invaluable in dealing with a strong city. There were at least three strong cities in the Old Testament-Jebus, Babylon and Jericho-and one in the New Testament, Ephesus. The story of how each was overcome by God's people shows that unless God led them they would not have succeeded.

In the case of Jebus, the Jebusites were so confident and cocky about the city's impregnability that they put the lame and the blind on the wall, taunting David by saying that those handicapped people were enough to defeat him. David threw a challenge to his officers and Joab went through the gutters and captured that city, which later became the seat of David's government.

Babylon was a masterpiece of architecture and its protection was carefully thought out. But Isaiah's prophecy in the 44th and 45th chapters of Isaiah, plus the hand of God that wrote on the wall of Belshazzar's palace MENE MENE TEKEL UPHARSIN, broke Babylon open for its fall to the Medes and the Persians. God had frustrated the nobility of Babylon, made their diviners mad, and turned the wisdom of the astrologers backward. In addition, he performed the counsel of Daniel, his messenger. Daniel was brought into the realm of the spirit to read that writing on the wall which spoke the doom of Babylon.

Jericho was a fortified city. But after Joshua was brought into the realm of the spirit, where he received the strategy to attack it, her defenses eventually could not avail. As a result of Joshua's conversation with God, the children of Israel obeyed all that they were told to do and this resulted in the fall of the seemingly impenetrable walls of Jericho.

Ephesus was so spiritually dense that the church in that city before Paul's visit was very weak, just 12 disciples who had only experienced John's baptism. Being the city where the temple of Diana was situated and having a hard core trade union led by Demetrius the silversmith, Ephesus was firmly in the hands of Satan. In addition there was much occultism practiced there. Paul taught for two years, ministered to them and gradually built a powerful church to whom he taught spiritual warfare (Ephesians 6). As time went on, God did special miracles by the hands of Paul. Handkerchiefs and aprons that touched his body were laid on the sick and demon possessed. The sick recovered and demons fled. From Ephesus the Gospel spread throughout Asia. The secret of the tremendous success in this strong city was that Paul had wrestled with beasts in Ephesus. After subduing them, the atmosphere, like in South Korea today, became clear. "I affirm, by the boasting in you which I have in Christ Jesus our Lord, I die daily. If, in the manner of men, I have fought with beasts at Ephesus, what advantage is it to me?...,'" (I Cor. 15:31-

32, NKJV). It would appear that Paul did much spiritual warfare with these beasts. It formed the basis of his teaching that we wrestle not against flesh and blood, but against principalities and powers in heavenly places.

Strong cities, spiritually speaking, abound in the world today. Intercessors need to be very much aware that it has taken the enemy many years to build up his fortifications, through covenants, altars, sacrifices, shedding of blood, satanism, sorcery, witchcraft and astrology. We must seek God to lead us into our cities in the spirit, to be able to overpower the forces of darkness. At this time across the world, God is speaking by the Holy Spirit to believers to take cities for Him. We need to realize that unless we approach the task spiritually we will only be scratching the surface as we have always done. The Argentinean church is making big strides in this area of dealing with cities spiritually and we need to learn from their example and experience as we seek the Lord to help us with our own cities. When God spoke to Joshua, it made all the difference in taking Jericho. We need to learn to hear the word of the Lord as we confront the enemy. Whenever we have heard the word of God in prayer warfare, we become excited, almost intoxicated with joy, regardless of the odds.

In 1977, I was teaching in a school located in Oshun State, Nigeria. Unknown to the education authorities, certain elements had carefully conspired to cause a riot in the town using the school children. These elements had briefed the prefects in each school and the plan was that the students at the school at the extreme end of town would start off by marching in a mob to the next school and then those students would join them, so that the mob swelled as they went from one school to another. This would go on until all the schools would go in one great mob to burn the market, the prisons, and the police station and cause other havoc.

The school where I taught was the fourth school on the route. A university lecturer, whose wife was a teacher in the school, rushed into the compound to alert his wife that a demonstration was surging toward the school. I overheard the agitated husband speaking to his wife through the window of the school library. As I stepped out to the corridor, we could hear the chanting of the approaching mob. In a matter of minutes our students would have joined them. But the Spirit of God spoke to me and said, "Bind the spirits controlling that mob and turn them back." I spoke aloud, "I bind the spirits controlling that mob in the Name of Jesus. I break your power and you will not take our students!"

Suddenly the advance guard of the mob stopped only a few feet in front of me. One or two went behind me to try to call our students out. Our students were riveted to the floor and could not move. Then the mob turned back, heading for the road, and as they moved their songs began to sound ragged. I remembered that our principal's house was directly across the road from the school. And so I spoke again with faith, "Lord blind their eyes from seeing that house and destroying it!" The mob broke the school signpost and took it away, leaving us, the staff and students, relieved. They went on to cause havoc in town, burning and looting, but our students were not part of it.

Obediently listening to God is indispensable in successful spiritual warfare. Joshua is an exemplary leader in warfare by his explicit obedience to the command of the Lord. He exhibited boldness as he and all the army came against the enemy forces suddenly. In Joshua 11, the troops of Israel attacked the coalition put together by Jabin, king of Hazor. The Lord delivered them into the hand of Israel who chased and slaughtered all of them. Joshua followed God's commands to the letter; he hamstrung their horses and burnt their chariots. God in his faithfulness, and an obedient commander, who demonstrated boldness, overcame the enemy in a situation that presented seemingly impossible odds. That could be our testimony as well as we listen to the Lord and go forth in obedience and boldness to wage spiritual warfare.

The Lord of Hosts is His Name.

Excerpted from The Lord is a Man of War by Emeka Nwankpa©1997, by permission of the author.

CHAPTER 7

THE HEALING OF THE LOCAL CHURCH

Neuza Itioka

Dr. Neuza Itioka dedicates her time to travelling throughout Brazil and abroad conducting seminars on spiritual warfare. She is an author and national coordinator of the Spiritual Warfare Network in Brazil. Dr. Itioka earned degrees in education and theology and received her doctorate of missiology from Fuller Theological Seminary. She has been a part of SEPAL's board of missionaries since 1985.

On a Personal Note...

Dr. Neuza Itioka is our coordinator of the Spiritual Warfare Network in Brazil. Evangelism has greatly advanced in that South American nation, and spiritual warfare has been a very key factor. Neuza's ministry incorporates a combination of very important elements, notably intercession and deliverance.

Personally I have witnessed how much Neuza's colleagues respect and appreciate her. She dedicates a great part of her time to minister to leaders in God's kingdom. An anointed teacher and skillful writer, Neuza has greatly impacted her country.

Neuza is well known for her ability to combine spiritual concepts and theories with practice. She is gifted at showing others, especially pastors, the path toward transforming their nation.

Harold Caballeros

During a training session for missionaries, one of the trainers shared a vision. She told me that some people did not accept her experience but, nevertheless, she still wanted to share it. This was a vision of an unusual bride. Her clothes were torn, she was dirty, fallen and drunk. A voice said, "She is drunk from drinking so much of this world."
This bride was the Church of Christ, filthy and wearing torn garments. She was so entangled with the things of this world she became intoxicated from drinking in so much of it. She had lost her holiness and purity, framing herself in the values of the world.
That night we wept when we understood that the bride of Christ was in that horrible condition. This is a reality of the Church of Christ. If the Bridegroom came today to claim her, she could not be received. How tragic is her situation! But God, being rich in mercy, is revealing His strategies to move His people into healing and holiness.
I will be dealing with the subject of the healing of the local church within a framework of personal liberation, family liberation, and the liberation of a city and a nation within the parameters of spiritual warfare. Our perspective is that, in the same way an individual may need deliverance, a local church also needs healing and freedom. Here is a true story to illustrate this point.

The Case of an Oppressed Pastor

A colleague in the ministry once shared with me regarding his pastorate. He told me he suffered much in his ministry. This church was marked by division, accusation and slander. There were conflicts and fights among the church officers. His wife had even had a miscarriage because of stress from the ministry.
The other churches in the area flourished but his did not; it was plagued with problems. By all indications there was a legal right for a principality to work in his church. I spoke with him about it and he called the church to pray, asking God to forgive the sins of the church itself. Those sins were opening a breach and giving opportunity for certain demonic spirits to destroy it.
During their intercession time, God led him to examine the minutes of the church. It was then that he saw something unusual. The church had an interesting history. During the previous 20 years, the church had changed pastors seven times. All of the pastors, without exception, had fallen into adultery and left the pastorate as a result.
Armed with this information, he understood the reason for some specific battles he fought even from the pulpit. Now it became clear why, while he preached, he smelled the cheap perfume worn by prostitutes. Other harassing distractions came against him while he was delivering his sermon. The

principality of adultery and prostitution was operating in that church. This evil force had been granted legal permission because of unconfessed sins in the past. This pastor stood in the gap, before the presence of the Lord, asking forgiveness for the adulteries committed by the pastors who preceded him. These sins had been judged by the church but they had never been bound as they should have been. This pastor's repentance began the healing of that community.

Twenty years before, when the first pastor fell into sin, the church was angry and fired him, but nobody came before the presence of God to ask forgiveness for the sin and removal of the guilt. The iniquity remained in the church all this time, giving strength to the spirit of adultery and prostitution. The second pastor fell in the snare of that same spirit, and he, too, was expelled from the church. Because nobody dealt with this sin through repentance, the spirit of adultery and prostitution became stronger and bolder and continued taking more victims, until it consumed six pastors! The seventh pastor could have fallen into the same snare. Because the sin had never been confessed, the evil spirit had not been identified and expelled. It was setting the stage to defeat a new victim. The mercy of God made it possible for him to discern and solve the problem.

Analyzing Churches Today

Every church should be healthy, acting in society as light and salt, but many of them have serious problems even to the point of closing their doors. Many of our churches need healing.

If we are satisfied merely with the church growing, supposing that the church that grows numerically is healthy, we are making a limited diagnosis.

Churches that have a healthy integrated life, should have the following characteristics:

1. Growth is based on new conversions and many people are being baptized.
2. The church leads the new Christian to maturity.
3. The church has a vigorous discipling program.
4. The church has a strong program of teaching the Word of God to its members and trains them to be good workers in various levels of service.
5. The church has an intense life of prayer and intercession.
6. The church is involved in spiritual warfare at different levels: ministering inner healing and deliverance to individuals, families and cities.
7. The church has a missionary agenda and program.
8. The church has community service outreaches for street children, beggars, prostitutes, the poor, and if possible, a school, medical clinic, etc.

9. There is fellowship and mutual respect among the members of the church through home groups and different departments.
10. The youth, children and women, have room to grow and use their spiritual gifts.

The perception I have of many sick churches is that they are divided (or the result of a division); others are bound and blind. Many churches do not show signs of spiritual health. It seems that the diagnosis Jesus made when He referred to the Laodicean church, refers to many of the churches of the twentieth century.

"To the angel of the church in Laodicea write: I know your deeds, that you are neither cold nor hot. I wish you were either one or the other! So, because you are lukewarm-neither hot nor cold-I am about to spit you out of my mouth. You say, 'I am rich; I have acquired wealth and do not need a thing.' But you do not realize that you are wretched, pitiful, poor, blind and naked. I counsel you to buy from me gold refined in the fire, so that you can become rich; and white clothes to wear, so that you can cover your shameful nakedness; and salve to put on your eyes, so that you can see. Those whom I love I rebuke and discipline. So be earnest, and repent. Here I am! I stand at the door and knock" (Rev. 3:14-20, NIV).

First, He says that the church is neither cold nor hot-it is lukewarm. Second He says that the church has an incorrect self-concept. She thinks she is rich and needs nothing. Is a church that is satisfied with her poverty, mediocrity and human control, totally annulling the action of the Holy Spirit?

The city of Laodicea was founded in 250 BC by Antiochos Epiphanes of Syria. It was strategically located in the intersection of three important roads; consequently, Laodicea was one of the richest cities of the Roman Empire. It was so rich that when it was destroyed by an earthquake in the year 61 BC, it was completely reconstructed with public money, without any outside help. The riches of the city originated in three sources. Its central industry was glossy black wool. It was also the financial center of all Asia, with an extensive gold exchange. In addition, it was a medical center specializing in ophthalmology. Many became rich by selling collyrium for eye disease.

The church of Laodicea is the only one among the seven churches in the Revelation that does not receive a compliment from Jesus, but only hard words of correction. How can a church receive a word so strong as: "you are repulsive; I will vomit you?"

From Where does Lukewarmness Come?

The church of Laodicea was being seduced and deceived with the illusion of the riches of its own city. Somehow, the spirit of the city had penetrated the church to give it the false sense of security and satisfaction. But truly, that church lived in a spiritual poverty that Jesus called pitiful. To get rich, she would have to buy the spiritual gold refined by the fire of the Holy Spirit and of trials. Jesus was telling them that unless the church was tried by fire, passing through the trials of criticism, the death to self, persecution and tribulation, it would continue to be poor. The raw material needed to build the spiritual building of the church has to be of gold and precious stones, not hay, stubble and wood (1 Cor. 3:12).

The church was naked, since the rich clothes of black wool that made the city so proud, were not covering its nakedness. She had been deceived, having confidence in a material covering. But God exposed the shame of her sin in order to give her white clothes of justification from the Lord Jesus.

She was blind. The collyrium provided by the city healed physical problems, but was incapable of developing spiritual perception. She had lost the ability to discern spiritual things from material things, and light from darkness.

The worst sin we see in this letter is that the church had dethroned the Lord, the Head of the Church. There was no place for the Lord to act. In a sense, He was absent; He had left the church because of the lukewarmness, arrogance and self-sufficiency, sin and spiritual blindness. And now He says that He is at the door of the church, knocking, asking that he who hears open the door and let Him come in, because He wants to dine with the one who opens the door. He wants to share the intimacy of dinner with the church.

For Jesus to enter through the door, the church had to repent. He says that in spite of her intolerable state, He loved her and that is why He would discipline her. That is why He appeals, "So be earnest, and repent."

True repentance is the condition that would allow Jesus to dine with the church. Jesus is not telling the world to repent, but He is saying it to the church. "Those whom I love I rebuke and discipline. So be earnest, and repent". To understand the spiritual dimension of the problem of the churches, we have to examine the situation and work with absolute honesty. If we want to see a church healed, there is a price to pay.

As we said before, we discovered that certain situations in the city can determine the attitude of the church. These are external situations influencing a Christian community. A city can be under the dominion of principalities and powers which, if allowed, can influence the lives of the people of God. We have seen that when discerning a problem of a church that has to do with pride and death, it was because those spirits were reigning in the city.

The Church as a Body

The analogy the apostle Paul used to explain the dynamics of a church, is the human body (I Cor. 12:12-14, 25-27). The apostle also refers to the Church as "the Body of Christ." Thus, the Church is a living organism. In the same way a single cell does not make up a body, a single person cannot make up a church. But as many cells make up a body, in like manner many followers of Jesus, make up the Church. The elderly, young children and adults comprise the Church. It is made up of rich and poor, black, white and indigenous, natives, foreigners and diplomats, educated and illiterate, scientists and technocrats; all of them have their place as part of the Church. There is only one condition: the person must be born again and know Jesus as Lord and Savior.

The body is a living organism and cells need each other to survive. One organ cannot be independent from the others. They are all intrinsically intertwined. "For the body is one and has many members..." (I Cor. 12:14). In this revelation of the body, Paul continues that "if a member suffers, all suffer with it" (I Cor. 12:26). If a member sins, it is as if all the members had sinned. If one member resists temptation and is victorious, his victory is shared by all.

This explains why we have to deal not only with an individual sin, but also with corporate sin.

Corporate Sin

I am part of a country called Brazil. One day I had to ask forgiveness for my country. A Colombian woman confronted me saying that Brazil was an exporter of explicit and brazen sex through music and soap operas. I was left silent before this accusation and I could do nothing but ask forgiveness for what Brazil has done.

We admit that, as a nation, we sin through our idolatry, witchcraft, "sexolatry," corruption, juvenile prostitution, poor quality of education, the endemic health situation, poverty and misery in certain regions of Brazil. I think I can affirm, without fear of being mistaken, that these are corporate sins of the nation of Brazil. Even if you and I, individually, have not committed sins of that nature, nevertheless as citizens of that nation we are part of those acts they practice, and we must repent as representatives of our country.

Examples of Corporate Sin in the Old Testament.

There are innumerable cases of corporate sins found in the Old Testament. We are going to analyze a few of them.

"I will set my face against that man and I will cut him off from his people; because he hath given of his seed unto Molech, to defile my sanctuary and to profane my holy name" (Lev. 20:3). God connects His people to the "sanctuary" in the context of the abominable sins. The idea is that, because of these abominable sins, all the people were contaminated, and even the place of God's habitation was contaminated.

The language used is evidence that we do not live an individual life of faith. We are indeed connected one to another. There is a corporate solidarity, in the sense of family, ancestors, peoples and nations. So, God does not just speak to us individually when He refers to commandments, promises, blessings, judgments, and prophecies. He is speaking to a people collectively, giving them a corporate responsibility. His language is almost always plural: "If ye walk in my statutes...then I will give you rain in due season..." (Lev. 26:3-4).

Achan's sin is another instance in which a sin was committed by an individual, but God considered it a corporate sin of the people collectively. This sin brought judgment upon the people of God. "But the children of Israel committed a trespass...for Achan...took the accursed thing and the anger of the Lord was kindled against the children of Israel" (Josh. 7:1).

The leaders of the people (especially Joshua) did not know what had happened. They waged war against Ai, believing that the city was relatively easy to conquer. They sent only 3,000 men. But the army of Israel, along with its great commander, was defeated (Josh. 7:5). When Joshua asked God why his army was humiliated by so weak an enemy, God's reply was, "Israel hath sinned...for they have even taken of the accursed thing..." (Josh. 7:11). Achan (one man alone) sinned, and his sin was considered corporate; thus he brought defeat to the entire people. The consequence of the sin did not only reach him but the whole nation.

Other examples of repentance from corporate sin are seen in leaders who take before God the sins of their forefathers to confess them. Nehemiah, Ezra and Daniel modeled corporate repentance. As part of the promises of blessing and cursing, God had told Moses that if the people did not carry out His commandments, both they and the king would be taken to a distant land and forced to worship gods of wood and rock (see Deut. 28:36).

Nehemiah's ancestors disobeyed God's commandments; thus fulfilling this prophecy, they created a situation which pushed God to raise up alien nations to conquer and take Israel into exile. Nehemiah, a prophet of God, was among the captives living in Susa.

When he heard that the people returning from captivity to the promised land were living in a miserable condition, that the city walls had not been rebuilt, and that there was no resemblance to the city's previous glory, he spent days in anguish and depression. He wailed and suffered for the fate of his people and the condition of the city. In his anguish, Nehemiah prayed and confessed before God, taking upon himself the corporate sins of his ancestors. "...I pray before thee now...and confess the sins of the children of Israel, which we have sinned against thee" (Neh. 1:6).

Daniel was another person who confessed corporate sins while in exile. Daniel had been taken to Babylon to serve Nebuchadnezzar, Darius and others. He lived a blameless life and prayed daily. When he read in the book of Jeremiah that the times of captivity were about to end, he began to intercede asking for the forgiveness of the sins of his ancestors. "We have sinned, and have committed iniquity and have done wickedly, and have rebelled..." (Dan. 9:5).

We can see in the text that the corporate sins refer to the iniquities of ancestors as well as to current sins that are committed by the collective people as a whole.

An Example of Corporate Sin in the New Testament

The apostle Paul declares that the gathering of the believers is the Body of Christ. We see that Paul also considered that the sins of individuals became problems for the entire fellowship of believers. When Paul wrote to the Corinthians about a man who sinned with his father's wife, he said, "It is reported commonly that there is fornication among you...ye are puffed up, and have not rather mourned..." (I Cor. 5:1-2).

A Case of Corporate Sin

I met John (fictitious name) a few years ago. He was part of a group of college believers who witnessed for Christ and evangelized people at the university. This group was excited. They felt the power of prayer and intercession over their fellow students who did not know Jesus. They saw students convert to the Lord. Through this same group, John had been led to Jesus out of Marxism.

He noticed that when there was unity among the group of believers, the Holy Spirit moved freely and the message they preached had sufficient authority to convict of sin, judgment and righteousness. But when there was sin and unresolved conflicts, he realized that the testimony was weakened and did not have a powerful effect.

The state of the church in his homeland was most striking to him. When he went back to visit, he was shocked to discover that the church his parents attended did not have the same enthusiasm as his group at the university experienced. John discovered that no one had come to the Lord for years in this church. He noted that exactly eleven years ago, the wives of two elders had had a quarrel and had not talked to each other since. Sunday after Sunday, they would attend the worship service but not talk to each other.
John connected these two examples and received revelation on the power of unity. The sin of the two women had become the sin of the fellowship, thus destroying the spiritual vitality and weakening the authority of their testimony about Christ.

Reciprocity in the Body

Paul frequently uses the phrase "one another" to teach reciprocity in church life. He shows us that we need each other and that a healthy spiritual life depends on our relationships within the Body of Christ. Like it or not, both our attitude of commitment and reliance on the Lord, as well as our negative attitudes of sin in interpersonal relationships, will affect the entire body (see Rom. 15:5; I Cor. 12:25; Gal. 6:2; I Pet. 1:22).

Dynamics of Corporate Sin

What happens when the pastor sins? When ministering at various churches in many cities, we have noticed that it is fundamental for the leaders and pastors of the church to live a faithful and righteous life.
When one notices widespread, repetitive behavioral problems in the congregation, such as difficulties between couples, financial problems, etc., the cause frequently lies in the church's leadership. A whole church can be affected by the sin of its leaders. It is corporate sin that must be faced.
If a leader acts dishonestly, robs, envies or plagiarizes the works of other authors, his own people will do the same, repeating the sin committed by the leader. What happens when the leaders, a group of elders or the whole group of ushers, are in sin, entangled in lying, thefts or corruption?
Depending on how important their position of authority is to the congregation, the same pattern of behavior will influence the rest of the church. In this case there will certainly be a transfer of spirits. What happens when a person in the congregation is in sin? When one sins, the whole body is affected by that sin; this is the principle of corporate sin. The weight of the sin of the leaders, the pastor or an individual sheep are all different. Nevertheless, the sin of a simple member will have an influence of its own,

although small. The leaders must always stand in the gap for the weaker ones and new believers by asking forgiveness of their sins. This is similar to Job's daily prayers of intercession for his children.

What does the Bible say about the body, the Church? As we have seen, it says that when one suffers, everyone suffers as well. When someone sins, the consequence of the sin will somehow influence everyone to suffer to some extent. Sin opens a door for the devil (Eph. 4:25-30). Both the sins of the individual and corporate sins give demons room to act.

I once attended a home cell in a congregation that was faring well. It was a typical group, with many youngsters and young newlyweds. They emphasized prayer and intercession; they were dynamic in their testimony to reach their community. Later I longed to see them again; I expected to find the same maturity, devotion and enthusiasm to reach unbelievers. I was shocked to discover that this previously healthy group was now very negative. Something went wrong. In a private conversation with the leaders, the Spirit moved me to ask, "What is wrong with the group? Do you know if a leader is in sin?" The answer I received was, "Yes! A young couple, part of the group, are living together." It was the sin of this couple that was becoming heavy and taking away the vitality of the group.

Later on, I had an opportunity to talk about the privilege of serving God. I mentioned that God is not limited to using a special group to do His work. If a group does not commit to God's standards, He can pass the anointing and calling along to another group. When I spoke to the group about the seriousness of sin, the people cried and confessed. Through pastoral care, confession and shunning of their previous sins, that group became healthy once more.

It is very sad that many who call themselves Jesus' disciples do not accept that a congregation can be influenced by evil spirits or that a church might open the door to demonic attack. We believe this occurs, based on both the Old and New Testaments and in Jesus' own words. In the book of Revelation, the Lord addresses a church who tolerated a woman with the spirit of Jezebel; He also addresses a church who permits Balaam's doctrine. The churches had allowed demonic infiltration. The apostle Paul teaches that the Church will need to resist seducing spirits and doctrines of devils (I Tim. 4:1). The apostle John warns us to test the spirits trying to deceive the Church (I Jn. 4:1-4).

The Soul of a Church

We know that, in a certain sense, cities have a soul that characterizes the overall behavior of its residents. Likewise, the church has a soul. In a manner,

the soul is molded by the attitude and conduct of its members, for good or evil. The church will be either well oriented by the Holy Ghost or afflicted by the powers and principalities of the city.
Robert Linthicum, in his book, City of God, City of Satan, writes, "each unity of a society is kept and directed by its protecting angel. Because of that, the letters in the book of Revelation are sent to the angels of the cities in Asia Minor and not to the cities themselves (Rev. 2, 3). Linthicum further describes the "soul" of a church. To illustrate it, he tells the story of one congregation: ¨I was part of a group of elders and was responsible for sorting out church difficulties. One of them was a congregation downtown, which has been great and prestigious but which was going through a difficult time. Its problems were greater than a decline in the number of members or the amount of offerings it received. For three generations, this church had rapidly changed pastors; some of them had been talented and successful in previous ministries.
¨I began to work with that congregation when it seemed ready to destroy one more pastor. I started to meet with leaders and review with them the story of the church. The problems had begun fifty years before…A leader said, `You know, we always blame our pastors for our problems. But it may not be always the pastor's fault. It's as if someone within us were always looking for a scapegoat.`…We do not know exactly what happened fifty years before, but something went wrong that began to feed on the church's soul, slowly diminishing its power, slowly becoming more demonic. In a particular manner, the transgression of the church's fathers seemed to be visiting its spiritual children in the third and fourth generation. They were trapped in a destructive cycle that could not be broken. It really was like there was `someone within us.` Not being acknowledged or expelled, it oppressed generation after generation of pastors and the congregation, until it finally destroyed that church.4

A Divided Church with a Divided Soul

One day a pastor asked me, "Why does my church not grow?" He had been transferred to that church and city shortly before. He had left a prosperous church to be appointed pastor at this new one. He told me, "My current church was founded 65 years ago and we have 25 members; why is this so?" I asked, "What is the story of that church? How did it start?" He replied, "It started as the result of a division." To make a long story short, the church had had a long history of conflict among pastors. It was a church with a divided soul.
I have heard the phrase, "The Brazilian church grows based on divisions." In

fact, we have seen fragmented churches everywhere. It is extremely difficult in some towns to unite the Body of Christ, because there is resentment between the pastors because of all the strife, conflict and divisions among them. Naturally, there are various reasons for division, ranging from rebellion to leadership conflicts. Subsequent groups repeat the same story in terms of behavior, sin, rebellion, criticism and cursing. The "soul" of the daughter church reflects the soul of the mother church because it was never healed.

The Purification of the Church

If I had to tell all my stories about the situation of the church, I would need to write book after book. I have seen the church of Christ with torn clothes. In several places the church seems to be terribly ill. It seems to be going through a rather delicate moment; it seems to be midnight. We will see clearly by dawn. But the darkness of night is also the preamble to a morning, to the dawn of a new day. I see here and there many signs of revival in Christ's Church.

While I was in Peru in 1996, a Chilean girl talked to me saying, "I had a vision of a bride." I was interested, although I initially thought that I would be given the same vision of a dirty and drunk bride with torn clothes that I had been told about before. I was surprised to hear that this bride was lovely, wonderful, splendid, glorious, worthy of her groom Jesus Christ. She told me that she had seen a very detailed bride; her face, hands, dress, hair ornaments and clothes were made of people, all of them sanctified.

Jesus Christ, the groom, is preparing a bride for Himself. In fact, Jesus Christ is committed to sanctifying the Church. He will purify her by the cleansing of the Word; Jesus Christ, the groom, will make her glorious, spotless, without wrinkle, holy and blameless (Eph. 5:25-27). We should cooperate with the groom and with the Holy Ghost, who glorifies Jesus. The message of Jesus to the angels of the seven churches in Revelation is: "Remember therefore from whence thou are fallen, and repent, and do the first works. . ." (Rev. 2:5). The Bible's recommendation is for us to repent; if we are convinced that there is corporate sin, we must always begin with ourselves. By learning the Church's condition, we are led into deep sorrow which produces within us repentance by the Holy Ghost (2 Cor. 7:10).

How Can we Diagnose our Condition?

We must seek God to properly diagnose our condition. We need to pray and fast, being contrite before God, asking him to show us through his Spirit of revelation. Along with prayer, we must research the history of the church.

Here are some questions we need to ask: Who founded it? What motivated them? Were there any difficulties in its foundation? Any participation in freemasonry or any other type of compromise with darkness? Was there any division or transfer of spirits? We must also search and identify corporate sins, either the church's or its members', especially pastors' and previous leaders'. We must look for common, repetitive behavior patterns, which are indicators of unconfessed sins; we must also identify the problems that the church and its leaders have undergone.

Finally, through spiritual mapping, we must analyze the church's context, determining the principalities and powers that act strongly in the region and which might be trying to oppress the church. Always assess where the gaps are that the principalities and powers might find to influence the church.

How to be Healed

I am impressed by the stories in the history of God´s people. God brings restoration, forgiveness and healing wherever there is an open heart. He has promised, "If my people, which are called by my name, shall humble themselves, and pray, and seek my face, and turn from their wicked ways; then will I hear from heaven, and will forgive their sin, and will heal their land" (2 Chron. 7:14).

We must always remember that Jesus took our guilt and redeemed us through his death (Col. 2:14-15). Also, repentance and confession of sins to one another are required for healing (Jas. 5:16; I Jn. 1:9). Based upon personal experience ministering at seminars on spiritual warfare, we can indicate several steps to reach true healing in our churches.

For example: A person who represents the church must repent. Even if the person who is standing in the gap asking for forgiveness did not commit the sin, the person will represent the church and those whose sin has been detected. It is ideal for this to be done by the leaders, such as pastors, governing boards or elders; it is best if the entire congregation participates as well in this time of repentance.

There must be repentance and confession of sins; if there were divisions, quarrels, strife, dissension, there must be a time of reconciliation, restitution and mutual confession, asking for forgiveness and releasing it. There must be reconciliation between people. If there were any words of cursing, these must be revoked and cancelled; if there were any divisions, the brothers and sisters must be forgiven and blessed.

Finally, the evil spirits that were coming against the church must be named, bound and expelled and forbidden to return. The temple must be consecrated to the Lord again, asking everything to be purified by the blood of the Lamb.

One Final Word

We must remember that the Church lives in a spiritual dimension; like her members, she also suffers the consequence of sins and can be enslaved by them. Therefore, it is necessary to constantly watch and seek holiness. The following verse may be applied both at an individual and collective level. "And above all things have fervent love for one another, for love will cover a multitude of sins" (1 Pet. 4:8, NKJV).

Given that we are prone to sin, we must constantly confess corporate sins. Leaders in particular must always stand in the gap, praying for forgiveness; they must cry out for forgiveness of the city and region, forbidding principalities and powers in the region to oppress the church. They must order them to release the captives.

The next important and fundamental step is to establish reconciliation and to obtain forgiveness. Churches that are the fruit of divisions must seek reconciliation with their mother church. We cannot forget restitution. If any buildings, furniture or any other items were stolen, they must be returned to their rightful owner. We must stay in God's presence, seeking His Word and His power; we must not have the Word without the power, and not have the power without the Word.

We must always lead everyone in our churches into the fullness of the Spirit. We must acknowledge the gifts within the body and release them, while watching for any spirits of deceit. Pastors in particular, must be accountable and have a leader to guide them spiritually. They must choose people with whom they can pray and confess their sins, and remain constantly in prayer (Rev. 3:14,19).

The testimonies I have seen of transformation in the church are evidence that God wants to prepare the bride, not only individually but also corporately. He wants, as we do, to see her sanctified, without spot or wrinkle, full of glory, splendid, worthy of the groom, Jesus Christ!

CHAPTER 8

PLUNDERING THE GOODS OF DIANA OF THE EPHESIANS

C. Peter Wagner

Dr. C. Peter Wagner is cofounder of the World Prayer Center in Colorado Springs, Colorado, and coordinator of the United Prayer Track of the A.D. 2000 and Beyond Movement. He is also a professor at Fuller Theological Seminary. He is the author/editor of more than 40 books.

On a Personal Note...

What we know today as the united prayer movement surely wouldn't exist if it weren't for Dr. Peter Wagner's leadership. It is not an exaggeration to say that he is the one who has provided us with the terminology we use today with ease. Time after time he has put himself in a difficult position in order to promote a concept he believes in, risking criticism in the process.

Peter has a gift from God to recognize the times and seasons of the Holy Spirit. He also has the talent to organize those ideas and concepts so the Church can optimize them for the glory of God.

We have had many experiences with Peter and his loving wife, Doris, but one of the most memorable ones was the day we were involved in an accident together. My wife, Cecilia, was five months pregnant when the plane we were flying in with the Wagners had to make an emergency landing because the landing gear wouldn't operate. Not only were we unharmed, but God's hand was so evident and powerful over us that (even though it sounds ridiculous to say so) we were almost unaware of the accident! It was not until we were out of the plane, and saw it half destroyed that we understood what happened.

The spiritual lesson came later. The Wagners' intercessors in the United States had felt the need to strengthen their prayers, because the Spirit was showing them something was going to happen. That day I understood the value of having intercessors. It was one of the practical lessons, among many, I have learned from Peter and Doris.

I do not have adequate words to describe how special this couple has been to us. I think you will be blessed by this chapter and that we will stand up as one to overthrow the power called the "queen of heaven."

Harold Caballeros

On the assumption that the Apostle Paul did not have a divine nature, as did Jesus, I am going to suggest that not everything he did in his career was equally successful. I am supposing that Paul, as a human being, made his share of mistakes and suffered the resultant setbacks. The main subject of this chapter is Paul's greatest missionary and evangelistic success, namely his ministry in Ephesus and the surrounding Asia Minor. Before I get to that, however, I also want to look into his greatest evangelistic failure, namely Athens. Both of these, in my opinion, are related to strategic-level spiritual warfare.

ATHENS: AN IMPREGNABLE ENEMY STRONGHOLD

After Paul left Philippi where he battled the Python Spirit (Acts 16:16), he and his missionary team had outstanding success in planting churches in Thessalonica and Berea. Then Paul, apparently contrary to their original plans, had to flee from Berea and he ended up in Athens, leaving Silas and Timothy behind.

Making the best of the situation, Paul energetically attempted to evangelize Athens, but with notably scant success. Luke seems to be scraping the bottom of the barrel when he finishes the story in Acts 17 by saying, "However, some men joined him and believed, among them Dionysius the Areopagite, a woman named Damaris, and others with them" (v. 34). A Christian church in Athens is never mentioned in Scripture.

How could this be? What were the variables? My hypothesis is that the territorial spirits assigned to the city of Athens were so powerful and so deeply entrenched that Paul was not able to overcome them. The strongholds that had furnished them the right to rule the city for centuries were awesome, at the time virtually impenetrable.

A City Given Over to Idols

The only place in the Bible where we find the phrase "given over to idols" (from the Greek kateidolos) is where Luke describes Athens in Acts 17:16. Athens was the idol capital of the ancient world. The literature of that day describes Athens as a forest of idols in which it is easier to find a god than a human being. One observer estimated that Athens contained more idols than the rest of Greece combined!

Because idols themselves are only made of wood or stone or metal, some are not concerned about their presence. These idols, however, were not just any piece of wood, stone or metal. They had been carefully and intentionally crafted by human beings as forms in the visible world through which the forces of the invisible world of darkness were invited to control the lives of people, families and the city as a whole, locking the people in spiritual darkness. That's why we read that Paul's "spirit was provoked within him" (v. 16). He knew that behind the thick cloud of evil over the city were conscious decisions that had been made, in the past and in the present, by human beings in rebellion against God.

Day by day the people of Athens were living their beliefs in the worship of idols, petitions to specific demonic spirits, sacrifices of all kinds and eight major, plus many other minor, public festivals to honor the highest ranking of the territorial spirits of the city. George Otis Jr. warns us about such festivals: "These celebrations are decidedly not the benign, quaint and colorful cultural spectacles they are often made out to be. They are conscious transactions with the spirit world. They are opportunities for contemporary generations to reaffirm the choices and pacts made by their forefathers and ancestors. They are occasions to dust off ancient welcome mats and extend the devil's right to rule over specific peoples and places today."[5]

Little wonder Paul had more than his share of problems trying to move the people of Athens from darkness to light and from the power of Satan to God, as was his heart's desire. Then a funny thing happened to Paul in Athens. He deviated from his tried-and-true evangelistic strategy of building the nucleus of the new church primarily with converted Gentile God-fearers who had been attending the synagogues, and then reaching out to win Gentiles at large through them. Instead, Paul himself decided to go out to the marketplace and the Areopagus and face the Gentile philosophers who had called him a "babbler" (Acts 17:18). Why Paul accepted their challenge to do this is not clear, but it is not beyond reason to suspect that some sort of powerful and perverse spiritual influence might have been at work. The result? He presented a sermon widely regarded as among his most brilliant discourses, but at the same time among his most ineffective.

What was the end result of Paul's experience in Athens? In The Message, Eugene Peterson translates Acts 17:32, "Some laughed at him and walked off making jokes." For Paul it was not a good day.

EPHESUS: AN ABUNDANT HARVEST

In Ephesus, by contrast, Paul not only had a good day, but many of them. There he took a different approach. Things changed considerably when Paul left Athens for his next stop: Corinth.

From Human Wisdom to the Power of God

As Paul reflected on his time in Athens, it became clearer to him that brilliant and true words, unaccompanied by the deeds that demonstrate openly the power of God, can be of little avail. After arriving in Corinth, he was ready to say, "And my speech and my preaching were not with persuasive words of human wisdom, but in demonstration of the Spirit and of power, that your faith should not be in wisdom of men but in the power of God" (1 Cor. 2:4,5, emphasis mine).

In Athens the word overshadowed the deed, but in Corinth the deeds of supernatural power supported and confirmed the word. In Athens Paul saw little fruit, but his evangelistic ministry in Corinth produced a great harvest of souls.

Paul had made an attempt to go to Ephesus years before he actually arrived there. Luke tells us that he and his missionary team did not go there at that time because

they were forbidden by the Holy Spirit to preach the word in Asia" (Acts 16:6). I believe a major reason they were not permitted to go to Ephesus was that they were not yet ready. Paul's defeat in Athens and his reassessment of priorities in Corinth was a major and necessary learning experience prior to Ephesus. So was his high-level power encounter with the Python Spirit in Philippi.

Paul and his team spent almost three years in Ephesus, much longer than usual, because the harvest was abundant. House churches, which were where Christians met for worship in those days, multiplied throughout the city and into its suburbs. Paul trained church planters, sending them out to evangelize other cities in Asia Minor. In summary, Luke says things such as, "So the word of the Lord grew mightily and prevailed" (19:20), and "all who dwelt in Asia heard the word of the Lord Jesus, both Jews and Greeks"(v. 10). As well, Paul's enemies were admitting "that not only at Ephesus, but throughout almost all Asia, this Paul has persuaded and turned away people (from worshiping Diana)" (v. 26).

Never before or after did Paul have an experience that matched the success of this ministry in Ephesus. This is what missionary work was all about. Paul had laid such a good foundation that vigorous church growth continued for a long time after he left. F.F. Bruce says, "The province [of Asia Minor] was intensely evangelized and remained one of the leading centers of Christianity for many centuries."6

Perhaps the strongholds of darkness in Ephesus were not as formidable as they were in Athens nothing we know of would equal Athens but they were not far from it. The major key to opening Ephesus and Asia Minor to the Gospel was not brilliant preaching or persuasive words of human wisdom, but spiritual warfare on all levels, including strategic-level spiritual warfare. Paul's experience in Ephesus caused him to write back to the believers there, saying, "For we do not wrestle against flesh and blood, but against the rulers of the darkness of this age, against spiritual hosts of wickedness in the heavenly places" (Eph. 6:12). Clinton Arnold, a Biola University scholar and a specialist on Ephesians, says that the Epistle to the Ephesians contains a "substantially higher concentration of power terminology than in any other epistle attributed to Paul."[7] Powerful action in "the heavenly places," or in the invisible world, prepared the way for the spread of the Word of God in the visible world.

Paul wrote I Corinthians while he was in Ephesus. Something he said there could be interpreted as referring to his strategic-level spiritual warfare in Ephesus. Paul said to the Corinthians, "If, in the manner of men, I have fought with beasts at Ephesus" (15:32). What does he mean by "beasts"? Were they literal beasts as in the coliseum in Rome? F.F. Bruce thinks we should take Paul's language figuratively, not literally,[8] and I would agree. Some commentators suggest that he might be referring to human opponents. That could be, but I think it is more likely that Paul was referring to fighting in "the heavenly places" because he clearly said that the battle is not against flesh and blood. If so, the "beasts" could well be territorial spirits or strongmen whom Paul had bound, thus clearing the spiritual environment for extraordinary church growth.

What, exactly, were the spiritual forces facing Paul in Ephesus? It was a large city, the fourth largest in the Roman Empire. According to Bruce Metzger, Ephesus was the magic capital of the whole ancient world. He says, "Of all ancient Graeco-Roman cities, Ephesus...was by far the most hospitable to magicians, sorcerers, and charlatans of all sorts."[9] As such, it is not surprising that Ephesus was a major producer of fetishes, which were key tools of the forces of darkness in almost all animistic societies. The silversmiths of Ephesus had developed a lucrative business in the manufacture and sale of fetishes. The so-called "Ephesian writings" were known throughout the Roman Empire. F.F. Bruce comments, "The phrase 'Ephesian writings' was commonly used in antiquity for documents containing spells and formulae...to be placed in small cylinders or lockets worn around the neck or elsewhere about the person."[10]

Diana Was Supreme

Supernatural powers of darkness were rampant in Ephesus when Paul arrived. He did not have to be an expert in spiritual mapping to discover that the highest-ranking spirit of all was Diana, sometimes called Artemis, of the Ephesians. Diana was extraordinarily well known not only in Asia Minor, but throughout the whole Roman Empire as well. The silversmiths who sold fetishes made in Diana's image used extravagantly blasphemous language when referring to her: "the great goddess," "her magnificence," "all Asia and the world worship (her)" (Acts 19:27). Their shout was, "Great is Diana of the Ephesians!" (v. 28). In other literature she was exalted as "greatest," "holiest," "most manifest," "Lady," "Savior," and "Queen of the Cosmos."[11] In the mind of anyone familiar with the operations of the kingdom of Satan, there could be little doubt that not only was Diana of the Ephesians a territorial spirit over the City of Ephesus and Asia Minor, but that her evil power exceeded that of most as well. Her influence had extended well beyond those boundaries. F.F. Bruce quotes a source indicating that she was worshiped in at least 33 places within the Roman Empire.[12] Diana was actually ruling her territory before the Greeks arrived. They gave her the name "Artemis," but that is not a Greek name. Her image is not a typical work of elegant Greek art, but a grotesque, many-breasted pagan idol of Asia. Clinton Arnold has discovered that Diana was "the only divinity to depict visibly her divine superiority with the signs of the zodiac."[13]

Paul, well experienced by now in evangelism, church planting and spiritual warfare on all levels, is ready to take on the fortress of Diana. He must have been stunned when he first saw Diana's temple, one of the most beautiful pieces of architecture in history. It was later classified as one of the Seven Wonders of the Ancient World. Its 93,500 square feet was four times the size of the Parthenon in Athens. Each of its 127, 60-foot-high columns had been donated by a different king, another indication of Diana's widespread influence. Its position in the visible world was evident to all, and its awesome standing as a power center in the invisible world was recognized by any who had eyes to see that dimension of reality.

LEVELS OF SPIRITUAL WARFARE IN EPHESUS

As far as we know from Luke's account in Acts, in Ephesus, Paul overtly engaged in spiritual warfare on the ground level and on the occult level, but not on the strategic level. He was falsely accused of provoking strategic-level encounters when the rioting silversmiths and others falsely testified that he had gone into the temple of Diana and insulted the spirit herself. The judgment of the political authority hearing the case was that Paul and his team "are neither robbers of temples nor blasphemers of your goddess" (Acts 19:37). We can surmise, then, that Paul did not have a head-on encounter with Diana in Ephesus, as he did with Python in Philippi.

Ground-Level Warfare

Luke's account in Acts 19 of doing ground-level spiritual warfare, that is, casting demons out of people, contains two parts: how to do it and how not to do it. He uses Paul as the example of how to do it, and he uses the seven sons of Sceva as examples of how not to do it.

One of the unusual events in Ephesus was that demons were expelled by carrying handkerchiefs or articles of clothing that Paul had physically touched and laying them on the demonized person (see Acts 19:11,12). Other than the story of the Python spirit in Philippi, this is the only other instance Luke gives us of Paul doing deliverance. I have already commented that this should by no means be taken to imply that deliverance was only a minor feature in Paul's career or that he didn't cast out demons regularly. It is noteworthy that Luke would attach one of his rare mentions of it to the use of objects, such as handkerchiefs.

We see here that Paul used healing cloths to a positive effect. In casting out demons with handkerchiefs, Paul wasn't doing magic, he was instead launching a frontal attack on the spiritual forces empowering the magic capital of the Roman Empire. The supernatural power operating through Paul was not the power of the demonic world on which magicians have drawn throughout history, but it was the power of the true God who had commissioned His emissaries to "Heal the sick, cleanse the lepers, raise the dead, cast out demons" (Matt. 10:8).

Occult-Level Spiritual Warfare

In Ephesus, perhaps more than most places, spiritual warfare at any level would necessarily have something to do with magicians. Occult-level spiritual warfare, by definition, involves such practitioners. Some of the most notable conversions in Ephesus occurred among magicians. The account has the characteristics of a people movement, especially considering the communal decision to burn magical books and other paraphernalia publicly. The magnitude of the bonfire is often overlooked because the phrase "fifty thousand pieces of silver" (Acts 19:19) does not register with most of us. The maximum value we might instinctively put on it would be $50,000 on the assumption they were silver dollars. Once we recognize that in those days a piece of silver was a day's wage and do some calculations, suddenly the value of the articles burned rises to around $4 million!

What prepared the way for such a massive prophetic act and public declaration of the lordship of Jesus Christ? Many things, but probably the major factor was the encounter with the seven sons of Sceva.

These Jewish exorcists practiced real magic and, like most magicians, they were always looking for more power. As they observed Paul, they noticed that he used what they interpreted to be a magic formula-"in the name of Jesus." The results were something they had never seen before, so they were interested. They tested the formula by approaching some demonized people, addressing the evil spirits and saying, "We exorcise you by the Jesus whom Paul preaches" (v. 13). Big mistake!

The sons of Sceva used the name of Jesus, but without previously having received authorization from Jesus to use it. The first ones who recognized their stupidity were the spirits themselves. One of them mocked them and said, "Jesus I know and Paul I know, but who are you?" (v. 15). A demonized man then jumped on the seven sons of Sceva, ripped off their clothes and chased them out of the house naked!

Interconnecting the Spirit World

Better than any other passage of Scripture, Acts 19 shows us clearly how the world of darkness is interconnected, overriding the somewhat artificial lines some of us have drawn separating ground-level, occult-level and strategic-level spiritual warfare. Casting out demons with handkerchiefs strongly influenced the people movement among Ephesian magicians, as did the foolish arrogance of the seven exorcists in Sceva's household. Both of these had their influence on the power of Diana of the Ephesians. Without overtly confronting Diana herself, Paul and the missionaries had weakened her authority so much that the silversmiths and others rioted. They, along with the general population of Ephesus, were alarmed that Diana's temple could be despised and her magnificence was being destroyed (see v. 27). Diana had been so powerful that many people thought the very fabric of their lives might be ripped apart if she were harmed.

The result was that the kingdom of God came to Ephesus and the surrounding area of Asia Minor in a more widespread and more notable way than any other place in which Paul had ministered. The strongman, in this case strong woman, had been bound, the spiritual blinders were removed from the multitudes, souls were saved, churches multiplied and Ephesus became a long-term center of gravity for the whole Christian movement.

THE DEFEAT OF MAXIMON

So as not to relegate such a spiritual victory as Paul had in Ephesus to some faded pages of yesteryear, let me relate a similar event I personally have witnessed. I have in my hand a copy of the Guatemalan equivalent to Time or Newsweek: Cronica Semanal (June 24-30, 1994). The cover story carries the headline, "The Defeat of Maximon: Protestant Fundamentalism Alters the Culture of the Altiplano and Turns the Native Religions into Tourist Attractions." Maximon was a territorial spirit similar to Diana, and he also was defeated essentially through ground-level spiritual warfare.

The small city of Almolonga is a three-hour drive over beautiful mountains west of Guatemala City. The population of 18,000, almost all Quiché Indians, are descendants of the vast Mayan Empire. Almolonga is known as the garden city of Central America, growing and marketing fresh vegetables from Mexico to Panama.

A central characteristic of the city, which is built on the hills overlooking a rich valley, is 17 evangelical churches. They are the most prominent features of the urban landscape. All of them are alive and well and relatively large. At least 80 percent of the people of Almolonga are born-again Christians.

It was not always like this. Prior to the late 1970s, Almolonga was little different from neighboring cities such as Olintepeque and Zunil. It was characterized by misery, poverty, immorality, corruption, violence, dissension, and disease. Men would typically receive their pay on Friday, spend it on drunken orgies and return home to distressed wives and children on Monday. According to one observer, "Drunks were laid out in the streets like cordwood." Many never awoke from their stupors.

The Gospel came to Almolonga in 1951. Three churches were planted, but made virtually no headway. Their spiritual power was minimal, and the community remained under the control of the god of this age. Then a pagan named Mariano Riscajché was saved in 1974, hearing a voice from God, as did Paul, on the day of his conversion, saying, "I have chosen you to serve Me." Soon afterward a sick and demonized man asked Mariano to pray for him and he was miraculously healed and delivered.

Deliverance from Demons

The word got out, more sick came and many were also healed. Churches began to grow. The opposition to evangelicals then intensified and the unbelieving merchants would not sell food to the Christians. The spiritual battle was on full force. In 1975 Mariano received a new filling of the Holy Spirit, began large-scale deliverance and soon had freed more than 400 people who had been held captive by demons in Almolonga. The spiritual atmosphere of Almolonga began to change radically.

Almost immediately the physical and social atmosphere of the community began to change also. Barrooms closed down. Restaurants and stores and businesses now carry biblical names such as "Bethany" and "Jerusalem" and "Shalom." Almolonga has become a city of entrepreneurs who purchase Mercedes trucks, paying cash, to deliver their vegetables on international routes. Families are together and happy. Schools are thriving. Mariano Riscajché has recently completed an elegant sanctuary accommodating 2,000 right next to the central plaza of the city.

Doris and I traveled to Almolonga in 1992 with our friends Harold and Cecilia Caballeros of the El Shaddai Church in Guatemala City. We had heard that the territorial spirit over the whole area was a notorious demon named Maximon. We wanted to see Almolonga, where his power had been broken, and also neighboring Zunil where a shrine housed the revolting idol that represented the principality.

Maximon did not want us to invade his territory. The private airplane we had chartered crashed on landing when the landing gear did not come down as the pilot thought it had. We thought we were goners, but God protected us from serious harm. An intercessor who was on the ground waiting for us to land reported he had been told by the Holy Spirit that Maximon was about to attack us, and he had been praying fervently for our protection. The plane was split open and mangled, so we had to take a bus back to Guatemala City. The shrine of Maximon had to be the threshold of hell itself. Five warlocks and one witch were hard at work when we paid our brief visit, invoking the activities of dark angels. It was the most revolting spiritual activity I ever want to see, and I do not care to record any more of the hideous details. Have these beings really come to steal, to kill and to destroy? In Zunil, disease, hunger, drunkenness, accidents, poverty, immorality and violence are part and parcel of daily life. Recent natural disasters have torn the town apart, but Almolonga, only 3 kilometers away, has remained unscathed. Maximon was in his glory in Zunil.

Maximon was on the retreat, however, and still is. The report of the Cronica Semanal cover story tells of a city such as Zunil, formerly under Maximon's perverse power, and it says, "The cult of Maximon and its followers has been reduced to a mere handful of individuals, and, due to his downfall, the men of the city no longer drink liquor because of their evangelical faith and therefore the annual festival to the idol...is now financed only by money collected from sightseeing tours of Japanese, Germans and Americans."[14]

The territorial spirit that had Almolonga bound in spiritual captivity for centuries was well known by name. His power over Almolonga and other places had been neutralized through the power ministries of Mariano Riscajché and other servants of the Most High God. As in Ephesus, the supreme spirit of the area had lost its authority through vigorous activity on the ground level, casting out large numbers of demons from people. As a result, the physical, social, material and spiritual blessings of the kingdom of God were able totally to transform the city. This helps us understand why we must never forget that Satan's kingdom is one, and that successful spiritual warfare on any level will influence all levels to one extent or another.

SUMMARY

The invasion of the territory of Diana constitutes the final episode of strategic-level spiritual warfare I believe we find in the New Testament. In Athens Paul learned that human wisdom is not enough to penetrate a city "given over to idols." He corrected it by moving in demonstrations of supernatural power in Corinth, and especially in Ephesus. Ephesus provides for us the most vivid example in the Bible that "we do not wrestle against flesh and blood, but against principalities, against powers, against the rulers of the darkness of this age, against spiritual hosts of wickedness in the heavenly places" (Eph. 6:12). Defeating the powers on the strategic level will clear the way for the vigorous spread of the Gospel, whether in the first century or in modern times.

Excerpted from Confronting the Powers by C. Peter Wagner, Regal Books, Ventura, CA 1996. Used by permission of Regal Books and the author.

CHAPTER 9

THE ROLE OF IDENTIFICATIONAL REPENTANCE IN THE CHANGING SPIRITUAL CLIMATE OF BRITAIN

Roger Mitchell

Rev. Mitchell and his wife, Sue, have been pioneers in evangelism and church planting for more than 20 years. They were members of the senior leadership team of Ichthus Christian Fellowship in London for many years and have just launched the ministry Passion to serve the Church in England and abroad in the areas of evangelization and reconciliation.

On a Personal Note...

Since we met Roger Mitchell at the Gideon's Army meeting in Korea in 1993 we have witnessed the way God has touched him and used his life.

Many times we have proven through our experience the depth of his point of view in relation to indentificational repentance and the remitting of sins of the nations. It is easy to appreciate those who have a prophetic burden for their nation, and those whose desire is to see Christ's redemption to their people. I am completely in agreement with Roger in this field and I believe that this chapter will make many people think deeply about their own nation. I pray that God will raise up many more such as Roger Mitchell for the healing of nations.

Harold Caballeros

In 1992, one of the most strategic conferences to be held in Britain in recent years took place. Held in Birmingham under the title of *Challenge 2000*, it was inspired by the principles and vision of the DAWN movement (Disciple A Whole Nation), encouraging a living church to be provided for every 1000 people on the planet by the year 2000. The unique strategic quality lay in the agreement of senior English church leaders across over 30 denominations and streams to propose the planting of 20,000 new congregations in England alone in an eight-year period. What impressed me most was not some new programme and system, but rather the new climate of expectation and faith that could only mean revival was in the air. By anyone's definition of revival, Britain has to qualify with this bold plan to plant 20,000 new churches in 8 years in the final decade of the 20th century.

Those of us from Ichthus Christian Fellowship, one of the new church movements in England, realised midway through our journey back home from the conference that we had just agreed to attempt the planting of 2,000 new churches in eight years, 10% of the entire goal for our nation. It so happened that I had recently agreed to accept the responsibility to lead the Ichthus church-planting department. As we had just consolidated from 46 to 30 the congregations we had taken 18 years to plant, I could hardly avoid taking the situation seriously! I was sure that the extraordinary goals set at the conference were not just the result of hype but rather the presence and wisdom of the Holy Spirit. But to achieve them was going to require major new revelation. Somehow the whole spiritual climate of England was going to have to change.

Early in 1993 a small band of leaders came together to consider our responsibilities within the wider DAWN vision: how could we achieve those 2,000 church plants we had agreed to? If ever we needed divine help it was now, and so we asked the Holy Spirit for a clear prophetic word. We received one. It consisted of a simple, and at that time, unexpected, even enigmatic statement: "The sin of England is Ireland." We all agreed it was from God, but we had little understanding of what to do with it. Frankly none of us knew enough historical data for it to be obvious. We agreed, however, that a good beginning point was to say sorry to God on behalf of England. Nobody present was Irish but there were representatives of the English, the Scots and the Welsh. The Scots and the Welsh had the grace to stand with us English as we began to repent for the sins of our fathers. Each of us was overwhelmed as we began to pray and became immediately aware that we were touching an undeniable and deep reality. Trying to analyse why we were so moved, one by one the three representatives realised that each had Irish forbears, despite their current national identities. Further reflection reminded us that not only were the Irish the ancestral fathers of these three individuals, but also the spiritual fathers of English and indeed British Christianity. For while there have been heated debates about the early history of the British church, no one disputes the heavy involvement of the Irish mission in the first half of the first millennium AD. It dawned on us that any English sin against Ireland was a sin against our spiritual fathers, and that such sins were foundational to the subsequent British experience and history.

We had embarked on a road with huge and far-reaching implications for the revival and salvation of contemporary Britain. Subsequent revelation and research uncovered what the less ignorant would have already known, that Irish Catholicism and Irish Protestantism were not spontaneous spiritual movements. They were inflicted on Ireland by the English with the sword and musket (Roman Catholicism in the 12th century and Protestantism in the 17th century) as a means of gaining religious and political domination. This is in no way to claim that there was no genuine spiritual life in the two expressions of Christian faith, but that the primary initiative and purpose led to the disinheritance of the Irish and control by the English. Increasing numbers of intercessors have come to see this over the recent years that followed and taken a variety of exciting initiatives, steps and prophetic acts. Some of us began to ask the Holy Spirit for even more specific revelation of the roots of this sin against Ireland which we had increasingly seen to have provided a shape for the ongoing oppression toward brother and sister nations in the centuries that had ensued.

A group of senior British intercessors was present at the Spiritual Warfare Network "Gideon's Army" conference in Korea in late 1993 and experienced for themselves the impact of Dr. Paul Ariga of Japan confessing the sins of the Japanese people against the Koreans. The impact was so great that it allowed the Holy Spirit to change the whole direction of the conference as intercessors from nation after nation began to confess the sins of their people. It left the British shell-shocked as we realised the huge backlog of British colonial history in which we have repeatedly mixed oppression with the undoubted blessings we have brought across the nations through our missionary endeavours. We came to see that what England had done to its closest national relative - our brother nation who had also been our spiritual father - we had then exported almost everywhere, to Scotland, to Wales and then throughout the nations of empire and commonwealth. While we knew we had to face these sins one by one as the Holy Spirit indicated, we needed a specific root to cut in order to do the rest more easily.

In September 1995, the Holy Spirit gave me an extraordinarily supernatural lead. I was on a prayer retreat and praying my way through Michael Mitton's helpful book *Restoring the Woven Chord (Strands of Celtic Christianity for Today's Church)*. His references to the Bede's A History of the English Church and

People written around AD730 sparked in me a conviction that something in that history would give us the insight we needed. I promised God I would make it a priority to purchase and read the Bede's book in modern English since my Anglo-Saxon is pretty nonexistent!

Two days later I flew from the UK to Omaha, Nebraska, in the Central USA. Imagine my amazement when my host, a U.S. attorney whom I had never met previously, asked me at breakfast whether I had any interest in the history of English Christianity. On my affirmative reply, he presented me with a copy of the *Bede's A History of the English Church and People* in modern English! As you can imagine, I didn't sleep that night, and there discovered the precise details of the original meeting between the first two great missionary thrusts into England, the meeting between the Celtic and the Roman bishops. It was that discovery that led a group of Christian leaders and intercessors representing North and South, Irish and English, Roman and Celtic traditions to descend in July 1996 on the ancient parish of Cricklade. Close to the source of the Thames, Cricklade was the almost certain site of the original conference which was held in the sixth century AD. There we repented for the sins on both sides, but particularly confessed and forgave the abuse of spiritual authority and spiritual gift that Augustine and his Roman mission displayed toward the Irish-originated Celtic bishops. The story is worth taking time to recount.

Augustine, who later became the first archbishop of Canterbury, was sent from Rome in 596 by Bishop Gregory, who had seemingly no expectations of encountering the existing missionary work of the Irish mission. Nevertheless, when Gregory heard of the situation, he was quite enlightened in his approach. His view was to bind the different forms of worship and tradition into "one sheaf" and evangelise the Saxons together. The one major exception was that the Celtic bishops had to submit to his authority! When they were uncertain, Augustine went for a display of apostolic power and healed a lame man that the Celtic leaders were unable to heal. Their response was to consult a hermit who said that it was all right to submit to a humble man and suggested the test that if Augustine stood up when they entered, then he was humble. He, however, remained seated. So they declined to submit. Augustine's response was to issue a "prophetic" warning (actually a curse), saying that if they would submit to his and Gregory's authority they would succeed in evangelising the Saxons. If not, they would be killed by them. The latter scenario was fulfilled soon after when 1200 intercessors were murdered by the Saxon king while they assembled to pray as the Celts and Saxons fought in the battle of Chester.

It's not hard to see the abuse of spiritual and apostolic authority of the Roman mission despite their missionary zeal, nor hard to deduce that this attitude to authority, so different to that of the Lord and the early apostles, was part of the cultural bondage of the Roman church to the Roman empire of the day. It was this damaged and controlling attitude to authority that characterised English Christianity in the ensuing centuries and explains how the British combined the blessing of the Gospel with an oppressive and controlling spirit that even the Reformation and many subsequent spiritual movements have failed to deal with. It was this that was at the heart of our repentance that day in Cricklade.

During this process we were learning a whole new outlook and approach to the sins of our fathers. But wonderfully the Holy Spirit opened the Scriptures to us step by step and we came to see how central the theme of national sin and indentificational repentance is in both Old and New Testaments. Among the many Old Testament passages, none was more revelational than 2 Samuel 21, a story opaque to us in the past but now crystal clear to so many people in this field. (It was this passage that Dr. Peter Wagner referred to at the commencement of the Reconciliation Walk in Cologne in 1996.)

The passage begins, "Now there was a famine in the days of David for three years, year after year, and David sought the presence of the Lord. And the Lord said, It is for Saul and his bloody house, because he put the Gibeonites to death." The implications of this single verse are massive. Injustice and bloodshed carried out by past national and spiritual leaders now dead, unjust because of covenants made some 250 years before that, can cause a famine at harvest time in the present day. The rest of the story unravels how atonement can and must be made once God brings sins to light. The hanging of the seven sons of Saul, which averted the famine and brought in the harvest, can only have worked because the curse came off of the land onto them. But this in turn can only have worked because of the vicarious atonement of Jesus one thousand years later, where He took the past curses onto Himself ("Cursed is everyone who hangs on a tree" Deut. 21:23).

This corporate aspect of the atonement, its ability to deal with the judgment and sin on a whole nation, people group or city, was clearly understood and underlined by the Lord. In Luke 24:45-49 we read how, after His resurrection, He "opened their minds to understand the Scriptures and he said to them 'thus it is written, that the Christ should suffer and rise again from the dead the third day, and that repentance for forgiveness of sin should be proclaimed in his name to *all nations, beginning from Jerusalem.*'" I was somewhat shocked to discover that there is only one place in the OT from which "the Christ suffering and rising again from the dead the third day" could possibly be inferred-Hosea 6:1-3. But no exegesis of those verses can avoid the conclusion that they primarily refer to the forgiving and healing of *national* sin and only secondarily can they be properly applied to the forgiveness of the individual who personally repents.

It is impossible to avoid the exciting conclusion that Jesus died for the sins of Jerusalem, Israel, and all the nations and cities of the world. If we can find a way to repent of the corporate sins of nations today and apply the power of Jesus' atonement to them, we can lift the curse and judgment off of our towns and cities and leave a spiritual climate in which individuals can respond personally to the Gospel. Because Jesus stood in the gap for the sins of Israel, the prophetic act of hanging seven sons of Saul some 1000 years earlier worked in removing the blood guilt and curse from the land. Similarly, when we stand in the gap and repent for the sins of our fathers today, the same powerful atonement can lift the blood guilt and curse off our city and nation and can avert a famine at harvest time. This is fantastic news for us here in Britain where revival is in the air and harvest time is on us but we have been experiencing a spiritual famine. In situations like ours, we need to seek the face of the Lord and discover the past sins of our fathers' "bloody house." This is precisely what has been happening to us as God has revealed the sin of England toward Ireland and the spiritual abuse between the original founding missions of British church history.

Obviously the story does not stop there. As a result of our experiences so far, some of us have been asking the Lord which sins against which nations are particularly grievous to Him and whether there is any more recent outworking of the abuse of authority and the oppression of people that would provide the kind of focus for repentance which would unlock other outstanding situations. The analogy here would be the way that confessing specific sin or sins by an individual can unlock all the rest, as the woman at the well experienced. Jesus focused only on her adultery, but she said "come see a man who told me all things that ever I did" (John 4:29).

In the end, many of us are concluding that World War I is the most complete example of British abuse of authority and power. This, because it was the time and place where the oppression that had been directed in the past onto our brothers and fathers, was now directed toward our sons. World War I, unlike World War II (which would arguably never have happened without it) was unequivocally a war which should never have happened, and where the sons of Europe were sacrificed on the altar of the national and imperial pride of a family of brother nations. 2 Kings 3 tells of how the king of Moab brought down great wrath against the people of God by sacrificing his son in pride "on the wall" (2 Kings 3:27). Great wrath has come against Europe in this century because of the pride of the fathers and leaders of Europe in the battles of 1914-18.

Nowhere is this described more clearly than in Wilfred Owen's revelational poem, "The Parable of the Old Man and the Young," written in July 1918, just four months before he died on the Somme in the last days of the war.15 Twenty-six years of age, he was the son of an intercessor and had been at the Keswick convention at the age of nineteen in the extraordinary years of blessing following the Welsh revival.

So Abram rose, and clave the wood, and went,
And took the fire with him, and a knife.
And as they sojourned both of them together,
Isaac the first born spake and said, My Father,
Behold the preparations, fire and iron,
But where the lamb, for this burnt-offering?
Then Abram bound the youth with belts and straps,
And builded parapets and trenches there,
And stretched forth the knife to slay his son.
When lo! an Angel called him out of heaven,
Saying, Lay not thy hand upon the lad,
Neither do anything to him, thy son.
Behold! Caught in a thicket by its horns,
A Ram. Offer the Ram of Pride instead.

But the old man would not so, but slew his son,
And half the seed of Europe, one by one.

We're currently seeking the face of the Lord on ways of standing in the gap for the overwhelming blood guilt of that war in which somewhere between one in four and one in five of all men of military age in Britain died, along with some six million of the rest of Europe's sons. Even secular historians agree that the reality of that war has been defining for the subsequent history and experience of the twentieth century. On the basis of God's verdict on Cain's murder of his brother, we have to conclude that Britain and our brother European nations are "cursed from the ground" by the blood of these sons of Europe. Pray for us!

CHAPTER 10

THE AGREEMENT OF HEAVEN AND EARTH

Cindy Jacobs

Cindy Jacobs is president and co-founder of Generals of Intercession, which is a missionary organization devoted to training in the area of prayer and spiritual warfare. It is the mission of Generals to see that every unreached people group of the world (about 6,000 people groups in all) receives strategic prayer by the year 2000 in order to see them reached with the Gospel.

On a personal note...

Cindy is an International Advisor-At-Large for Women's Aglow Fellowship and serves as a member of Aglow's International Prayer Council. She is currently the coordinator for the U.S. Spiritual Warfare Network. She is the author of three books: Possessing the Gates of the Enemy (Chosen Books); The Voice of God (Regal Books); and Women of Destiny (Regal Books).

It has been a big blessing to have Mike and Cindy Jacobs as friends. God united our hearts from the moment we met. We have shared very special moments, and my wife, Cecilia, and I have come to love them very much.

When we received the text of The Agreement of Heaven and Earth, once again it was evident to me the gift God has given Cindy. In a time when prophetic intercession is needed more than ever, this chapter is a great inspiration. Personally, I believe that the time has come for a marriage between the priesthood and the prophetic. The Church is absolutely prepared to take its place of authority in Jesus Christ and "legislate in heavenly places."

Thank you, Cindy.

Harold Caballeros

"Your kingdom come, Your will be done on earth as it is in heaven" (Matt. 6:10, NKJV). This is a profound scripture from the Lord's Prayer, which most Christians not only read, but also memorize. One day while reading this verse I began to meditate on its meaning. I had always assumed that it meant that the will of God would be done on the earth as it is in heaven only after Christ's return. I don't know why I thought that was so, because obviously there are many ways that God's will is being done in the earth today; i.e., people getting born-again, etc.

Since Jesus taught His disciples to pray this prayer while He was on earth, He must have done so because part of their role in intercession was to believe that those things, which are His will in heaven, will be done on earth. I believe that this was to have happened in each generation since the time of Christ. In other words, each generation is responsible to pray for God's will to be released into the earth from heaven for their generation.

As intercessors it is important to understand our part in this role of intercession and know what to release from heaven to earth in prayer. There are also specific weapons of warfare that we have been given to cause this to happen.

First of all, how do we know what God's will on earth is? This is fundamental to coming into the agreement of heaven to earth. God's will is revealed through His Word. I like to say that it is important to not only read God's Word, but to read His world in the light of His Word. By this I mean that we are to use His Word as a plumb line for everything that happens in the earth. Part of God's Word reveals to us not only what is happening on earth, but also what is in heaven.

There are keys to fulfilling God's will on earth which can only be seen from a heavenly perspective. In fact, the Bible states that we are seated in heavenly places with Christ, (Eph. 2:6). Therefore, we are directly linked with heaven as we pray.

A strategic verse in this understanding of the link between heaven and earth in intercession is Matthew 18:18: "Truly, I tell you, whatever you forbid and declare to be improper and unlawful on earth must be what is already forbidden in heaven, and whatever you permit and declare proper and lawful on earth must be already permitted in heaven" (AMP).

In other words, whatever has already been declared unlawful in heaven should be declared unlawful on the earth, and whatever is permitted in heaven is what should be permitted in the earth.

As one studies the two words used here, "bind" and "loose", (NIV; KJV) it is important to note that these words were legal court terminology in the time of Christ. The courts of the day would pass judgment on a matter, and either rule that it was forbidden or unlawful and would bind it legally, or rule that it was loosed or permitted or lawful.

I like to refer to this type of prayer as legislating in the heavenlies. This is where we literally convene the court of heaven through our prayers; we judge something to be lawful or illegal in the earth, and declare through intercessory prayer that it will or will not be permitted.

As we look around our cities and nations today, there are many issues that we need to pass judgment on in prayer-matters such as abortion, sexual immorality, idolatry, etc. Rather than just throw up our hands and complain about how bad things are, we can actually change them through intercessory prayer.

How does one convene the court of heaven and legislate in the heavenlies? The intercessors in the Philippines have a good grasp on this concept. They used to have violent storms called typhoons that would lash their coasts each year. Utilizing the understanding that they were gate keepers for what comes in and out of their nation, they went to the weather bureau and got a list of the names given to the storms for the coming year. Then, they convened the court of heaven, legislating these storms (by name) as bound, forbidden, and illegal, declaring there would be no devastation from violent storms the following year. Guess what? There were no violent typhoons that hit the shores of their country the following year.

This principle was picked up by the intercessors in Argentina. A youth group leader and his wife, Claudio and Nidia Cabrera, found out that a satanic rock group was booked to perform in their city. They decided that they would legislate in the heavenlies and declare that that group would not pollute their city. The youth group did some binding and agreed with heaven that God's will would be done on the earth, and that particular form of unrighteousness would not come into the lives of the youth of their city. They later shared with me that the rock group members got violently sick and they were not able to hold their concert. Amazing, isn't it?

Since our perspective for this is a heavenly one, we need to understand what is happening in heaven that should be declared into the earth as the will of God. In order to do this, we need to understand the intercession of heaven.

This may sound unusual to you or it might even be an entirely new thought. However, for this portion of this chapter, we will focus on the basic understanding that there are not two bodies of Christ-there is only one. There is not one body of Christ in heaven and another that exists on earth.

For some time I have felt that one of the most important ministries that believers in heaven are taking part in is that of intercessory prayer. Prayer is eternal. It is not limited to earth. This is

patterned after Hebrews 7:25, "Therefore He is able also to save to the uttermost (completely, perfectly, finally and for all time and eternity) those who come to God through Him, since He is always living to make petition to God and intercede with Him and intervene for them" (AMP).

I believe that one of the most important jobs of the saints in heaven is intercession. If this is so, then what is the focus of their intercession? What is the Body of Christ interceding to see happen?

This links us back to the Lord's Prayer: "Your will be done on earth as it is in heaven." This year (1998) I fasted for an extended period of time. One of the things I was seeking the Lord for on a personal level was an increased measure of revelation from His Word. One day I opened my Bible to the book of Revelation and it was as if the words opened up to me in a way I had never seen before. I'd never heard them taught quite in that light. (I know that others have probably thought about these things I'm going to share, but it was a new paradigm to me.)

I want to interject an important principle that my father, who was a minister, taught me to practice as I study the Word of God: Always ask God to help you to put aside preconceived notions of what the scripture says and pray that the Holy Spirit will guide you into His truth.

Of course I am not saying that all of the things that I have learned from others are bad or erroneous. What I do mean is that there may be depths to scripture passages that we have read over and over, and the Holy Spirit wants to amplify them in a new light for this present season in which we are living. This method of studying Scripture has opened up new teachings to me, such as the healing of nations. When I first started teaching on this beginning in 1985, I had never heard another person teach on the subject that nations could be healed. However, Revelation 22:2 leapt out at me one day. It says: "....the tree of life with its twelve varieties of fruit, yielding each month its fresh crop; and the leaves of the tree were for the healing and the restoration of nations" (AMP).

Prior to this time I didn't think that nations could be healed in this dispensation. However, we are seeing the Lord bring tremendous healing and restoration to nations today. Many other Christian leaders began to teach on this passage in a similar way, independently of each other.

Now, to many believers, the thought that nations can be healed is not foreign to their thinking at all.

The teaching on healing of nations was the first glimpse that I had of a connectedness between heaven and earth. Another one came around the same time when the Lord gave me a vision of a tremendous river and started opening my understanding that the river of God from heavenly places flowed into the earth through us, (Rev. 22:1, John 7:38). My pastor, Dutch Sheets, does an excellent teaching on the golden censors of heaven, (Rev. 8:3-4). These censors are filled with the prayers of the people of God which are mingled with incense in heaven. What a powerful revelation to think that as we intercede, our prayers are filling these bowls or censors. To add a note of my own, there also is a heavenly-given ingredient of fragrant spices and gums (AMP) which makes a perfume. This mixture of perfume and prayers (symbolic of heaven and earth functioning together as one body) is then released to the earth. What a beautiful picture of the agreement of heaven and earth!

As I was meditating on heaven's intercession I prayed a prayer (based on Revelation 4:1) that the Lord would open a door in heaven to me. I cried out to Him to take the scales off my eyes concerning the intercession taking place before the throne. This began a path of intense study for me in the book of Revelation. You might be aware that I am a prophetic intercessor, so I look at scripture through this understanding. While reading Revelation, it suddenly occurred to me that what was transpiring before the throne of God was a massive prayer and praise meeting. The next major, eye-opening insight I received was that there were things in heaven which needed to be released into the earth through intercession so that God's will would be done on earth as it is in heaven. This was startling to me.

While searching the scripture, I came to the realization that there were two major types of intercession taking place in the throne room of heaven-prophetic praise and prophetic declarations. "And when He had taken the scroll (book), the four living creatures and the twenty-four elders (of the heavenly Sanhedrin) prostrated themselves before the Lamb. Each was holding a harp (lute or guitar), and they had golden bowls full of incense (fragrant spices and gums for burning) that are the prayers of God's people—the saints" (Rev. 5:8, AMP).

This passage goes on to say that they sang a new song. What were they singing? "You have redeemed us to God by your blood out of every tongue and tribe and people and nation and have made us kings and priests to our God and we shall reign on the earth" (Rev. 5:9,10).

The saints in heaven were declaring something that was future tense at the time of John's vision. In fact, we still haven't seen the manifestation of this in the earth as of this writing. However, I do believe and fervently pray that this will happen. We work with major prayer organizations whose whole thrusts are to see that all will hear and know about the Gospel of the Lord Jesus Christ.

How do we reign on the earth? At present we can reign in intercession. We become God's lawful body functioning in the earth. One day we will literally reign with Him in ways that I don't think any of us fully understand.

Note that this new song cannot be sung by one nation or people group alone. The new song comes out of times when the body in the nations of the earth comes together. We have yet to sing the new song in its fullness. Why? Because we still do not have every tongue, tribe, and nation represented before the throne.

I believed for many years that God was only going to save a few people from certain unreached nations. This certainly displayed a small opinion on my part of the supreme Creator! Today I have changed my thinking. One day I took a moment to meditate on the thirty million or more intercessors who have been praying for the unreached people groups. My next thought was introduced through the whispering of the Holy Spirit in my ear, "Cindy, do you think I am too weak to bring a sweeping revival to the Islamic countries? How about those who are bound in Hinduism, or Buddhism?" I think the Lord was saying to me, "Why are you praying if you don't want me to answer those prayers?"

Truthfully, I never put my end-time belief system next to the thought that we were praying for worldwide revival. I had this escapist mentality that things were going to get blacker and blacker until God was going to rescue us from the terrible wickedness of the age. But today I believe that we are getting ready to see a massive harvest of souls in the coming hour.

This doesn't mean that I don't know that the last days will be punctuated with tremendous spiritual warfare. We, as prayer leaders who are on the front lines, live with a measure of warfare almost every day. Believe me, we realize that Satan has come down with great wrath because he knows that his time is short (Rev. 12:12).

The next type of intercession we see pouring forth from the throne of God into the earth is that of prophetic declaration. The Bible says that ten thousand times ten thousand, and thousands and thousands, (and that's a massive amount of people praying), are saying with a loud voice:

"Worthy is the Lamb who was slain to receive power and riches and wisdom, and strength and honor and glory and blessing!" (Rev. 5:12).

Imagine the releasing of these things into the earth and our agreement that the will of God will be done here as it is in heaven. What does this mean? As we get in alignment with God's heavenly will, we will take back the power and riches of the earth for the King of Glory. This cannot be accomplished through political means. It has to happen through intercession and God touching hearts to release the wealth of the sinner which has been laid up for the righteous.

As this wealth is taken back, we will present it from earth as an offering to God in heaven. The money we need will be available to finance this great end-time harvest of souls. I have been in nations such as Argentina, Guatemala, and Colombia that have experienced great revivals. These revivals cause the churches to have to build much larger buildings and rent stadiums for their services. You can imagine the other financial pressures that come from these mighty moves of God. The churches need to pay more staff members and they need larger Bible schools to train more leaders, etc.

There are other aspects of anointing that God wants to release to earth from heaven. One of these is the release of kingdom authority. The Bible clearly states that there are 24 elders that fall down before the throne of God and cast their crowns before Him who lives forever (Rev. 4:10). There are elders in heaven and God also wants eldership to be established in the earth.

What is the earthly type of this heavenly eldership? I believe that it is the apostles that God is raising up in the nations. As apostolic, kingdom authority structures are recognized over whole nations, a mighty move of the Holy Spirit will be released into the earth that will affect the physical governmental systems. Revival will sweep whole nations and the kings of these countries will cast their earthly crowns before Him who sits on the throne.

Many other aspects of heavenly anointings need to be prayed into the earth realm. We need to agree on earth that our nations will see a sweeping move of holiness, honor, etc. Prophetically, we come into agreement with heaven when we pray, "Your kingdom come, Your will be done on earth." It is possible to establish our nations as holy unto the Lord, set aside for His glory through intercessory prayer.

Where is this all heading? I believe that we are going to see a tremendous harvest of nations across the 10-40 window of the world's most unevangelized nations. Just as we've seen Communism fall, we will see Buddhism come down, a collapse of Islam and Hinduism. Sound impossible? It very well could be that we have set our sights way too low in what we ask God to accomplish in the nations of the earth. Now I realize that not everyone will be saved, but it is my desire that all be saved and come to the knowledge of the Lord. By this, I mean it is my heart for the people of the world as I intercede.

What do I believe will happen as this all wraps up? One day God will look down at the nations which have prepared themselves for His return and say to His Son, "Son, go get your bride. She is a glorious bride, beautiful to behold. Go, get her and bring her home! The marriage feast is ready." After this time there will be a time of great darkness on the earth with the coming of the anti-Christ, etc.

Let's come into agreement with heaven for the harvest of the nations. *Father, we your people cry out to You, we are longing for that wedding day. Give us the nations for our inheritance. Lord, now let Your kingdom come, Your will be done in my nation and the nations of the world. Amen.*

CHAPTER 11

SOULWINNING

Dr. T.L. Osborn

Dr. T.L. Osborn is regarded as one of the greatest soulwinners of this century. He is a prolific writer whose series of 18 gospel tracts has been published in more than 130 languages and distributed at the rate of over a ton a day for many years. He has ministered in 73 nations. This humble man of God most recently ministered in Poland, Russia, and Estonia where he distributed thousands of copies of the powerful books he has authored.

As young missionaries, Dr. Osborn and his

wife, Daisy, determined to take the Gospel to unreached multitudes. In the years that followed, they pioneered many effective methods and tools which have enabled them and thousands of other Christian workers to accomplish this goal.

Early in their ministry overseas, when first confronted by immense crowds, the Osborns introduced the concept of successfully praying for the sick en masse. In one of those early crusades, 125 deaf mutes and 90 totally blind people were miraculously healed by the power of God.

On a Personal Note...

During August 1980, when I had known the Lord less than one year, I had the opportunity of hearing Dr. T.L. Osborn for the first time. That day through his preaching, God spoke to my life and called me into the ministry. I will never forget that at the end of the service, my wife, Cecilia, and I were kneeling and crying as we dedicated our lives to the service of God.

The message that Dr. Osborn gave on that occasion has been like a spiritual compass for our lives. Every time we hear this message, which we do every three or four years, I am astonished at how careful God is with us. A great portion of the message has been fulfilled but it thrills me to think that we have not yet reached even the halfway point and that the most exciting part is still to come.

Two years later, Cecilia and I had the great privilege of being ordained for the ministry, and we received the laying on of hands from Brother T.L. and Daisy Osborn.

I have never met a representative of Jesus Christ like Brother Osborn. His life is an example of what God can do when a person decides to "live" the Word of God. There are many things I could say about this man of God that I admire so much, but let me use the words of another man of God, Rev. Benson Idahosa, who shared the same feelings for Brother Osborn. Idahosa said, "Osborn is a citizen of the world, a person who can cross all the cultural barriers to preach Christ and demonstrate the Gospel with signs, healings, and miracles." In addition, he has the very special gift of inspiring others so they can also accomplish the same results.

When one studies the theme of evangelism, it is imperative to study the ministry of Brother Osborn. In many nations, including ours, frequently you hear of the history of the Church in terms of "before and after" the Osborn crusade. This great ministry has impacted more than 70 countries! Nobody is more qualified to present to us what the Word says about winning souls for Christ.

Harold Caballeros

What is the difference between revival and evangelism? Revival is reviving something that had life before. You cannot revive what never lived. But evangelism is giving new life to those who are "dead in trespasses and sins" (Eph. 2:1)-who have never had God's real life before.

Revival is for Christians. Evangelism is for non-Christians-for the unbelieving world.

Christians received life from Christ when they believed the Gospel and accepted Him. But since they may become "lukewarm" (Rev. 3:16) or may have "left their first love" (Rev. 2:4), they may need revival.

Inside the church building is the place for revival. Outside the church building is the place for evangelism.

Evangelism has been greatly impeded by a notorious mental block that assumes that if unsaved people can be persuaded to come into the church building, then they can be influenced to embrace Christ and be saved!

So a special speaker is brought to the church. Advertisements appeal for the public to come to hear their invited guest. Announcements are sent out by radio, television and the newspaper. But, alas, only a few respond.

Why? Because non-Christians are not interested in going into church buildings.

Outdated Mentality

But the out-of-date Christian mind-set ignores this fact. Church members love their sanctuary, their freshly carpeted aisles and newly padded pews. Their choir is well trained and they are proud of their pastor. They believe that if enough advertisement is done, the unconverted will come into their church and be saved.

So more musicians or singers or performers or speakers are scheduled. More advertisement and more promotion are scheduled. Believers are urged to more earnest prayer. Again the church doors swing open. And thank God for those who do come because any souls won to Christ are worth every investment.

But, in general, few unconverted people respond. The groundwork is well laid. The believers spare nothing, yet the efforts made are not productive. Christians ask in bewilderment: "Why?"

The lost world has been trying to tell Christians something for a long time: "Your pastor may have a Ph.D., you may air condition your building, carpet your aisles, cushion your pews, invite us to your church via radio, television, phone calls, letters, church bulletins, newspaper ads, or personal visits; you may bring preachers, lecturers, prophets, teachers, evangelists, musicians, entertainers, or singers, but we are not interested in coming to your church!" So churches that have not updated their philosophy ask in dismay, "What then is to be done?" And the answer has proven to be quite simple: Abandon the traditional mental block.

Where the Need is Obvious

If the testimony of Christ is only shared within the sanctuary, then the majority of unconverted people will never be saved because they will not be present.

There are millions of needy, despairing, lonely, fearful, unloved and neglected people who are ripe for harvesting. They are waiting right outside the sanctuary. They need salvation, they want forgiveness, they search for knowledge about Christ, they fear to die as they are, they are encompassed with problems and they yearn for God, but most of them will never come to church.

When Christian believers go to them and give them the Gospel, out where they are, they gladly accept Christ and receive His grace and salvation.

Then they follow those believers back to their churches where they grow in grace and in the knowledge of Christ. They know that someone cared for them, came to them and helped them to receive Christ on their own terrain.

Two Words that Count

The most timid Christian who witnesses of Christ to an unconverted person says two of the most powerful words in our language before he or she ever opens their mouth: They say, "I care!" And human persons want to be loved; they want to know that someone cares for them.

There is a church that wins more people to Christ than any other one in its denomination. The pastor was asked: "Do you win people by getting them to attend your Sunday School?"

He answered, "No, we win almost no one that way. We live in an area of strong religious loyalties and almost no one will visit our church. We go to the people's homes and workplaces and win them there. Then they come to our church and become strong believers."

First, to Christ; Then, to Church

Most churches teach their members how to invite people to their sanctuary. First century believers were skilled in inviting people to Christ. New

Testament Christians testified and taught people "publicly and from house to house" (Acts 20:20), making new disciples out where the people lived and worked and played.

Their focus was to get people to Christ, then to their meeting place-to win them out where they are. That concept is limitless. The very meaning of evangelism is the grand theme of biblical ministry-to "preach the gospel to every creature" (Mark 16:15).

As Christians share Christ with unconverted people-on their own territory like first century believers did-the most rewarding ministry that Christ ever committed to His followers is rediscovered.

Two Kinds of Evangelism

In the book of Acts, the first century believers witnessed of Christ and shared His teachings, both publicly and from house to house. They practiced mass evangelism and personal evangelism. Occasionally, multitudes came together to hear one of them speak or preach, especially if some outstanding healing miracle had occurred (Acts. 3:1-11; 5:12-16; 8:5-8; 9:33-34; 14:8-11), but each individual's own ministry was in person-to-person encounters with people.

The book of Acts begins with a reminder of "all that Jesus began both to do and teach" (Acts 1:1). His life was their inspiration and model. He had told them, "Whoever believes on me, the works that I do shall he [or she] do also; and greater works than these shall they do; because I go to my Father" (John 14:12). And they believed His words. Their focus was to continue doing and teaching the same Gospel that He had represented. They understood that He was living and ministering through them. They were His voice, His feet, His body. He was continuing what He had begun and He was doing it through them.

Just before Christ ascended, He told His followers where to go and what to do: "You shall receive power, after that the Holy Ghost is come upon you; and you shall be witnesses unto me both in Jerusalem, and in all Judea, and in Samaria, and to the uttermost part of the earth" (Acts 1:8).

A first century map can clearly indicate what this means: Jerusalem represents your hometown. All Judea suggests your state, province, or nation.

No Discrimination

But why did He specify Samaria? It was part of Judea and He had already said "in all Judea." He specified Samaria because it was a segregated area. Remember how the woman of Samaria remarked to Jesus, "The Jews have no

dealings with the Samaritans" (John 4:9). And the Jews slandered Him saying, "Say we not well that you are a Samaritan, and have a devil?" (John 8:48).
Jesus told His followers to reach all Judea, then He specified and Samaria-the forgotten, hurting, unloved people. Samaria could be Indian or Aboriginal reservations, minority communities, migrant settlements, ghettos, rehabilitation centers, immigrant and refugee communities or any place that is considered inferior or is segregated from the mainstream of society.
Jesus specified these places, then He added, and unto the uttermost part of the earth. In other words, He was saying, "at home and abroad." Soulwinning is a worldwide ministry.

The Way to Reach Everyone

Human population can only be reached by personal evangelism. It is the only way to reach every creature with the Gospel. Even those who are not won to Christ in this way can at least be given a personal witness about His love.
The Moody Bible Institute has estimated that less than five percent of Christians have ever led a soul to Christ and that only about ten percent of the people in so-called Christian nations attend church. God gets more cooperation from non-Christians than from Christians. Many unbelievers come to God's house, but there are not many Christians who go share Christ in non-Christian homes.
God never said, "Go, you unconverted, to my house and be saved, lest you die." But He did say, "Go you [believers]...to every creature" (Mark 16:15).
Paul the apostle was that kind of a believer. "He reasoned...with the Jews and with the Gentiles...and in the marketplace daily with those who happened to be there" (Acts 17:17, NKJV).

From the Gallery to the Arena

Personal soulwinning transforms Christian believers from the grandstand of spectators, lifting them out of the gallery of hearers of the word and places them out into the arena of action as doers of the word (Jas. 1:22-25).
There is nothing as exciting as coming to church and looking across the aisle at a new believer whom you have personally led to Christ. You allowed Christ to win that soul through you. No church can be ineffective when members like that are scattered throughout its congregation.
The first century Church was born in a blaze of personal soulwinning. A revival of that passion is sweeping the world today as Christians are writing the last chapter of the Acts of the Believers before Christ's return.

Seven Reasons Why We are Soulwinners

The remainder of this chapter will share these seven reasons why we are soulwinners:

1. Because Jesus was.
2. Because the harvest is so great.
3. Because the laborers are so few.
4. Because Jesus said to do it.
5. Because of the unfulfilled prophecies concerning Christ's return.
6. Because we do not want the blood of non-believers on our hands.
7. Because of what we have experienced.

The Greatest Calling

We are soulwinners because Jesus was. The Bible says, "This is a faithful saying, and worthy of all acceptation. That Christ Jesus came into the world to save sinners" (I Tim. 1:15). It also says, "The Son of man is come to seek and to save that which was lost" (Luke 19:10).

Jesus came to save people. That is His mission. First and last, He was a soulwinner-the greatest soulwinner the world has ever known!

The first group that Jesus chose to follow Him were told: "Follow me, and I will make you fishers of people" (Matt. 4:19). The last group who followed Him out to His ascension heard Him say these words: "Go make disciples of all nations" (Matt. 28:19). "You shall be my witnesses unto the uttermost part of the earth" (Acts 1:8).

First and foremost, Jesus was a soulwinner. That is why He came to save people. That is why He lived, died, rose again, and sent the Holy Spirit to His followers, enabling them to witness for Christ with signs, miracles and wonders to confirm that He is alive and real.

The word Christian means to be like Christ. He came to save people, to seek out the lost. To be Christians, we are to be soulwinners like Him.

Christ is born in us and He wills to do the same things in and through us that He did when He walked on this earth. Yet, there are hundreds of thousands of Christians who have never known the joy of allowing Christ to win even one soul through them. There are even preachers and Bible teachers who have never won a soul to Christ. Missionaries have told us that they never won a soul to Christ during their term of ministry abroad.

If the majority of Christians have not yet discovered this truth, could it be the reason the Church has not yet given the Good News to every creature?

Out Where the People Are

We are soulwinners because the harvest is so great. No one can look into the faces of the masses of people who are bewildered by superstitious religions, as we have done, without doing their utmost to win souls.

For over a half century Daisy[16] and I have stood on crude platforms out in the open air, before multitudes of underprivileged people interspersed with lepers, demoniacs, witch doctors, and the hopelessly diseased. We have preached Christ to them when it was all one could do to hold back tears of human emotions.

Worldwide, there are millions who have not yet been reached. They constitute the vast, ripened harvest of souls waiting to be reaped.

This is the second reason why we are soulwinners: because the harvest is so great.

The Bible says, "When Jesus saw the multitudes, he was moved with compassion on them, because they fainted, and were scattered abroad, as sheep having no shepherd" (Matt. 9:36).

Pondering these needy multitudes, He said, "The harvest truly is plenteous" (Matt. 9:37).

What did He do about it? He called 12 disciples, gave them power to cast out devils and to heal the sick, and sent them out to help reap this harvest. Later, He called 70 more. Then before His ascension, He conferred upon all believers the power to witness with evidence-with signs following (Mark 16:20), in His name.

The fact is that He did something about this ripened harvest. He did not just sit and ponder it and pray about it. He set about getting laborers out into these harvest fields.

Since Christ was **moved with compassion** when He saw the multitude and since we are like Christ, we also can be moved with compassion for or toward those who are untouched by the Gospel. If we are, then, like Christ, we become involved doing something about sharing the Gospel with them.

This truth cannot be overemphasized: We are Christ's body; He can only reach people through us.

Here Am I! Send Me!

We are soulwinners **because the laborers are so few**.

"Also I heard the voice of the Lord, saying, 'Whom shall I send, and who will go for us?' Then said I, 'Here am I; send me,'" (Isa. 6:8).

World population is increasing at the rate of over 70 million per year. Do you know that less than three million of that increase is being touched by the

Gospel?
It is a fair estimate that there are perhaps two billion souls alive today who have never heard the Gospel-and many sources put the number much higher. This represents nearly half the world's population, including tribes who speak over a thousand different languages.
The golden opportunity for Christians is to reap this vast human harvest with renewed enthusiasm and dedication.
Jesus said, "Lift up your eyes, and look on the fields, for they are white already to harvest" (John 4:35).
Again He said, "The harvest truly is plenteous, but the laborers are few; pray ye therefore the Lord of the harvest, that he will send forth laborers into his harvest" (Matt. 9:37-38).
We have looked upon these vast harvest fields. We have prayed for more laborers. But above all, we are giving our lives to help reap this harvest.

The Choice to Win

We are soulwinners because of the Great Commission of Jesus Christ.
The last thing Jesus authorized His followers to do before He went away was: "Go into all the world, and preach the gospel to every creature" (Mark 16:15).
This is His authority to each of His followers. This is the greatest opportunity He ever offered believers. This is every Christian's privilege, calling, purpose, and ministry.
When God's love overflowed to the point that He gave His only begotten Son, it was for the whole world, so that "whoever believes in him will not perish, but will have everlasting life" (John 3:16).
Christ left us no privilege greater than to announce the Gospel to every creature. This is the believer's guarantee of happiness.
If you had walked on to the grounds of our campaigns back in the late 40s and 50s, and then if you had attended one of our most recent mass crusades of the 90s, you would have heard the same Gospel presented with the same simplicity. You would have observed the same strategy, heard the same prayers, witnessed the same spiritual and physical miracles that always confirm the proclamation of the Gospel.
We live and breathe for one purpose: to share the Gospel with the maximum number of people, by every means possible. We do not only use our voices as Christ speaks through us, but also we use the channels of mass media, of reproduction, of duplication, and every form of gospel dissemination that we can utilize.

The Forgotten Ones

We are soulwinners **because of the unfulfilled prophecies concerning Christ's return**.

For centuries, it has been traditional for Christians to live in anticipation of the Lord's imminent return. Many Bible teachers emphasize that all of the prophecies of events which are to precede His second coming have been fulfilled.

But is this true? Perhaps the most significant prophecy concerning our Lord's return has not nearly been fulfilled. It is the sign that concerns you and me. It involves us as Christians and our ministries as His witnesses.

Jesus specified several signs of His coming; among them He specified false christs, wars, nations in conflict, famines, pestilences, earthquakes, persecutions, deceit, and lack of consecration (Matt. 24:4-12).

Then He added, "And this gospel of the kingdom shall be preached in all the world for a witness unto all nations; and then shall the end come" (Matt. 24:14).

Christ's last words, before He returned to the Father, were, in essence, "Go now to all nations and proclaim the good news to every creature. As soon as you do this, I shall return." This enormous and significant task has not yet been accomplished.

"Come on, Let's Hurry!"

I can imagine impetuous Peter nudging John and saying, "Come on, John. Let's hurry. This won't take long. Then Christ will come back."

The first century Church understood their mission. They knew that Christ was not dead, but that He had risen and had returned to live in them, continuing the same works which He did before He was crucified. They remembered His promise to return as soon as the Gospel was "preached in all the world for a witness to all nations" (Matt. 24:14).

What might have happened if this original zeal and passion for souls had continued in the Church? But it did not.

It was hundreds of years later before the great Reformation took place. The Church began her rediscovery of the truths which had been so cardinal to first century Christians and to their evangelistic success.

Finally, in the mid-1700s, the Wesleys proclaimed the message of spiritual sanctification. Later, there followed the 20th century rediscovery of the baptism of the Holy Spirit. These were significant steps in the reemergence of effective Christianity.

These vital truths were being unveiled afresh so that Christians might be empowered to witness in **all the world, among all nations** (Mark 13:10; Luke 24:47), **to every creature** (Mark 16:15), and bring back their King.

Top Pr iority

We are soulwinners because we do not want the blood of the unconverted on our hands.

As a young Christian, one of the Bible portions which impressed me was in the third chapter of Ezekiel. God specifically speaks about the purpose of sharing His message with people so that everyone can have a chance to be blessed.

"I have made you a watcher...give warning from me. When I say to the wicked you shall surely die; and you give no warning...to save lives; the wicked shall die in their iniquity; But their blood will I require at your hand" (Eze. 3:17-18).

"**Their blood will I require at your hand**." Each time Daisy and I read these words, we review our priorities. That scripture has motivated us since we were teenagers. We do not want the blood of the unconverted required at our hands.

This is another reason we are soulwinners. This is why we share the Gospel. This is why we have given, and continue to give, our lives to worldwide gospel crusades. This is why we have consistently done everything we can, using every tool for evangelism available to share Christ with the unreached. It is why we have led this ministry in sponsoring so many thousands of qualified national preachers as gospel messengers among the unchurched masses.

This Century

We are soulwinners *because of what we have experienced* conducting mass evangelism crusades for over a half century. In 73 nations, the response has been the same.

Even though we human beings come and go, the Gospel is the same in any generation, when proclaimed in the power of the Holy Spirit.

Around the world, we have proven that people of all races, religions, and creeds want to know God. They have their forms of worship, their superstitions and their religions. But their spirits are not satisfied without Christ. They search for reality but are unable to find the peace they seek. They pray in many different ways, but without receiving answers. They seek God but do not experience Him in reality.

We have proven that once people are offered an opportunity to hear the Gospel in simple language and "in demonstration of the Spirit and of power"

(I Cor. 2:4), they eagerly rush to receive Jesus Christ.

Sometimes we have had to carry bags of charms and fetishes away from the campaign grounds and burn them, as Paul did (Acts 19:18-19). As the people receive Christ, they no longer cling to fetishes or worship graven images for protection from evil spirits. He is enough.

Our Open Doors

The unconverted world is hurting. They have problems without answers, diseases without remedies, fears without faith, guilt without pardon. They afford us our golden opportunity and they guarantee our success, self-esteem and total happiness in life.

As we lift them, we are lifted. Healing them, we are healed. Loving them, we are loved. In serving them, we are truly serving the Lord.

As believers go outside their sanctuary walls-out where the people are, out among the traffic and din of humanity, out in public places and in private homes-there the Holy Spirit will guide them into encounters where they can lead needy and lonely human persons to faith in Jesus Christ.

Today, believers face the most unique and formidable epoch of Christian history. Never before have so many unevangelized millions been reachable with the Gospel. And never before have Christians had access to such potentially effective means of witnessing to these millions.

When we stand before Him, He will commend us: "I was hungry and you gave me meat. I was thirsty and you gave me to drink. I was a stranger and you took me in; Naked and you clothed me. I was sick and you visited me. I was in prison and you came to me

...Inasmuch as you did it unto one of the least of these...you did it unto me" (Matt. 25:35-40).

Excerpted from T.L. Osborn, Soulwinning (Tulsa, OK: OSFO Books, 1993). Used by permission of the author.

CHAPTER

12

GOD'S END-TIME DESTINY FOR HIS CHURCH

Morris Cerrullo

Chairman and President of Morris Cerullo World Evangelism, Dr. Morris Cerullo is the author of more than 60 books. During more than 50 years of ministry, he has trained over 1,000,000 nationals in more than 130 different nations to minister the Gospel to their own countries and indigenous peoples.

The ministry of Morris Cerullo World Evangelism includes miracle crusades around the world, schools of ministry, global satellite Network Schools of

Ministry, the Victory Miracle Living publication, the Jewish World Outreach, the daily "Victory" broadcasts, and the New Inspirational Satellite Network.

On a Personal Note...

The chapter you are about to read will bless you in a great way. It is a classic example of Brother Cerullo's ministry, the affirmation that God has no limits, and consequently, the Church should not have limits either.

It seems to me that we need to read this message time and again. I am persuaded that the Church is going through a very special season. Everywhere I look, even in the most unlikely places, the Holy Spirit is manifesting Himself in the Church with power.

The teaching of the believer's authority in the Name of Jesus is more necessary than ever because the challenges of the Church have been multiplied. A prophetic voice loaded with authority and unction is necessary to guide the Church to victory. This is, precisely, Brother Cerullo's ministry.

I would like to take this opportunity to mention a story about this servant's humility and great respect for the Holy Spirit. Brother Cerullo, his assistant, my wife, and I were having dinner one day and I had in my heart a question for Brother Cerullo. I am sure this was not the first time somebody asked for this special advice. He carefully listened to me, but he didn't answer immediately; on the contrary, he answered slowly and deliberately. During our conversation he told me, "You probably noticed that I did not want to answer you right away. Morris could have answered you, but you do not need Morris Cerullo to answer your question. I am trying to put myself aside in order to let the Holy Spirit answer." His attitude greatly blessed me.

It is a privilege to include Brother Cerullo's contribution in this book. I pray to God that you take part in "the Church without boundaries."

Harold Caballeros

Knowing that we are a people of destiny, and that God planned to fulfill His divine purposes in and through His Church in this end-time hour, we must refocus our attention and efforts upon being all He has destined us to be, and completing all that God has called and anointed us to do.

Throughout the ages, the Church became sidetracked and diverted from the original purpose God intended it to fulfill. Instead of being the indestructible, powerful force God intended and a full manifestation of Christ to the world, it became splintered...divided by denominationalism and bound by man-made traditions and doctrines.

The major focus of the Church turned inward. Instead of focusing upon ministering to the desperate needs of the world around us in a demonstration of the power and anointing of the Holy Spirit, we have placed our major focus upon building large sanctuaries and buildings, filling them with people, and ministering to the needs of the believers inside the Church.

The vast majority of Christians within the Church today have become satisfied and are content just warming a church pew. The average Christian has a very limited vision for the lost within his community, and an even more limited vision and burden for multiplied millions of lost souls around the world.

When God gave birth to the Church He never intended the ministry of the Church to remain within the four walls of what we call the Church today.

God didn't send forth the Holy Spirit...the blessed Third Person of the Trinity...and release His immeasurable, unlimited power within the Church just so believers would be able to soak up God's blessings, speak in tongues, shout, dance and sing the praises of God while thousands are dying daily...going into an eternity without God ...forever damned in the pits of hell.

When God breathed His life and power into the Church, He intended every believer to proclaim the message of salvation, healing and deliverance and meet the desperate needs of the world in a demonstration of power!

I call upon all Church leaders, pastors, evangelists, ministers and Christians everywhere who are hungry to experience God's power flowing through the Church to the fullest extent in this end-time hour, to join me in repenting before God for the current condition of the Church.

It is time for the true Church of Jesus Christ to wake up, to rise up from where we are and take the position God has ordained for us.

The power that was released in Jerusalem on the Day of Pentecost has not diminished! It has not stopped flowing within the Church. This is the key. We must understand...because when you look at the denominations and the structure that is to represent the Church, you can have every right to question the absence of the manifestation of the power of Pentecost.

The Church is not the denominations we see today as a whole.
The Church is not the physical structure of the buildings we see today.
The Church is Christ's Body. It is the representation of Who God is. It is His people of every walk, race, color, creed, and denomination.
Each of us knows the sense of what is in us that unites us to each other-the spiritual, mystical cord that has "deep calling unto deep."

It's Time for the Church to Wake up and to Grow Up!

That same dunamis, miracle-working power that was manifested in Jesus' life, and was demonstrated in the Early Church, to heal the sick, open blind eyes, make the lame walk, and to raise the dead, is still flowing today within the Body of Christ.
Pentecost did not end two thousand years ago. It never stopped!
Within the Body of Christ there has been a lack of understanding concerning the true power that was released at Pentecost and its purpose within the body of Christ. This is one of the major reasons why we are not seeing more of God's miracle power manifested within our churches.
One of the biggest lies Satan will use to block the flow of the fullness of God's power through your life is to tell you that it's impossible for the miracle power of God to flow through you as it did through Peter, Paul and the disciples in the Early Church. He will try to make you think God's miracle power is released only through great "spiritual giants"...well-known evangelists, ministers or teachers.
Remember, God's power is not limited by who you are or by your own limited talents and abilities.
His power is not dependent upon you.
God will manifest that same miracle power through you as you begin to understand the power He has already given you through the Holy Spirit. Then, as you dare to step out in faith and expect Him to release that power to heal the sick, cast out devils and proclaim deliverance in His Name, He will do it!
What is God's end time destiny for you?
There would be absolutely no need for God to give us the promise of power if it were not for service and ministry.
Jesus came to earth for a divine purpose. He said, "My meat is to do the will of him that sent me, and to finish his work" (John 4:34).
It's time for the Church to wake up and to grow up! We must completely refocus on fulfilling the will of God in this end-time hour. Jesus said, "I didn't come to do my will but I came to do the will of the my father."
The manifestation and power of the Holy Spirit is to give us the ability to

accomplish His purposes. The power of the Holy Spirit was given to equip the Church and give us the ability to fulfill the Great Commission.

God knew we could not do it in ourselves. That is why He sent the Holy Spirit with power to remain in us! We cannot accomplish the will of God in our own limited strength and natural abilities. There is no way that we can take our lives and lay them on the altar as a one hundred percent sacrifice. No way!

We must have an experience, a personal, divine encounter with God...where He implants His Spirit within us, giving us the power and ability to completely submit and yield ourselves to Him in obedience to His will.

What is God's Purpose for His End-Time Church?

In light of the fact that we are the end-time generation and believe Christ is coming soon, what is the major focus we must have before Christ returns for His Church?

With all my heart I believe this is God's time to bring the Body of Christ into an experience of power that will shake the world before Jesus comes!

The Church is at a point of destiny!

God's purpose for this end-time Church is the same as it was for the believers in the early Church. The divine charge Jesus gave the disciples before He ascended into heaven has not changed.

We face the enormous task of reaching the world with the Gospel before Christ returns. With our population nearing six billion and multiplied millions upon millions who have not yet been reached with the Gospel, we must have a supernatural manifestation of the true power of Pentecost.

The future success of this twentieth century Church lies within the hands of those who will grasp hold of the two great truths Jesus declared:

"You will receive power!"

"You will be witnesses unto Me!"

Without the same enduement of power, the same demonstration of God's power that was released within the early Church...there is no hope for this world!

There is only one way that we will be able to evangelize the world before Jesus comes. We must have an experience of power, where we have been baptized ...immersed...completely saturated...with the Holy Spirit so that we will be witnesses of the resurrection power of Jesus Christ to the world.

The true power of Pentecost was the power to proclaim the Gospel of Jesus Christ with evidence...by signs and wonders manifested through the disciples and believers.

This purpose has not changed.

We have Christ's promise: "...Ye shall receive power after that the Holy Ghost has come upon you; and ye shall be witnesses unto me..." (Acts 1:8). Through the Holy Spirit living within us, we have power to proclaim the Gospel in the same demonstration of power that was manifested in the early Church. Christ has equipped and empowered us. And it is the responsibility of every born-again believer to accept this charge and fulfill it in the power of the Holy Spirit.

The Church Must Refocus on its True Purpose!

God is calling His end-time Church to refocus upon the purpose He has for us. One of the most important end time signs that Jesus said would occur before His return is that there will be an incredible end time witness of the Gospel to the world. Jesus said, "This gospel of the kingdom shall be preached in all the world for a witness unto all nations; then shall the end come" (Matt. 24:14). This is the true purpose for the Holy Spirit being outpoured upon the Church today.

Just as the believers in the early Church were witnesses of Christ's resurrection through the signs and wonders which God manifested through them, God has called and chosen us to be His end-time witnesses...to produce proof through the miracles God has planned to manifest through us to meet the desperate needs within the world today.

The last thing Jesus did to prepare His disciples to fulfill the Great Commission was to refocus them upon their true purpose. Once they were focused and experienced the Holy Ghost, they never again looked to the world. They never again looked to the physical or the material things of the world.

Once they experienced the coming of God's Spirit into their beings, they never again asked about earthly power. Experiencing the power of God within their lives was the utmost experience of their lives. Nothing else was ever needed.

Once God's Spirit truly takes up residence within a person, that person is fully satisfied. Nothing else can ever satisfy...not position...not recognition...not fame...nothing else!

When they were baptized with the Holy Spirit, their focus changed to service and ministry. Instead of focusing upon themselves their focus was changed to the purpose God had given them to evangelize the world!

It is time for the Church to once again set our focus on fulfilling the purpose God has given us of proclaiming the Gospel of Jesus Christ in a demonstration of power to the nations of the world as an end-time witness. It's time for the Church to get back to preaching the simple Gospel of Jesus

Christ...crucified...risen...coming again.

The world doesn't need man-made doctrines...gimmicks...get rich schemes...or a watered-down, sugar-coated gospel.

The world desperately needs to hear and see a manifestation of God's power preached with signs and wonders accompanying it!

A New Release of God's Supernatural Power is Coming!

Two thousand years ago, the Church was born with a unique characteristic that gave it a divine capability to produce the proof of the resurrection of Jesus Christ, the Son of the living God.

After the third century, the Church lost that experience. Today when we get the mask off and look at the condition of the Church, we cannot find a true demonstration of that same manifestation...the fire of Pentecost...the same demonstration of the Holy Spirit that gave birth to the Church.

It's missing!

Over the years, we have had a small taste of it. The outpouring on Azusa Street...glossolalia...the moving of the Holy Spirit breaking through denominational barriers with the Charismatic movement.

We have seen recent unusual outpourings of God's Spirit, and have experienced awesome moves of the Holy Spirit in our meetings in the nations of the world.

However, what we have experienced is only a foretaste of what God has in store for His Church in this end-time hour. We haven't seen anything yet compared with what God is about to do in this end-time hour before Jesus comes!

We still have not seen the fullness of the true breakthrough of the power of Pentecost, the true baptism of the Holy Spirit.

But now something is about to happen! God is saying, "I'm going to do a new work among My people! There will be a new release...a new demonstration of my supernatural power!"

Since the third century, the Church has tried to contain the Holy Spirit within old wineskins...outmoded, man-made traditions...man-made philosophies.

The old wineskins of the Church structure have placed limitations upon the free moving of the Holy Spirit. Instead of following the leading of the Holy Spirit, Christian leaders, pastors, evangelists and ministers are bound by church politics. They are bound by tradition and their loyalty to their denominations.

Men have tried to confine the working of the Holy Spirit to their narrow concept and limited understanding of how the Holy Spirit should operate within the Church.

Over the years, the Church has "quenched" or tried to restrict the moving of the Holy Spirit because it does not fit within the framework of their doctrinal beliefs or organizational structures.

But, today is a new day for the Church!

The "old wineskins" of the Church structure, which have been binding and hindering the flow and demonstration of the power of God, are going to give way to the new!

God wants to do a new work in your life...to take you beyond your limitations...beyond your preconceived ideas...beyond your mental barriers and hang ups!

God never intended His power in your life to be limited. Believe me when I tell you there is no limit to the power God desires to release within you. NO LIMIT!

You are only limited to the degree you fail to accept God's promises and act on them.

God will do "exceeding abundantly above all that we ask or think, according to the power that worketh in us" (Eph. 3:20). Paul said that God would far exceed ALL our expectations and our limited natural abilities to think or ask. How? According to His power working in us!

Paul was not talking about some remote force or power far removed from us somewhere in the heavens. He was referring to the dunamis miracle-working power of God Almighty residing within us by the Holy Spirit!

He was not referring to some latent, inactive power that fluctuates or changes from one day to the next, or that is dependent upon man's abilities. He was talking about the immeasurable, unlimited power of God that is an active force working within us to transform and empower us.

Through the indwelling of the Holy Spirit, the same mighty power that raised Christ from the dead is in you! God's power that is working for you and in you is according to the unlimited power God manifested in Christ when He raised Him from the dead. The resurrection power of Almighty God is in you!

A True Manifestation of God's Power and Glory is Coming to the Church!

God has shown me that a new manifestation of true Pentecostal power is coming upon the Church to restore us to the position of power and authority He planned us to have. The greatest outpouring of God's Spirit is yet to come!

In the next few years, there will be greater manifestations of the power and glory of God than we have ever experienced!

Thousands upon thousands will be saved, delivered and healed on a gigantic scale!

God will work within the Church to bring us to a new level of maturity...a new level of spiritual authority and power...so that He can use us as a channel through which He can pour out His miracle-working power.

In 1996 when God showed me that this Decade of the Holy Spirit was about to close, He said to me, "Son, My people do not know My true Pentecostal experience."

When we get the mask off and look at the Church as it really is today, we see that we have a lot of joy, laughter, and other manifestations of the Spirit. These manifestations are wonderful. We need them. But, they are not evidence of the baptism of the Holy Spirit.

Ninety-nine point nine percent of the Christians sitting in our church pews have stopped at what I call "the point of blessing."

For years the Church has had a limited understanding of the ministry, the work, the power and the relationship of the Holy Spirit God intended for believers to experience. We have so much to learn about the ministry of the Holy Spirit, the blessed Third Person of the Trinity.

Within the Pentecostal and Charismatic churches, the major emphasis has been focused upon the gift of tongues and the other manifestations of the Holy Spirit's power. However, too often we have not gone far enough to discover the depths and fullness of the relationship and inner working of the Holy Spirit.

We need to repent for the way we have treated the Holy Spirit. We have misunderstood Him, overlooked Him, quenched His power and grieved Him.

Within the body of Christ there has been a lack of understanding concerning the true Pentecostal experience and its purpose within the Church. This is one of the major reasons why we are not seeing more of God's miracle power manifested within our churches.

Something must happen to the Church of Jesus Christ!

We have form.

We have tradition.

We have "head knowledge." But the power is missing!

We must have a fresh outpouring of His Spirit that will give us an experience of power like the early Church experienced. Without this, we will not be able to reach the world!

We Must Press Through until We Have an Experience of God's Power to Shake the World!

The majority of Christians sitting in our church pews do not believe it is possible for God's miracle power to be released through them to heal the sick, open blind eyes, unstop deaf ears or make the lame to walk.

Others have limited the experience of God's power to a manifestation of speaking in unknown tongues or some other outward manifestation.

Within the Church, we have placed limitations upon the working of God's Spirit in our midst according to how we think He should manifest His power.

If there is an unusual move of the Spirit, or if we don't understand a particular manifestation of God's Spirit, we refuse to acknowledge or accept it.

Before we can experience the fullness of God's power working within us in the dimension He has purposed for us, we must have a fresh revelation of God's power working in us through the Holy Spirit.

"Head knowledge" is not enough! We can know all the Scriptures on God's power and the power we have in Christ by heart, quote them every day for the rest of our lives, and it won't get the job done.

"Head knowledge" of God's power will never heal the sick, open blind eyes and break the bondage of drug and alcohol abuse!

It wasn't "head knowledge" that enabled Peter to say to the crippled man, lame from birth: "Silver and gold have I none; but such as I have give I thee: In the name of Jesus Christ of Nazareth rise up and walk" (Acts 3:6).

No. It wasn't "head knowledge" that enabled that man to leap and walk. Peter had an experience of the dunamis power of God!

It's time for the Church to go beyond "head knowledge" to an experience where God's power and anointing is gushing forth out of our lives to heal the sick and break the bondage of sin in our cities.

We don't have time to play church!

We must press through in the Spirit until we have experienced a breakthrough of the power of God that will shake our world, as did the early Church.

What Happened To Get Us So Far Off Course?

Church, the question we must answer is...

Why don't we see God's power flowing through us in the powerful dimension He has destined for us?

When we look at the experience of the Church today and compare it with what God has planned and all He has provided for us, we must ask ourselves what has happened to get us so far off course?

Nobody knows the pain of facing the reality of the issues of life today in our twentieth century more than we do.

When we look at the history of the Church and the things which brought it to such a weakened condition, we see that the greatest danger the early

Christians faced was not the intense persecution, lasting 300 years. It was during those years, in the first three centuries, the Church experienced its greatest growth.

It wasn't until the Church began to compromise with the world, organize, substitute man-made traditions, and depend upon its natural abilities instead of following the leading of the Holy Spirit, that the flow of the Spirit began to diminish.

My heart is so grieved...so burdened when I look at the true condition of the Church today. To think of the awesome price Jesus paid so that His Church would overcome every obstacle, every Satanic assault and fulfill His will upon the earth, and then to look at where we stand today!

Jesus defeated Satan...handed him over into our hands...

He has anointed us with the same Holy Spirit that was upon Him...

He equipped us with powerful spiritual weapons and sent us forth to make disciples of all nations.

But, after two thousand years, with all the tremendous technological breakthroughs...radio, television, satellites, computer technology...we still don't have the job done!

It's going to take a supernatural intervention of God on behalf of the Church to bring us from the position of weakness where we are today to the place of power He has planned.

Jesus is coming!

And, He is not coming for a lukewarm, wishy-washy, weak Church with an outward appearance of holiness and power, but in reality, is impotent...powerless...unable to manifest the reality of the Gospel.

Only God knows the pathetic condition that exists in the Church today!

We are living in the midst of a modern-day Sodom and Gomorrah. Sin, corruption, perversion, sickness and death surround us. Yet, the Church has fallen asleep. Our eyes have been diverted from our goal.

A spirit of compromise...

A spirit of complacency...

A spirit of worldliness...

A spirit of self-promotion...

A spirit of indifference...

A spirit of covetousness...

...has entered the Church of Jesus Christ.

We must not be afraid to acknowledge our weaknesses and failures, repent of them and ask God to bring us to a new position of strength and power greater than we have ever known before!

It's time for us to stop playing church!

We don't have time to keep making excuses or to keep sweeping our weaknesses under the carpet!

God Gave Birth to a Church That Would Know No Limits!

This is our hour and we must step into our destiny!

The message God wants to break forth into your spirit is that when He gave birth to the Church 2000 years ago, he never planned for it to know any limits...not one!

When He gave birth to the Church, He never intended for members of the Body of Christ to depend upon their own limited abilities or natural resources.

When He breathed the Holy Spirit upon the 120 disciples gathered together in the upper room, He imparted a part of Himself, the Third Person of the Trinity, to live within them giving them His unlimited, immeasurable power to fulfill His will upon the earth.

God has implanted His Spirit within us giving us His unlimited, immeasurable power to fulfill His end-time plan!

Christ has given us His power and authority to do the same works He did and greater!

He has planned for the Church to be invincible...the most powerful force upon the earth!

Christ has destroyed the works of the devil and He has planned for us to manifest His power in ministering to the desperate needs of the world...healing the sick...casting out devils...proclaiming the Gospel in the nations in a demonstration of His unlimited power.

Why have we allowed compromise into the Church?

Why have we compromised concerning divine healing?

Why have we limited and denied the Almighty power of God to heal?

There is probably no other doctrine that has been so attacked...both from within the Church and from without. The Church denies the power to heal and the world ridicules those who lay hands on the sick.

There are many Christians who do not believe divine healing is for today. They believe the gift of healing was only manifested within the early Church. Then, there are those who preach it, but do not see the results manifested.

The God you and I serve is a God Who knows no limit!

He is a healing God!

He is the same yesterday, today and forever!

There is not one Scripture that reveals God ever planned for His healing power to ever stop flowing through His Church.

Jesus paid a 100 percent price so that the Church would have 100 percent victory over 100 percent of the enemy 100 percent of the time!

The time has come for God's people to practice what they preach! It is one thing to preach divine healing and to say we believe God heals today, but an altogether different matter to go beyond head knowledge to see God's power released and healing manifested.

God's destiny for His Church is that we will be a full manifestation of Christ to the world.

He plans for us to be His witnesses...to produce proof, through the manifestation of His power flowing through us, of His power to save, deliver and heal all manner of sickness and disease.

How can we be a full representation of Christ to the world if we fail to proclaim divine healing in His Name, and have His power flowing through us to heal the sick and cast out devils?

No More Excuses...No More Compromise!

God never intended for His healing power to be limited or to cease flowing in the Church. In this end-time hour as He brings the Church to full maturity, He will release His healing power through members of the Body of Christ. There will be a wave of healing power that will encompass the world resulting in a great harvest of souls.

The time has come where the Church must stand and declare "thus saith the Lord!"

No more compromising the Word! Either we believe divine healing is provided for all in the atonement or we don't.

We must stop denying the power of God, stop making excuses for our failures, and have an experience where we are baptized with the same power that was flowing through the early Church!

It's Time to Stomp on the Devil!

It's time for the Church of Jesus Christ to take a stand and boldly declare to the world that there is healing in Jesus' Name! Instead of becoming intimidated and backing up when the world doesn't understand and starts criticizing and ridiculing us for praying for the sick and casting out devils, we must fearlessly proclaim the truth.

Ninety percent of the Church today retreats and is afraid of the criticism and ridicule. When the news media criticizes us, the Church gets confused and starts to accuse each other. They begin to point their finger and criticize. "If that brother was in the will of God, he wouldn't be persecuted. If that brother was in God's will, the newspapers wouldn't be tearing him apart."

How are we in the Church today going to stand against the powers of

unbelief?
How are we going to stand against the ungodly forces that are permeating our society?
We aren't going to stop homosexuality by getting on a soapbox or marching down a street carrying a sign.
We aren't going to stop abortion, alcohol and drug abuse, or pornography by having marches, signing petitions or picketing outside abortion clinics or X-rated movie theaters.
We aren't going to win the battle using carnal weapons. We aren't going to win using our natural abilities. We are going to use the mighty weapons of warfare God has given us that are mighty through God to the pulling down of strongholds.
We are going to win the battle through the unlimited power of God flowing through us! God never intended to use our natural abilities.
Its time for us to move from the natural into the supernatural!
It's time for the Church to take a stand. No more compromise! No more intimidation! We're growing up to full maturity.
Instead of backing down, we need to let the enemy know we are a militant Church.
We are an army of God!
It's time for us to start stomping on the devil!
The weapons God has given us are not the weapons of this world. They have divine power to demolish strongholds and destroy arguments.
"For though we walk (live) in the flesh, we are not carrying on our warfare according to the flesh and using mere human weapons. For the weapons of our warfare are not physical (weapons of flesh and blood), but they are mighty before God for the overthrow and destruction of strongholds, (inasmuch as we) refute arguments and theories and reasonings and every proud and lofty thing that sets itself up against the (true) knowledge of God; and we lead every thought and purpose away captive into the obedience of Christ, the Messiah, the Anointed One" (2 Cor. 10:3-5 AMP).
We don't argue.
We proclaim the unadulterated, uncompromising Word of God!
We must not be afraid to preach against the sins of lust, homosexuality, hatred, covetousness, and other sins that have infiltrated every area of our society and call for repentance.
We must not be afraid to proclaim to the humanistic, idolatrous society we live in that there is only one God...not Buddha...not Shinto...not Mohammed...He is God Jehovah, the God of Abraham, Isaac and Jacob. And, there is only one way to salvation...Jesus Christ, the Son of the living God!
We must not be afraid to preach divine healing, deliverance and the baptism

of the Holy Spirit with the manifestation of His unlimited power.

We must cast down everything that exalts itself above the knowledge of God and take captive every thought and make it obedient to Jesus!

We must continue to heal the sick!

We must continue to cast out devils!

We must continue to tear down the enemy strongholds over our neighborhoods, cities and nations in Jesus' Name!

Are you ready?

This is our time! We are going to rise up to our spiritual destiny and be the powerful force in this world God intended us to be!

CHAPTER 13

A VISION AND STRATEGY FOR CHURCH GROWTH

Lawrence Khong

Reverend Lawrence Khong graduated with a degree in business administration from the University of Singapore in 1976 and received his master's degree in theology at Dallas Theological Seminary in 1981. Rev. Khong is deeply committed to a strong pulpit ministry of expository preaching as well as to the ministry of healing through the supernatural work of the Holy Spirit. Filled with a consuming zeal to reach the lost for Christ, Rev. Khong preaches, as would a Bible teacher, but projects through the fervor of an evangelist. He is the senior pastor of Faith Community Baptist Church and also the chairman of the Spiritual Warfare Network, Singapore.

On a Personal Note...

One Sunday morning in September 1994, I preached four consecutive services in the Faith Community Baptist Church in Singapore. I must tell you that the church and its pastor, Lawrence Khong, made a deep impact on me. His leadership gifts, the militant attitude of the church members regarding evangelism, and their servant attitudes were just some of the elements that we could see in the great work the Holy Spirit is doing through that ministry. The organization and aggressiveness of the cells or family groups are exemplary.

When we were discussing who the authors of this book were to be, the name of Lawrence Khong came up immediately as an authoritative voice on the subject of leadership and assimilation of new believers. As you will see, he has a gift to tell the truth and challenge us while keeping humility and simplicity of the heart.

Without a doubt Asia has been rewarded time after time with great ministers of God. May God give us many more visionaries, like Lawrence, to evangelize Mainland China and Southeast Asia.

Harold Caballeros

On August 17, 1986, I stood on the platform in a rented auditorium in Singapore to preach in the first worship service of a brand new congregation. As I approached the pulpit, the Holy Spirit spoke clearly to my heart: "Son, today the new baby is born!" Then the words of Haggai 2:9 flooded into my mind: "'The glory of this present house will be greater than the glory of the former house,...And in this place I will grant peace,' declares the Lord Almighty" (NIV).

I was too emotionally worn out to be excited about the "greater glory." I simply took comfort in the fact that in this new church there will be peace. I had just emerged from more than a year of leadership struggle in my former church. I had grown up in this church-a Bible-believing congregation that had been growing consistently. This had been my spiritual home throughout my teenage years. The leadership of the church had clearly and lovingly affirmed my calling into the ministry. They sent me to pursue my theological training in the United States. I returned to be the pastor of the church. Within five years, it grew from 350 to 1,600 under my pastoral leadership.

A CAREER-CHANGING EXPERIENCE

During the fifth year of my pastorate, I had an unexpected encounter with the Holy Spirit that opened my heart to the reality of God's power. In that encounter, I began speaking in a new tongue. It was something I had always told my congregation would not and should not ever happen in this day and age. I clearly taught them that this particular gift, together with other power gifts of the Holy Spirit, had ceased at the end of the apostolic age. I taught them so well, in fact, that the leadership of the church rejected the validity of my experience and its theological implications immediately. I realized they were doing the very thing I would have done if I were in their shoes.

I was confused. My experience completely devastated my neat and tidy theology. I could not at that point give a clear biblical understanding about what happened. On the other hand, I could not deny the reality of that experience without compromising the witness of the Holy Spirit in my heart. Meanwhile, my ministry began falling apart. Before long, theological differences within the leadership degenerated to attacks on my personal integrity. After many months of painful struggles, I was finally asked to relinquish my role as the senior pastor of the church.

In the midst of this agonizing process, the Lord gave me a clear word from Scripture: "A woman, when she is in labor, has sorrow because her hour has come; but as soon as she has given birth to the child, she no longer remembers the anguish, for joy that a human being has been born into the world" (John 16:21).

The Lord told me He was bringing forth a "new baby" in my life that would launch me into a new ministry. The painful struggles I was going through were the labor pains needed to bring forth this new birth.

THE NEW BABY IS BORN

When the Lord said, "Son, today the new baby is born!" on August 17, 1986, Faith Community Baptist Church (FCBC) began. It brought unspeakable joy to my spirit. Since then, the promise of God has been true. The glory of this ministry has far exceeded what I would ask or think. Indeed, in the last 10 years of our church, there has been peace.

As I am writing this, the baby has grown considerably. The attendance in our weekly worship services has reached close to 8,000. In the past 10 years, we have baptized more than 6,400 new believers. During the same period, some 16,000 persons have made professions of faith for the first time. Most significantly, in my mind, almost every person who worships with us is also part of a cell group ministry during the week. In these small groups, we train every member to be a minister of the gospel, calling forth a higher-than-average level of commitment.

As I reflect upon the grace of the Lord in Faith Community Baptist Church during the last 10 years, the Lord has impressed me with four major factors that have contributed to the phenomenal growth in this local congregation. These four factors include (1) a clear vision and strategy for growth; (2) a cell church structure; (3) a reliance on the supernatural work of the Holy Spirit; and (4) one strong and anointed leader.

A CLEAR VISION AND STRATEGY FOR GROWTH

During the first 12 months of FCBC, I had the leaders of the church join me in seeking the Lord for a clear vision and strategy for growth. We were determined not to be another church that religiously maintained traditional programs. With all our hearts, we sought the Lord for a blueprint that would enable us to take our city for God. The Lord showed us that to do this, we must move in unity, we must share a common vision and we must agree on the appropriate strategies to fulfill the vision. As early as 1987, we developed a three-part vision that has guided our programs ever since. This three-part vision has seen refinements through the years. Today, it stands as follows:

By God's grace, we will, by the year 2000 (1) establish integrated ministries of outreach, discipleship and service that encompass the whole of Singapore; (2) be a model cell group church that provides quality pastoral training and equipping resources for transitioning cell group churches in Singapore and around the world; and (3) establish 50 cell group churches around the world by sending out teams to reach hidden or responsive people groups.

To achieve this vision, we have adopted the following strategies:

1. Develop an exciting and meaningful celebration every Sunday through music and the pulpit ministry;
2. Minimize committee meetings by decentralization of operations to full-time staff;
3. Commit to active staff recruitment to establish a multiple-staff ministry;
4. Establish a discipleship network for evangelism, prayer and Bible study;
5. Provide lay leadership training for all leaders of the church;
6. Develop and establish specialized ministries of outreach;
7. Train, equip, send and fully support missionaries from the church to the mission field;
8. Build a "Touch Center" consisting of an auditorium seating some 3,000, including other ministry facilities for both the church and the community;
9. Develop within every member a deep commitment to regular, disciplined and intense warfare prayer for spiritual revival in Singapore and around the world;
10. Strengthen the family so as to provide a solid base for reaching the unsaved with the love of Christ.

From the beginning, we were filled with a sense of excitement that God was going to fulfill these visions among us. In FCBC, every one of us is given a corporate challenge to fulfill the vision the Lord has given us. We believe that "everybody's job" becomes "nobody's job." Members of FCBC believe that if no one else will do it, we will assume the responsibility of winning our nation to the Lord. Before long, most of us would begin to realize that we could no longer possess this vision. Rather, this vision has now totally possessed us with a consuming zeal from the Lord!

COMPLETELY STRUCTURED AS A CELL GROUP CHURCH

In the last five years, FCBC has organized an annual "International Conference on Cell Group Church." Thousands from around the world have come to learn the principles and operations of a cell group church. Every year, I begin the conference by proclaiming a statement that has become a major landmark of my teaching about the cell church. My statement is: There is a heaven and earth difference; an east and west difference between a CHURCH WITH CELLS and a CELL GROUP CHURCH.

Just about every church in the world has some kind of small groups. Some of these groups are Bible study groups, fellowship groups, counseling/therapy groups, prayer groups and many others. However, these are churches with cells and not cell churches. The major difference between the former and the latter is a structural one. Hence there is a fundamental, not a superficial, difference between them.

In a church with cells, the cell ministry is only a department within the total ministry of the church. Members of the church have many options. They can choose to serve in the missions department or the prayer department or the Christian education department or the fellowship department. They can choose between the Sunday School or the adult fellowship. The cell ministry is just another one of the options.

This is not so in a cell group church. In a cell group church, the cell is the church. No menu of options is open to every member except that they be in a cell group. Every department of the church is designed to serve the cell ministry. Departments do not have any constituency of their own. All are designed to support the ministry of the cells.

In FCBC, every believer is assimilated into cell groups, similar to military squads. Each cell is trained to edify one another and to evangelize so that it will multiply within a year to a maximum size of 12 to 15 people. These cell groups are not independent "house churches," but basic Christian communities linked together to penetrate every area of our community. Approximately three to four cell groups cluster to form a sub-zone, and a volunteer zone supervisor pastors the five cells and its cell leaders. Five sub-zones cluster to create a zone of about 250 people pastored by a full-time zone pastor. Five or more zones cluster to form a district, and a seasoned district pastor shepherds as many as 1,500 people.

From the start, we created zones that were geographical (north, east, west) and generational (children, youth, military). Later, we added our music zone for those participating in our choirs, bands, orchestras, drama and dance. Even these music cells are constantly winning people to Jesus Christ. Every year, more than 2,500 make first-time decisions for the Lord in the cells.

FOUNDATIONS FOR MINISTRY

In the early years, we worked hard to create the foundations for our ministry. Pastors who had no previous experience with cell church structures were trained and cell leaders were equipped. Nonexistent equipping materials had to be written. Soon we had a nickname: "FCBC-Fast Changing Baptist Church"! Every experimental step helped us learn how to equip and evangelize in the new paradigm. We were determined to discard anything that did not help us achieve our goals, so we revised our strategy again and again as we gained experience. Indeed, we are still doing so!

Like other cell churches, our life involves three levels: the cells, the congregations (a cluster of five zones) and the celebration on Sunday. We quickly had to go to two and then three celebrations of 1,000 people to accommodate the growth in the cell groups. We presently have one evening service on Saturday and four services on Sunday of two hours duration each. A completely different congregation of people worships in the Saturday evening service. We have studiously avoided advertising "seeker-sensitive services," choosing instead to grow through the ministries of our members in the cells. Our cells are seeker-sensitive, but our celebration is not. For us, the celebration is an assembling of the Body of Christ rather than a means of attracting the unconverted. Nevertheless, many profess faith in Jesus Christ as a result of the intense anointing that comes through worship, as well as my pulpit ministry that focuses on down-to-earth life issues.

THE YEAR OF EQUIPPING

What we call "The Year of Equipping" has become an important part of our cell group life. Each incoming member is visited by the cell leader, who assigns a cell member to be a sponsor for the new person. A "Journey Guide" is used to acquaint the cell leader and sponsor with the spiritual condition of the person. Guided by private weekly sessions with the sponsor, this person will complete a journey through the "Arrival Kit" and then be trained to share Christ with both responsive and unresponsive unbelievers.

Another major part of The Year of Equipping consists of three cycles of training for evangelism and harvest meeting in the cells throughout the year. One such cycle begins in January, where new members of the cell are sent for a weekend of evangelism training. This is followed by further practices during the cell meetings, leading up to the Good Friday weekend.

In these months, every member of the cell is asked to pray for unsaved people whom they would invite to a special Good Friday evangelistic cell meeting. On that one Good Friday evening, we will have as many as 4,000 unsaved people in all our cell groups spread throughout the city. More than 10 percent of them will give their lives to the Lord for the first time. In that meeting, every member of the cell shares the gospel with unsaved friends. We do this three times a year. In this way, equipping for evangelism is an ongoing lifestyle of every cell. It is my intention that every cell become a fit fighting unit in the army of the Lord!

COMMUNITY SERVICE

Because of our strong desire to penetrate the society around us, we have formed the Touch Community Services. This is the neutral arm of our church designed to relate to the community. Through this separate corporation, we conduct childcare, legal aid services, after-school clubs, marriage counseling, a workshop to train the handicapped and many other social ministry areas. This has earned the respect of unbelievers around us and has provided openings for the gospel we would not otherwise experience. It has established good will for us among the many racial groups that live together in harmony in our nation.

Our community services have found so much favor with government authorities that much of our service ministry is actually funded by the government. As of now, the juvenile courts make it mandatory for their offenders to seek counseling from our youth counseling services. The registry of marriage has invited us to conduct premarital counseling for all who are getting married in Singapore! This is our "root system" into the unconverted world.

RELIANCE ON THE SUPERNATURAL WORKS OF THE HOLY SPIRIT

The structure of the cell church is nothing but a conduit for the power of the Holy Spirit. Unless the living water flows, the cells are lifeless. A major spiritual breakthrough came for us in those early years as we began to recognize the place of the gifts of the Holy Spirit in our midst. As our cell groups were confronted by the need for spiritual power in caring for people, we saw a gracious outpouring of His presence in our midst.

I shall never forget a certain Sunday when the Lord visited us powerfully. We were then conducting four worship services in a rented auditorium that seated about 800. On that particular Sunday, I preached a message about repentance. Many came forward to repent of their sins. As I prayed for them from behind the pulpit, the Holy Spirit came into our midst. Most of them fell under the power of the Spirit. This was something we had never experienced in our church. It surprised everyone in the auditorium, especially the people who found themselves lying on the church floor for the first time in their lives, completely unable to move.

The presence of the Lord was so overwhelming that by the beginning of the third service, members who were just walking into the auditorium for worship fell under the power of the Spirit, having no idea what had been happening in the preceding services!

This visitation of the Holy Spirit brought about a six-month period of deep repentance among the members of the church. The anointing of the Spirit filled every cell meeting. The sick were being healed. The demonized were set free. The church grew rapidly as our cell groups learned to minister in the power of the Spirit.

ONE STRONG AND ANOINTED LEADER

At the risk of misunderstanding me as being arrogant, I have always told audiences around the world that one of the main factors that has contributed to the growth of FCBC is the gracious gift of leadership the Lord has entrusted to me. FCBC has grown rapidly because of my strong and anointed leadership. In the early years of the church, the leadership team carefully studied a chapter written by Oswald J. Smith in his book Building a Better World. He began his chapter with these words:

"Behold, I have given him for a witness to the people, a leader and commander to the people" (Isa. 55:4). God's plan is that His flock should be led by a Shepherd, not run by a Board. Committees are to advise, never to dictate. The Holy Spirit appoints men. To Bishops and Elders is given the care of the churches, never to Committees. They are to be the Overseers, the Shepherds. Each one has his own flock. Because men have failed to recognize this, there has been trouble. When God's plan is followed, all is well. 17

The cell group church is vision driven. It needs a strong leader to rally the people toward a God-given vision. It is also structured like the military. It calls for a strong commander to instill a sense of strict spiritual discipline needed to complete the task. At the inception of the church, my core leaders asked, "Pastor, what sort of leader will you be?"

My answer was unequivocal, "I believe I will be a strong leader, one who believes what the Lord wants me to do and who pursues it with all my heart."

Traditionally, the church has been suspicious of strong leadership, especially when it is centered in one person. As a result, many man-made systems of checks and counterchecks have been built into traditional church polity to ensure that there can be no one-man rule. Although I agree that there is a need for mutual accountability, these checks have more often become major roadblocks for God's appointed leaders to lead His people into victorious ministry. Many lay leaders have expressed great fear of so-called "dictatorship" behind the pulpit. After 20 years of ministry, however, I must say that I have seen more "dictators" sitting in the pews than those standing behind pulpits.

WHAT IS LEADERSHIP?

One day I was praying about this issue of leadership and the Lord impressed upon me to write down these words about leadership:

Leadership Is Not Dictatorship

Leadership is rallying people to pursue a vision. A leader successfully instills in those he is leading a deep desire to fulfill that vision. He gains the trust of his people by virtue of his character, his integrity, his resourcefulness, his zeal, his good judgment, his people skills and, most importantly, his anointing from God. As a result, the people grant him the freedom to decide and the authority to supervise and control. Such leadership can never be provided by a committee or a board. If, indeed, such leadership is provided by a group, it is because within that group someone can provide such strong leadership first to the group and through that to the rest of the people.

We often talk about New Testament leadership as if it is completely different from Old Testament leadership. I believe that biblical leadership is consistent throughout the New and Old Testaments. Whenever God wants to do a work, He chooses a man. We have leaders such as Moses, Gideon, David, Elijah and others in the Old Testament. In the New Testament, we have leaders such as Peter for the Jews and Paul for the Gentiles.

In FCBC, I assert my clear leadership in three areas:

Casting the Vision

I lead the people by casting a clear and concrete vision for the church. In the early years, I spent countless hours sharing, discussing, praying and formulating the vision and strategies of the church. I realize that a vision is only powerful when it is fully owned by the people. Our vision and strategies were clearly set by the third year. Since that time, I have constantly shared and reinforced this for my leaders and members. I speak to every new member of the church about this vision in our new member orientation called "Spiritual Formation Weekend." I challenge every member to consider seriously our vision before joining our church. If someone is not able to subscribe to the vision, I strongly recommend that the person join another church.

Once the vision and strategies have been forged, I expect every leader in the church to support them. This is especially so for pastoral staff. They are selected on the basis that as lay cell leaders and group supervisors they have demonstrated their commitment to the vision of the church. Today, the church has a paid staff of almost 200. In the last 10 years, we have had a staff turnover of fewer than 10 persons. There is a tremendous sense of unity on the team. The reason for this is that I have clearly provided leadership in casting for the people a clear vision and articulating specific strategies from the Lord.

Creating an Environment for Growth

As leader, I am concerned about creating an environment conducive to growth. We have written a clear mission statement and we have agreed upon specific core values that define the uniqueness of FCBC, both in terms of belief and of practice. I will reproduce the mission statement here:

We seek to fulfill God's role for us in bringing the gospel to the world by developing every believer to his full potential in Jesus Christ within a vision & value driven environment and a God-centered community.

Preaching and Teaching from the Pulpit

The main vehicle by which the growth environment is established comes through dynamic teaching and preaching during the celebration. Some think that the cell church consists of only cells. This is not true. Although the cell is the church, the church is more than just cells. The cells come together in the celebration meeting, absorbing the apostolic teaching that shapes the direction, commitment and spiritual atmosphere for the whole Body. The church in Acts 2 met in homes, but they came together to listen to the apostles' teaching. I spend some 20 hours every week preparing my sermon. The sermon each week is more than teaching the Bible. Every sermon conveys a passion for God and communicates His purposes for His people.

There is no doubt that the growth of FCBC is the result of God's special grace in and through my life. As long as I walk humbly before the Lord in intimacy, the Lord will lead us from glory to glory. I realize that as I promote and support strong apostolic leadership, there is always the danger of abuse. It is altogether possible for apostles to abuse the authority God has given us as His apostolic leaders. Nevertheless, this apparently is a risk God is willing to take with us because, in His grace, He has chosen to do just that. God is more than able to bring down His erring servants just as quickly as He raises them up. Meanwhile, I believe in affirming God's appointed leadership over His people.

AFFIRMATION WITH HUMILITY

I believe that God's leaders need affirmation and encouragement as they agree to take positions of leadership. Yet they must have the humility to serve. Strong leaders have often been misunderstood to be dictatorial and proud. For my part, though, I would rather affirm them, pray for them and release them to become a blessing to the Body of Christ.

When FCBC started, my heart was completely shattered by the rejection of the leaders of my former church. The issues that finally brought about the split of the church turned personal. I was attacked for being controlling, dictatorial and even dangerously influential. At the inception of FCBC, I had lost my confidence to lead. Thus I became laid back, relinquishing the leadership to my core leaders who, together with me, started the church. In the beginning of 1987, a few months after the church had started, we invited Pastor Bill Yaegar from the First Baptist Church of Modesto, California, to speak to us about leadership. Pastor Yaegar was in his 60s and since then has retired.

In his visit with us, Bill Yaegar noticed how discouraged I was. I could never forget his parting words to me at the Singapore airport. He said, "Son, I was praying for you this morning. The Lord told me He was giving you a new name. Your name shall be called 'Ari.' This is a Jewish name that means 'lion.' Lawrence, the Lord tells you that you are the 'Lion of Singapore.' You are to stand up and roar. And whenever others forget that you are the 'Lion of Singapore,' stand up and roar again!"

No one had ever previously affirmed me that way. It was an extremely important moment in my ministry career. I realized in that instant that through all my years of Christian ministry, people were constantly warning me to go slower, to be more cautious and to be more "humble." This was the first time a seasoned servant of God had actually encouraged me to take charge, to lead and to press on. Something burst forth within the depths of my spirit. I have been roaring ever since for the glory of God and the advance of His kingdom!

Excerpted from The New Apostolic Churches edited by C. Peter Wagner, Ventura, CA, Regal Books 1998, used by permission of Regal Books and the author.

CHAPTER

14

THE NEW APOSTOLIC REFORMATION

C. Peter Wagner

Dr. C. Peter Wagner is cofounder of the World Prayer Center in Colorado Springs, Colorado, and coordinator of the United Prayer Track of the A.D. 2000 and Beyond Movement. He is also a professor at Fuller Theological Seminary. He is the author/editor of more than 40 books.

On a Personal Note...

As I said before, Peter Wagner has a supernatural gift to recognize what God is doing and to guide the body of Christ in order to maximize its resources within the move of God. We have felt the need to include this chapter because it discusses something we really need-the new wineskins to receive the new wine of the Holy Spirit.

After reading it, you will understand that God is establishing a whole new structure for the expansion of His Kingdom in the earth. This is the result of many factors, among which these are emphasized: the Holy Spirit's guidance, exercise of authority in the Name of Jesus, a strong expression of leadership, and a special emphasis on praise, worship and evangelism. I should add that this is happening everywhere. This is not a human movement, but the manifestation of God's sovereignty.

I like to call what He is doing, "the establishment of the structure of God's government in the Church."

Harold Caballeros

I will soon complete 30 years as a professor of church growth on the graduate level. During these 30 years, I have studied countless Christian churches of all sizes, in all kinds of locations, from new church plants to those hundreds of years old, spanning virtually every theological tradition, and rooted in varieties of cultures on six continents. I have reported my research the best I have known how in an average of one or two books a year.

I have never been more excited about a book dealing with church growth than I am about The New Apostolic Churches, from which this chapter is reprinted. I will begin with a personal testimony of how God has brought me to the place where I am now; it will explain why I am so excited.

Seasons of Research

During my decades as a scholar, God has seen fit to focus my research energies on certain aspects of church growth for certain periods of time. As I have done that, I have tried to use what I have learned to develop new courses for my students at Fuller Theological Seminary, and many of the lessons eventually become books.

My mentor in church growth research was Donald A. McGavran, the founder of the whole field of church growth. He is now with the Lord, but for years I have had the singular privilege of carrying the title of the Donald A. McGavran Professor of Church Growth. One of the most basic lessons I learned from McGavran was that the best way to discover what makes churches grow is to study growing churches. As a result, my first season of research, spanning the 1970s and into the 1980s, was spent doing exactly that. In retrospect, I now look at this as researching the technical principles of church growth.

During that time, I began to notice something I obviously did not have the mental equipment to understand or to assimilate into my analysis of church growth. I noticed that the churches worldwide that seemed to grow the most rapidly were, for the most part, those that outwardly featured the immediate present-day supernatural ministry of the Holy Spirit.

My mentor for helping me make a paradigm shift into what I now call the spiritual principles of church growth was John Wimber, founder of the Association of Vineyard Churches and Vineyard Ministries International. This began my second season of research, focusing first of all on the relationship between supernatural signs and wonders and church growth, then on prayer and spiritual warfare. This began in the early 1980s and continued to the mid-1990s.

My third season of research is now focusing on the New Apostolic Reformation, the subject of this chapter. I am very excited because the new apostolic churches, better than any I have previously studied, combine, on the highest level, solid technical principles of church growth with solid spiritual principles of church growth. I will tell more about that later.

Unity + Gifts = Growth

One of the most explicit Scripture verses about church growth is Ephesians 4:16, which says that the Body of which Jesus is the head, "joined and knit together by what every joint supplies, according to the effective working by which every part does its share, causes growth of the body" (italics added). A formula for growth, then, is: Unity (joined together) + Gifts (every part does its share) = Growth.

Paul tells us in verse 7 that each one of us has a "measure" of grace, just as Romans 12:3 says we have a "measure" of faith, the measure being our spiritual gifts. Then Ephesians 4:8 says that Jesus, when He ascended, "gave gifts to men," and it goes on to tell us that He gave gifted people to the Church on two levels: (1) the government level (apostles, prophets, evangelists, pastors, teachers) in verse 11, and (2) the ministry of the saints in general in verse 12. When the government is in its proper place, biblical unity of the saints emerges and "every part can do its share."

How do these biblical principles unfold in real life? For 2,000 years, the Church of Jesus Christ has grown and spread into every continent. Jesus said. "I will build My church," and He has been doing it. As we review those 2,000 years, however, it is quite obvious that Jesus does not always build His Church in the same ways. He did one way in the Roman Empire before Constantine; another way after Constantine; another way in the Middle Ages; another way following the Reformation; another way during the era of European colonization; and yet another way post-World War II, just to name a few.

Growth: a Story of New Wineskins

Every time Jesus began building His Church in a new way throughout history, He provided new wineskins. While He was still on earth, He said that such a thing would be necessary: "Nor do they put new wine into old wineskins, or else the wineskins break, the wine is spilled, and the wineskins are ruined. But they put new wine into the new wineskins, and both are preserved" (Matt. 9:17). The growth of the Church through the ages is, in part, a story of new wineskins.

Because this is the case, a crucial question not only for professors of church growth, but also for Christians in general, is this: *What are the new wineskins Jesus is providing as we move into the twenty-first century?*

Four Crucial Questions

My experience as a church growth scholar has led me constantly to ask four crucial questions:

1. Why does the blessing of God rest where it does?
2. Churches are not all equal. Why is it that at certain times, some churches are more blessed than others?
3. Can any pattern of divine blessing be discerned?
4. Do those churches that seem to be unusually blessed have any common characteristics?

As I have tried to answer these questions, it is important to realize that I am a very traditional Christian. For decades I have been an ordained Congregational minister, and I still am. We Congregationalists came over on the *Mayflower*! I find myself in one of the oldest wineskins on record. Furthermore, I am a conservative Congregationalist (ordained in the Conservative Congregational Christian Conference). This was definitely an obstacle to my early church growth research because while I was a missionary in Bolivia I was anti-Pentecostal, and the fastest-growing churches in Latin America at the time happened to be Pentecostal churches.

I finally overcame my biases, however, and, in 1973, wrote *Look Out! The Pentecostals* Are Coming! (Creation House). At that time, Pentecostal churches were one of the new wineskins, and their growth was showing it.

Wineskins of the 1990s

That was back in the 1970s. What, however, are the new wineskins of the 1990s? Where does the blessing of God seem to be resting today?

The answer to this question began coming into focus in 1993. As a professional missiologist, I had picked up certain bits and pieces of information through the years, but until then, at least in my mind, these bits and pieces were unrelated. Then, however, I did begin to see a pattern among three amazing church growth movements:

1. The African Independent Churches. These roots go back to the turn of the century when large numbers of contextualized African churches began breaking away from the traditional mission churches. Throughout the century, the growth of the independent churches in Africa has far exceeded the growth of the traditional churches.

2. The Chinese house churches. Particularly since the end of the Cultural Revolution in the mid-1970s, the multiplication of house churches under a hostile Marxist government in China has been a missiological phenomenon.

3. Latin American grassroots churches. During the past 20 years, the largest churches that have been launched in virtually every metropolitan area of Latin America are largely those that are pastored by individuals who have had no formative experience with foreign missionaries or mission-initiated institutions.

I would put these three together with the rapid growth of the American independent charismatic churches I researched for the *Dictionary of Pentecostal and Charismatic Movements*, published by Zondervan in 1987. My article, entitled "Church Growth," pointed out that this was the fastest-growing segment of Christianity in the United States in our times.

What happened in 1993, then, was the realization in my mind that, indeed, a pattern of divine blessing today on certain identifiable groups of churches is discernible (Question #3). The next question then becomes (Question #4): What are their common characteristics?

A Churchquake!

In the balance of this chapter, I will outline the nine most common characteristics of these churches I have been able to discern to date. My exposition and comments about each will, of necessity, be brief so as to keep the size of this chapter proportionate to the others in this book.

I am simultaneously working on my textbook about the subject, which will provide abundant details. The title I am considering for the textbook is Churchquake!, which, to me, reflects the magnitude of change these new wineskins are bringing to the Body of Christ. In fact, I am sure we are seeing before our very eyes the most radical change in the way of doing church since the Protestant Reformation.

Let's take a brief look at nine components of the new wineskins that are shaping the Church for the twenty-first century.

1. A New Name

When I began researching the Pentecostal movement years ago, it already had a name. This new movement, however, did not have a name. Because I was planning to teach a seminary course based on it, I needed a name for my course. For a couple of years I experimented with "postdenominationalism," but strong protests from my denominational friends persuaded me that it might not be the best name. Besides many of the new apostolic churches have remained within their denominations. "Independent charismatic" does not seem to fit either because (1) these churches see themselves as interdependent, as opposed to independent, and (2) they are not all charismatic in orientation.

The name I have settled on for the movement is the New Apostolic Reformation, and individual churches being designated as new apostolic churches.

I use "reformation" because, as I have said, these new wineskins appear to be at least as radical as those of the Protestant Reformation almost 500 years ago. "Apostolic" connotes a strong focus on outreach plus a recognition of present-day apostolic ministries. "New" adds a contemporary spin to the name.

Although many people were begging for a definition of the New Apostolic Reformation from the beginning, I resisted formulating one until I believed I had a more mature grasp of the movement. Now that I have taught my first Fuller Seminary course about the subject, I believe it is time to take the risk of a definition, hoping that it will not have to be revised too frequently in the future:

The New Apostolic Reformation is an extraordinary work of God at the close of the twentieth century that is, to a significant extent, changing the shape of Protestant Christianity around the world. For almost 500 years, Christian churches have largely functioned within traditional denominational structures of one kind or another. Particularly in the 1990s, but having roots going back for almost a century, new forms and operational procedures are now emerging in areas such as local church government, interchurch relationships, financing, evangelism, missions, prayer, leadership selection and training, the role of supernatural power, worship and other important aspects of church life. Some of these changes are being seen within denominations themselves, but for the most part they are taking the form of loosely structured apostolic networks. In virtually every region of the world, these new apostolic churches constitute the fastest-growing segment of Christianity.

Infinite creativity seems to be the watchword for assigning names to local churches. The "Crystal Cathedral" and "Community Church of Joy" are among the most prominent congregations in our country. "Icthus" churches are multiplying in England. On a recent visit to the Philippines I came in contact with "The Warm Body of Jesus Church." One of my favorite churches in Argentina is "Waves of Love and Peace." In Kenya, Thomas Muthee pastors "The Prayer Cave." A friend told me of a church in Zimbabwe called the "Dodge the Devil and Go Straight to Heaven Church"!

2. New Authority Structure

In my judgment, views of leadership and leadership authority constitute the most radical of the nine changes from traditional Christianity. Here is the main difference: The amount of spiritual authority delegated by the Holy Spirit to individuals. I have attempted to use each word in that statement advisedly. We are seeing a transition from bureaucratic authority to personal authority, from legal structure to relational structure, from control to coordination and from rational leadership to charismatic leadership. This all manifests itself on two levels: the local level and the translocal level.

On the local church level, the new apostolic pastors are the leaders of the church. In traditional Christianity, the pastors are regarded as employees of the church.

It is a question of trust. New apostolic congregations trust their pastor. Traditional congregations trust boards and committees. The difference between the two is enormous. The most passionate description of this difference I have yet seen is Lawrence Khong's chapter in this book.

On the translocal level, one of the most surprising developments for those of us who are traditionalists is the growing affirmation of contemporary apostolic ministries. Our English "apostle" is a transliteration of the Greek apostolos, which means one who is sent out with a commission. This is an important dimension of what we are seeing, but the more surprising feature is the reaffirmation, not only of the New Testament gift of apostle, but also of the office of apostle.

3. New Leadership Training

Although new apostolic pastors are fervently dedicated to leading their churches, they are equally dedicated to releasing the people of their congregations to do the ministry of the church. A characteristic of many new apostolic churches is an abundance of volunteers. Church members are normally taught that part of being a good Christian is to discover the spiritual gifts God has given them and to minister to others through those gifts as well as through any natural talents they might also have.

Members of the paid pastoral staff of typical new apostolic churches are usually homegrown. As all the believers in the congregation become active in ministry, certain ones tend to rise to the top like cream on fresh milk, and they are the ones who are then recruited for the staff. Because for many this involves a midlife career change, the possibility of their enrolling for two or three years in the residence program of a traditional seminary or Bible school is extremely remote. Therefore, academic requirements for ordination, so long the staple in traditional churches, are being scrapped. New apostolic ordination is primarily rooted in personal relationships, which verify character, and in proved ministry skills.

Continuing education for leaders more frequently takes place in conferences, seminars and retreats rather than in classrooms of accredited institutions. Little aversion is noticed for quality training, but the demands are many for alternate delivery systems. A disproportionate number of new apostolic churches, especially the large ones, are establishing their own in-house Bible schools.

One of the most notable features of new apostolic churches, which traditional church leaders soon discover to their amazement, is the absence of nomination committees (to place lay leaders within the congregation) and of search committees (to locate and recruit new staff members).

4. New Ministry Focus

Traditional Christianity starts with the present situation and focuses on the past. New apostolic Christianity starts with the present situation and focuses on the future.

Many traditional churches are heritage driven. "We must get back to our roots. We need to pray for renewal"-meaning that we should once again be what we used to be. The founders of the movement are often thought of as standing shoulder to shoulder with the 12 apostles.

On the other hand, new apostolic church leaders are vision driven. In a conversation with a new apostolic senior pastor about his church, I once asked, "How many cell groups do you have?" I think that was sometime in 1996.

He replied, "We will have 600 by the year 2000!"

I can't seem to recall ever finding out how many cells he did have in 1996. As far as the pastor was concerned, though, that apparently didn't matter at all. In his mind, the 600 cells were not imaginary, they were real. The 600 was what really mattered

5. New Worship Style

In only a few exceptions, new apostolic churches use contemporary worship styles. Contemporary worship is the one characteristic of the New Apostolic Reformation that has already penetrated the most deeply into traditional and denominational churches across-the-board. Many churches that would not at all be considered new apostolic are now using contemporary worship in at least one of their weekend services.

Worship leaders have replaced music directors. Keyboards have replaced pipe organs. Casual worship teams have replaced robed choirs. Overhead projectors have replaced hymnals. Ten to 12 minutes of congregational singing is now 30 to 49 minutes or even more. Standing during worship is the rule, although a great amount of freedom for body language prevails.

As you scan a new apostolic congregation in worship, you will likely see some sitting, some kneeling, some holding up hands, some closing their eyes, some clapping their hands, some wiping tears from their eyes, some using tambourines, some dancing and some just walking around.

"Performance" is a naughty word for new apostolic worship leaders. Their goal is to help every person in the congregation become an active "participant" in worship. Frequent applause is not congratulating those on the platform for their musical excellence, but it is seen as high tribute to the triune God.

6. New Prayer Forms

Prayer in new apostolic churches has taken forms rarely seen in traditional congregations. Some of this takes place within the church and some takes place outside the church.

The actual number of prayer times and the cumulative number of minutes spent in prayer during the worship service of new apostolic churches far exceed the prayer time of the average traditional church. Worship leaders weave frequent times of prayer into singing worship songs. Many of them argue that true worship is, in itself, a form of prayer, so blending the two seems natural. A considerable number of new apostolic churches practice concert prayer, in which all the worshipers are praying out loud at the same time, some in a prayer language and some in the vernacular. At times in some churches, each one will begin singing a prayer, creating a loud, harmonious sound not unlike the sound of the medieval Gregorian chant.

New apostolic leaders have been among the first to understand and put into practice some of the newer forms of prayer that take place in the community itself, not in the church. For many, praise marches, prayerwalking, prayer journeys and prayer expeditions have become a part of congregational life and ministry. For example, 55 members of one local church, New Life Church of Colorado Springs, recently traveled to Nepal, high in the Himalayas, to pray on-site for each of the 43 major, yet-unreached people groups of the nation.

7. New Financing

New apostolic churches experience relatively few financial problems. Although no vision-driven church believes it has enough resources to fulfill the vision adequately, and although financial crises do come from time to time, still, compared to traditional churches, finances are abundant. I think at least three discernible reasons explain this situation.

First, generous giving is expected. Tithing is taught without apology, and those who do not tithe their incomes are subtly encouraged to evaluate their Christian lives as subpar.

Second, giving is beneficial, not only to the church and its ministry in the kingdom of God, but also to the giver. Tithes and offerings are regarded as seeds that will produce fruit of like kind for individuals and families. Luke 6:38, which says that if we give, it will be given to us in greater measure, is taken literally.

Third, giving is cheerful. It is not yet a common practice, but I have been in new apostolic churches in which the congregation breaks out into a rousing, athletic-event kind of shouting and clapping the moment the pastor announces he is collecting the morning offering. They are cheerful givers and they want everyone else to know it. I rarely hear the complaint in new apostolic churches I often hear in traditional churches: The pastor talks about money too much.

8. New Outreach

Aggressively reaching out to the lost and hurting of the community and the world is part of the new apostolic DNA. The churches assiduously attempt to avoid the "bless me syndrome" as they try to live up to their apostolic nature and calling. They do seek personal blessings from God, but usually as means to the end of reaching others. A worship song I frequently hear in new apostolic churches says: "Let your glory fall in this room; let it go forth from here to the nations."

Planting new churches is usually an assumed part of what a local congregation does. The question is not whether we should do it, but when and how. The same applies to foreign missions. One of the more interesting developments for a missiologist like me is that a large number of congregations are becoming involved, as congregations, in foreign missions. This does not mean they are necessarily bypassing mission agencies, especially new ones such as Youth With A Mission, but it does mean that they are expanding their options for influencing their people to participate in a more direct and personal way in world outreach.

Compassion for the poor, the outcast, the homeless, the disadvantaged and the handicapped is a strong characteristic of most new apostolic churches. Many other churches do a lot of talking about helping unfortunate people, but new apostolic churches seem to find ways to actually do it. The Vineyard Christian Fellowship of Anaheim, California, for example, distributes almost $2 million worth of food to hungry people in their area every year. The Cathedral of Faith in San José, California, has constructed a million-dollar warehouse facility and it has become one of the largest food distribution centers in the state. Other local churches are doing similar things.

9. New Power Orientation

I mentioned earlier that the New Apostolic Reformation seems to be combining the technical principles of church growth better than any similar grouping of churches I have observed. Even those new apostolic churches that do not consider themselves charismatic usually have a sincere openness to the work of the Holy Spirit and a consensus that all the New Testament spiritual gifts are in operation today.

The majority of the new apostolic churches not only believe in the work of the Holy Spirit, but they also regularly invite Him to come into their midst to bring supernatural power. It is commonplace, therefore, to observe active ministries of healing, demonic deliverance, spiritual warfare, prophecy, falling in the Spirit, spiritual mapping, prophetic acts, fervent intercession and travail, and so on in new apostolic churches.

A basic theological presupposition in new apostolic, as contrasted to traditional, churches is that supernatural power tends to open the way for applying truth, rather than vice versa. This is why visitors will frequently observe in these churches what seems to be more emphasis on the heart than on the mind. Some conclude from that that new apostolic churches are "too emotional."

Conclusion

The more I have studied the New Apostolic Reformation during the past few years, the more convinced I have become that we have a major transformation of Christianity on our hands. Don Miller titles his excellent new book on the subject Reinventing American Protestantism (University of California Press). By extension, I believe we are witnessing a reinventing of world Christianity. If that is the case, it is all the more reason to give God thanks for allowing us to be alive and active in His kingdom in these enthralling days.

Excerpted from The New Apostolic Churches edited by C. Peter Wagner, Ventura, CA, Regal Books(1998, used by permission of Regal Books and the author.

CHAPTER 15

EVANGELISM BY DISCIPLESHIP "THE FIELDS ARE WHITE UNTO HARVEST"

Don D. Pretty

Dr. Petry is an accomplished consultant, administrator, lecturer, and teacher in education and educational administration. He has worked in education for over 35 years, and was the founding vice president of Regent University in Virginia Beach, Virginia. He was an advisor for the establishment of three other universities, including one in Africa.

As president of Teled International, which he founded in 1984, Dr. Petry has served as a visionary for education throughout the world. His international conferences to train teachers, administrators, and educational leaders have resulted in schools being established (or in process of being established) in 35 nations around the world.

Dr. Petry received his doctorate in education in 1969 from the University of Missouri, Columbia.

On a Personal Note...

For a long time we talked about reaching our cities. Then the phrase "taking our cities" became popular. I think it has been a beautiful vision, but I have always believed that it stops short. We need men and women of God who have an even broader vision and burn with the desire to see God impact their nation. The time has come for the "nation claimers." After all, we are children of a very big God to whom nothing is impossible.

When a person is impregnated with a vision to claim his nation, he will probably start searching for those factors of change that can be used by God in order to bring the desired transformation. Within the sequence followed in this book, we now approach a critical moment; we need to be aware that Christian education is a basic element of change.

In order to accomplish our task of being salt and light it is necessary that we do the same thing the founding fathers did in the United States: establish schools where God's Word is the foundation.

Praise God that we hear "the sound of many waters" in this sense. A very big movement in opening Christian schools and universities is coming, especially in places like Latin America and Africa.

Dr. Don Petry is a person that is being used by the Lord throughout the world to bring this awakening. Through his educational conferences and the implementation of "model schools," as well as through the masters in education program at Oral Roberts University (of which I am a part), Dr. Petry is influencing the nations and mobilizing human resources to serve in the transformation of nations.

It is a special honor to include Dr. Petry's chapter. I have said before, "I deeply admire people that have a great vision," and in the case of Dr. Petry, I have seen a man with an immense vision that embraces all the earth.

Recently Dr. Petry conducted a series of seminars and made recommendations to the highest directors in the office of the Secretary of Education of Mainland China. Time after time the United States government has organized these encounters between the Chinese officials and Dr. Petry.

I pray that we receive the vision of Christian education because God has certainly called us to make disciples.

Harold Caballeros

Evangelism is our supreme task and discipleship is our supreme strategy. Many national churches as well as international missions groups that conduct crusades, Bible schools, tract distribution, witnessing, etc. have focused on getting people "saved," "converted," "born again," and as a result inside the Kingdom door. Too often efforts have stopped there…with eternity secured…just inside the door. The Apostle Paul would call them "babes" who still must be fed milk.

Salvation is a necessary and needed first step. With salvation comes the mind of Christ but now we must learn to use it. As Christians, we can never be overcomers, leading victorious lives, until we advance in our relationship with the triune God. Godly knowledge, understanding and wisdom are essential in building a relationship of trust and faith.

Many Christians today can be identified with the researcher who concluded that one reason children fall out of bed is that they stay close to where they get in! Christians who do not advance in the Kingdom stay as baby Christians never experiencing much of what God has for them.

This treatise is about discipleship. It is about the Bible's strategies, principles, and precepts foundational to being and becoming spiritually mature men and women of God; but it is more than that, it is also a call to God's people everywhere to follow biblical mandates and models in making a "people of God." Now is the time for the Church to respond to the call of Christ, the Great Commission, and make disciples (taught ones) of all nations.

Let there be no misunderstanding as to our mission-this is a call to the Church worldwide to begin discipling (making taught ones) at all ages in order to develop God's people "to be in the world but not of the world." The organizational structures to do this will involve Sunday Schools as well as Monday Schools-Christian preschools, Christian primary, junior secondary and senior secondary schools, Bible colleges, Christian community colleges, and Christian universities.

PART I: SURVEYING AND PREPARING THE SOIL

The plan of God for each of us, as was true for Jesus and the Church universal, has some unique characteristics. First, God's plan originates from Him (Jer. 29:11); is irrevocable (Rom. 11:29); and God Himself will bring it to pass (1 Thess. 5:24). God's plan for us is both spiritual and vocational (Eph. 4:1). God's plan is answered by "why" and "what:" "why was I born" and "what am I to do."

Jesus knew "why" He was born and "what" He was to do. Everything else surrounding the plan of God is "strategy" which answers the questions, "how," "when," "where," "with whom," "how much," etc. Since the Holy

Spirit is the Supreme Strategist, it becomes essential that we be filled and led with and by the Holy Spirit in order to be led into godly wisdom (action). The plan of God for one's life can be known and living it daily must be done in tandem with the direction provided by the Holy Spirit.

Jesus' Strategy-Disciples for His Great Commission
Did Jesus Commission Me?

Since Jesus started the first "School of Disciples," it can also be said that He started the first Christian school, perhaps more precisely, a Bible school. This strategy of learning and teaching was not unknown to Him since He Himself was undoubtedly taught in the temple school. Luke 2 reminds us of His visit at age 12 to the temple in Jerusalem where He entered into discussions and teaching with the teachers-scribes and Pharisees.

The emphasis here upon Jesus' own educational preparation until the time of His ministry focused upon receiving instruction from His home and His "church." He was not enrolled in the Roman school or Philistine school but received godly instruction in both spiritual and vocational matters (remember, He was a carpenter by trade) by His parents and church (temple).

During Jesus' ministry He was known as Rabboni, or teacher. He spent perhaps five to ten percent of His time preaching to the masses of people but most of His time was spent teaching His disciples ("disciple" literally means in Greek, "taught one").

Because Jesus understood the biblical principles of unity and multiplication, Jesus selected 12 disciples into whom He would invest His life and ministry. The Apostle Paul understood this principle of discipleship quite well as he reminded Timothy. "And the things which thou hast heard of me among many witnesses, the same commit thou to faithful men who shall be able to teach others also" (2 Tim. 2:2). Jesus' strategy for evangelism was discipleship.

Teaching the Children of Israel-the 8 Day Plan,
The 18 Month Plan, or the 40 Year Plan
Which Plan Have I Chosen?

When Moses was called to deliver God's people out of slavery and bondage in Egypt, God made Moses both pastor and director of a school. Moses' most important responsibility was not as tour leader but was as preacher/teacher to make a people of God who had not known their God. I am going to rehearse this story of deliverance for you using contemporary terms.

For nearly 400 years the people whom God had chosen to be His own people-the sons and daughters of Abraham, Isaac, and Jacob-had lived in the land of Goshen in Egypt. After Joseph died a new pharaoh came into power and was concerned about how these Hebrews seemed to prosper and multiply. The pharaoh was fearful of their potential power, so he enslaved them.

Generation after generation passed and now the time spent in Egypt was 430 years. The Hebrew people were surrounded by Egyptians. They lived in Egyptian houses. They practiced Egyptian religions. The Hebrews became Egyptians except in name and perhaps some oral history of their heritage. This point was to be reemphasized later on their journey because when adversity came their way on their pilgrimage to the Promised Land, they resorted to Egyptian ways. They longed for their Egyptian food; they reminded Moses they were better off in Egypt, they worshipped an Egyptian idol (the golden calf); they were willing to return to Egyptian slavery rather than change.

God would like to have led His people along the Mediterranean coast to the Promised Land, but God knew His people were not ready to face an enemy. In the face of danger, they would have run back to Egypt. God realized that He may have chosen these people but they had not chosen Him. The eight-day plan would fail. The people were not ready. They had not been taught. They did not know their God and, therefore, could not possess His blessings in the Promised Land.

Moses led the children of Israel by the way of the wilderness and Mount Sinai where He could teach them. So he started an adult Bible school. For 18 months Moses taught them. The time was filled with many setbacks, much complaining, open rebellion, and desires to return to Egypt, but finally Moses led them to an oasis on the edge of the land of Canaan, the Promised Land, to Kadesh-Barnea.

Since none of the children of Israel had been in this new land, Moses sent 12 scouts, or spies, to go into this new land and return with reports.

All 12 of their reports of observation were the same-God had prepared a great blessing for them in this new land with wells they wouldn't have to dig, houses they wouldn't have to construct, cities they wouldn't have to build; vineyards they wouldn't have to plant, etc., but...there were giants in the land.

Ten of the 12 spies failed the final exams of their adult Bible school. They did not believe nor trust in what Moses taught them about their God. They resorted to human reasoning and satanic fears.

Only Joshua and Caleb passed the test. The teaching and learning was effective. They had developed a relationship with God and trusted Him and

His promises to them regardless of the appearance of the situation. "And Caleb stilled the people before Moses, and said, 'Let us go up at once, and possess it; for we are well able to overcome it'" (Num. 13:30).

The teaching program by Moses for the adults had failed and once again the Hebrews' worldly education in Egypt became more real than the things which Moses had taught them in the adult Bible school on their way to receive God's blessing. "Let us make a captain and let us return to Egypt" (Num. 14:4).

The 18-Month Plan had Failed

Moses began a new plan to develop a people who would trust their God. This plan started with a preschool, a primary school, and junior and senior secondary school, a Bible school, a community college, and even a university with continuing education courses. The organizational structure may not have been as I have stated but the implications are still there. Moses taught those who did not have worldly minds to overcome. He began with them as children (all under the age of 20-Num. 14:29) and taught them for 40 years.

The plan was a great success. The plan worked even though it took 40 years. All of the older ones had to die before a new generation could receive God's bountiful blessings as a result of their trust in Him. Read the first three chapters of Joshua and you will find no doubts, fears, or distrust of God expressed by the children of Israel in those chapters. God's own people now also chose Him and moved forward boldly to accept His blessings.

The third chapter of Joshua is a particularly poignant one as preparation and positioning take place for the children of Israel. Even a river at flood stage could not dissuade them from moving to possess what God had ordained with blessings in abundance.

When Joshua said, "Go!" they went. The priest's feet had to touch the water before it became dry land. They did not doubt. They did not waiver. God said they would go across on dry land. The command to proceed had been given so the priests moved in obedience despite what they saw and God fulfilled His promise as they all crossed on dry land!

The 40-year plan worked!

This story of the journey of the Hebrews from Egypt to Canaan is an excellent example of God's desire to have a people He can call His own-a people who will trust Him and love Him despite circumstances, appearances, or seemingly impossible situations.

I believe it was God's desire for the people He had chosen to make a quick trip to His blessings in the Promised Land, but the 8-day plan would not work. God Himself realized that. The people were not yet prepared.

The 18-month plan to teach the adults seemed reasonable and Moses was diligent in carrying it out but it, too, was marked with failure. God then instituted the 40-year plan starting with the children and grew up a people who would trust and love God.

How I wish that the foregoing story were fictional but it is historical and unfortunately it also describes tribes and even nations today. Most people have not been taught the "ways of God" and some not even "His acts" (Ps. 103:7). Many Christians today still operate with worldly minds. They think as they were taught by the world. "Born again" Christians have the mind of Christ. The problem is that most don't think God thoughts. They still think as they were taught in the world.

Paul in the writing to the Romans said, "And be not conformed to the world; but be ye transformed by the renewing of your mind, that ye may prove what is that good, and acceptable, and perfect, will of God" (Rom. 12:2).

The Current Destruction of Civilization-Present Condition of the World What Must I Do?

The President of an African nation said in a statement on national television, "In 1995 there were virtually no orphaned, abandoned children in our country. The extended families absorbed them. But today (1998) there are thousands of such children in our streets. The traditional family and traditional economic systems are being destroyed."

According to an international network of relief and children's agencies headquartered in England, by the year A.D. 2000 one half of the world's population, 2.5 billion, will be children 15 years of age and younger. Of that number over 2 billion (80 percent) will be at risk-malnourished, disease-ridden, or abused, and 200 million orphaned and abandoned. In 1995, the orphaned and abandoned figure was 100 million but in just five years it was expected to double to 200 million, with a child dying of starvation every 2.5 seconds.

Mexico City has 2 million orphaned children. San Salvador has over 200,000. One out of 100 people in Mongolia is an orphaned, abandoned child under the age of ten.

Of every two babies conceived in this world today, one will die of abortion. In the United States when three babies are conceived, one will die by abortion. Of the two remaining children one will grow up in a single parent family.

Isaiah 47 is a prophetic chapter about the conditions of the world today. It describes the results of a humanist mind, and humanist people who make themselves their own god and serve themselves. But there is judgment upon a people who make themselves "I am."

"Therefore hear now this, thou that art given to pleasures, that dwellest carelessly, that sayest in thine heart, I am, and none else beside me; I shall not sit as a widow, neither shall I know the loss of children. But these two things shall come to thee in a moment in one day, the loss of children, and widowhood; they shall come upon thee in their perfection for the multitude of thy sorceries, and for the great abundance of thine enchantments. For thou hast trusted in thy wickedness; thou has said, None seeth me. Thy wisdom and thy knowledge, it hath perverted thee; and thou hast said in thine heart, I am, and none else beside me" (Isa. 47:8-10).

Two acts of judgment-loss of children and widowhood-will come upon a people, a nation, that declares itself "I am" God.

These two conditions exist throughout the earth today-loss of children (abortion kills 50 percent of all babies) and widowhood (the destruction of families leading to orphaned/abandoned children).

The Psalmist wrote, "If the foundations be destroyed, what can the righteous do?" (Ps. 11:3).

The foundations are definitely being destroyed. The very foundations of life, the foundations of the infrastructure of nations, spiritually, morally, economically, educationally, and politically are being destroyed. What can the righteous do? Paul wrote to Timothy that the teaching that was destroying Ephesus "...only ministers questions" (1 Tim. 1:4). Nations have few, if any, answers, only questions, about this present-day destruction. God's people, however, have answers both in logos and rhema.

Paul, in writing to the Corinthians, reminded them of the answer. "For other foundation can no man lay than that is laid, which is Jesus Christ" (1 Cor. 3:11). There are answers for the nations of the world. These answers are found as principles, precepts, practices, and truth from God's Word. The foundation for and learning (education) process must start from God's Word. The following illustrations of foundational truth from God's Word give only a small glimpse of biblical principles that will both revolutionize and re-relationize God's people. Study these truths and allow the Holy Spirit to speak to you regarding their application.

PART II SOWING AND WATERING THE SEED

No harvest will be gathered until first the seed is sown, watered, and cultivated. This seed is from God's Word which always produces in abundance.

Spirit, Mind and Body-God Made Man with Three Parts Which Part Controls Me?

Man is spirit, made in the image of God (Gen. 1:26; Jn. 4:24). Man was made with a mind. It is the place of God's values barometer-a conscience. Man was clothed, housed in a physical body. God made man into three parts-spirit (heart), mind (soul), and body (flesh). The Bible has many scriptures that address the characteristics, functioning, and control of these parts. The Bible reminds us in Hebrews that the soul (mind) and spirit are so intertwined, so closely aligned and allied, that only the Word of God can separate them. "For the word of God is quick and powerful, and sharper than any two edged sword, piercing even to the dividing asunder of soul and spirit..." (Heb. 4:12).

Man's tripartite nature becomes foundational to his walk with God. The central question becomes "Who is in control?" Will it be the body or flesh? Will it be the mind in soulish or humanistic thinking? Will it be the spirit (heart) in control of mind and body? If the spirit controls, then the mind must operate as the mind of Christ, renewed, thinking God thoughts. The body or flesh must submit itself to the dictates of a godly heart and a renewed man.

Spirit, Mind, and Body-the Philosophy and the Meaning of Life What is Truth?

Basic questions concerning life that have always been asked by man are such fundamental questions as, "Who am I?", "Why was I born?", "What is the meaning or purpose of life?", "What is truth?", etc. These questions have been answered in God's Word. We just need to know what God's Word says about them, believe them, and do them.

Down through history philosophers have struggled with these questions and have postulated a variety of answers. But a quick analysis would reveal a very interesting observation. Despite all the wide variety of answers possible to these foundational philosophical questions (there are as many responses as there are philosophers), there are only three philosophical roots.

If man is a tripartite being, then one of the three parts is going to control the other two. These three philosophical roots either lead to identifying the control of man and the meaning of life, truth, etc. from the heart, the mind, or the body.

If the heart (spirit) truly controls then the mind must be renewed and the mind of Christ is used. The body (or flesh) is brought unto subjection and must submit and obey the renewed mind (the mind of Christ) and the heart (spirit). This is a **theistic** philosophy.

If the mind is in control, not the spirit or body, then man himself becomes the measure of all things. Logic, reasoning, self-serving actions and thoughts make man his own shaper of his destiny-his own god. This philosophical position is **humanism.** Chapter 47 of Isaiah is a graphic/prophetic discourse of what happens to a people who make themselves their own god and take authority and responsibility for their own lives. Humanism rejects moral and ethical questions built upon absolutes and embraces situational ethics, relativism, and even existentialism. "Eat, drink, and be merry, for tomorrow you die!" There is not eternity. There are no established answers for conduct or anything else in life. A devout humanist rejects even God.

Adam and Eve became humanists when they disobeyed God and ate of the tree of knowledge of good and evil. In that act of disobedience they decided to take their lives in their own hands and make their own decisions about what was going to be "good" for them and "bad" for them. They took God's job.

If they had not disobeyed God by giving into their desire to control their own lives, then they would have continued to be led by the Holy Spirit, Who would make all things work toward their "good" because they loved the Lord and were called and fulfilling His plan for their lives (Rom. 11:29). Christians can still get back to that position as God intended and still desires today, but it is a conscious act of daily submitting one's will to God's will and allowing and using the mind of Christ to prevail.

James wrote that "faith without works is dead" but the reverse is also both dead and humanistic and that is works without faith. Unfortunately many, if not most, Christians fall into this humanistic trap and do not let the Spirit control their mind and therefore do not have a "renewed mind" but a "soulish," "humanistic," "self-centered" mind. They may be a new creation in the spirit but they still use the same humanistic mind in a lustful, unsubmitted body.

There is a third philosophical position and this one emanates from the body (the flesh). This philosophy is named in contemporary circles as "new age." There is nothing new about "new age." It is "old age" and has been around since Eve carried on a conversation in the Garden of Eden with a snake. "Who changed the truth of God into a lie, and worshipped and served the creature more than the Creator…" (Rom. 1:25).

In every part of the world since the beginning of man, his first desire to worship has brought him to his world around him. When he couldn't understand nature and the principles of God's laws in making it work, then he turned to worship the creation, nature, the physical world. The Chinese philosopher who established Tao did it. The pagan world did it. The Ancient

Egyptians, American Indians, Aztecs, Mayans, Incas, Africans, Druids, all worshipped the created world and in many parts of the earth they still do. The sun has often been the center of such worship. It was for the Israelites as they would turn their backs on God and worship the rising sun. Such worship was called Baal or Baalim worship. The goddess, Astoreth, was also called upon as the Israelites practiced planting groves of trees for the worship of life in the trees. Temple prostitutes, both male and female, were part of temple worship for, after all, if man were only part of the evolution of nature, then he was also like the animals. Sex was to be a natural, pleasurable act without marital restraints and, like the animals, was to be freely given and received.

Pagan temples were to be constructed with the entrance or door in the west so that worshippers would face the rising sun in the east. Ezekiel was told, "Son of man, hast thou seen what the ancients of the house of Israel do in the dark, every man in the chambers of his imagery? For they say, 'The Lord seeth us not; the Lord hath forsaken the earth.' ...and he brought me in to the inner court of the Lord's house, and, behold, at the door of the temple of the Lord, between the porch and the altar, were about five and twenty men, with backs toward the temple of the Lord, and their faces toward the east; and they worshipped the sun toward the east" (Eze. 8:12-16).

Today, many people have come to the conclusion that they are only a part of an evolutionary process. There is no meaning to life. Since we have evolved into a higher order of mammal, then we have a responsibility to our environment; hence, baby whales become more important than baby people- and living in communion with nature, the created world, is essential since there is no creator.

In all countries of the world today, all three philosophies can be found- theism, humanism, new age. All philosophical roots started in the beginning in Genesis with man, and man has always chosen one part of his triune nature to control the other parts. Christians who do not use the mind of Christ probably don't realize that they are thinking and living humanistically or new age when they do not use the mind of Christ and allow the Spirit of God to lead their every thought and deed. "My people are destroyed for lack of knowledge" (Hos. 4:6).

The Bible clearly reveals to us what our response should be. The Spirit of God must control our spirit, mind, and body. Anything less or different is not of God.

As Christians, we must have renewed minds and God told us in Genesis to be fruitful, multiply, replenish, have **dominion** and **subdue** the created world. Man's first job in the Garden of Eden was as caretaker, conservationist. We are stewards of what God created.

To have dominion does not carry with it reckless, selfish domination. Dominion, authority, carries with it responsibility. We are to be environmentalists, but we don't worship the environment.

We have a responsibility to **subdue** creation; therefore, we must learn to master it. To tame a wild beast, one must understand it. To master a subject or information, one must understand it.

We need to discover God's principles, truth, laws, and character in the created world. We must be investigators, researchers, explorers. God mandated it when He said to **subdue** creation. The Christian's war is not against science, medicine, or technology but is with its godly or ungodly use, the interpretation of ultimate meaning, and the origin of the laws, principles, and characteristics by which and in which it was created.

Christians should lead in the research of God's creation and give God glory for His creation, for God Himself declared, "...it was good" (Gen. 1:4,10,12,18,21,25,31).

Which part of you is going to control you-
the spirit, the mind, or the body?

Spirit, Mind, and Body-Curriculum Considerations

What Must I Learn?

There are four major groups of study to be known and understood if the Christian is going to do *(wisdom)* what God expects.

The written Word of God *(logos)*, the revealed Word of God *(rhema)*, studies of man, and studies of nature *(created world)*, these are the four essential yet comprehensive areas of study. The Christian should have some knowledge and understanding about all four of these areas and should be an expert in the written and revealed Words of God. The studies of man and creation are likewise important and should be pursued in accordance with God's vocational call on one's life.

The Bible is foundational to the study of God's "acts and ways," His deeds and character, throughout this written Word of God.

The revealed Word of God *(rhema)* is essential in our personal relationship with God through Jesus Christ, as led by the Holy Spirit. Man's experiential or personal relationship with the Father, Son, and Holy Ghost are foundational to having the mind of Christ and being equipped to develop a renewed mind so as to think God thoughts and thereby live a Christ-emulated life.

Studies that are foundational to understanding man are guided by both the written and revealed Word of God-the Bible and the Holy Spirit. These studies of man, if from a humanistic or new age perspective, are going to arrive at a very different conclusion than what is stated and guided by God. Again, it is not the area of study that is misguided but its conclusions-not the findings but the credit for its origin.

Studies related to man include the fine arts-music, drama, dance, etc.; the language arts-literature, language, speech, etc.; and the social sciences-psychology, sociology, anthropology, history, etc.

The studies of the created world embrace all areas where we must discover God's truths, principles, and laws in the physical world. Such areas of study include the sciences-astronomy, biology, botany, zoology, chemistry, physics, etc.; the mathematical sciences-algebra, geometry, calculus, etc.; and the areas of technology-computers, engineering, electronics, etc.

The major problems of civilization today can be traced to a lack of understanding of God's work that prioritizes and gives direction for all areas of study and problems confronted in life. God is first; man is second; and the created world is third!

Man has answers (principles and priorities) about his relationship with God. Man has answers (principles and priorities) about his relationship with other men. Man has a mandate from God about his relationship with the created world.

Man is struggling in every country of the world today. World conditions are at a most critical stage. Civilization stands at the brink of destruction. Man is ignoring God, warring with other men, and destroying the created world. At such a time, the world has no answers, only questions-but Christians have answers, if they would only search the scriptures and apply their principles and practices.

The five major areas of worldwide need today are in the areas of study-spiritual, educational, economics (business), communications, and government. Did you notice that all five areas are concerned with either the knowledge and understanding of God or with man?

For too long, the evangelical Church has focused on studies of the heart (spirit) and not on a renewed mind. The Church wanted to get people saved so they would have the mind of Christ, but then failed to help them use it and gain a renewed mind.

If we learn what we know from the world, then we will think worldly thoughts. The first generation of the children of Israel who came out of captivity in Egypt had Egyptian minds, and their Egyptian minds would not let their newly discovered spiritual knowledge control them. Every time it really mattered, every time it was essential for them to respond by godly, Spirit-controlled minds, they failed.

The second chapter of the book of Judges tells the heartbreaking story of what happened to the children of Israel after Joshua and the generation died who had been taught for 40 years in the wilderness. The people now possessed the Promised Land. They had finally received God's blessings for a prepared people.

"And also all that generation were gathered unto their fathers; and there arose another generation after them, which knew not the Lord, nor yet the works which He had done for Israel. And the children of Israel did evil in the sight of the Lord, and served Baalim; and they forsook the Lord God of their fathers, which brought them out of the land of Egypt, and followed other gods, of the gods of the people that were round about them, and bowed themselves unto them, and provoked the Lord to anger. And they forsook the Lord, and served Baal and Ashtaroth" (Judges 2:10-13).

The past must not be prologue. We must not forget to learn our lessons from history-even the history of God's people. Every generation must be taught. Every generation must be born. The great man of God, David du Plessis from South Africa, once said, "*God has no grandchildren, only children.*"

Each generation must be discipled. Who is going to do that? The world? The government? The state? And when they do, what will be in the hearts and minds of those being taught? Renewed minds? Godly thoughts? Great faith? I don't thing so!

"A disciple [student] is not above his teacher, but every one when he is fully taught will be like his teacher" (Luke 6:40, RSV).

Spirit, Mind, and Body-Educational Goals
What Goals Must I have to be Fully Taught?

God's Word is not difficult. His ways are not complex. His great mysteries are simply stated. But the natural mind, the unregenerated mind, and even the unrenewed mind, have great difficulty with the simplistic and even paradoxical nature of God's ways and will. (Read 1 Corinthians 1).

In one verse of Scripture, a summary of Jesus' life from 12 to 30 has embodied the four major educational/learning goals of life. "And Jesus increased in wisdom and stature, and in favor with God and man" (Luke 2:52).

Jesus grew in (knowledge, understanding) wisdom. Jesus grew in stature. Jesus grew in favor with God. Jesus grew in favor with man.

Jesus grew academically, physically, spiritually, and socially.

One can search the scriptures and never find a better summation about the education, the learning goals, the growing goals for man. Even worldly educators would embrace these goals-perhaps substituting "moral" for "spiritual."

Please look carefully again at these educational goals describing Jesus. Jesus grew in His *mind*, in His *body*, in His *spirit*, and in His relationship with *others*. What does this passage of Scripture say to the Church today? In all of these areas of growth, the Church has a responsibility. Jesus' parents and the temple priests and scribes did this for Jesus. The temple had what were called "teaching priests." Ezra was one. "For Ezra had prepared his heart to seek the law of the Lord, and to do it, and teach in Israel statutes and judgments" (Ezra 7:10).

Spirit, Mind, and Body, and My Neighbor
The First and Second Commandments
How Must I Respond to These Commandments?

All of us want to know what is the most important thing. With so many things, ideas, philosophies, meanings, information, and opinions, we still want to know and ask, "Help me with priorities."

A lawyer came to Jesus and asked, "Master, which is the greatest commandment in the law?" "Jesus said unto him, 'Thou shalt love the Lord thy God with all thy heart, and with all thy soul, and with all thy mind.' This is the first and greatest commandment. And the second is like unto it, 'Thou shalt love thy neighbor as thyself.' On these two commandments hang all the law and the prophets" (Matt. 22:36-40; Mark 12:28-34; Luke 10:25-28).

Did you see the four education goals? Did you see the tripartite nature of man? Did you see the roots of all philosophical thought?

The first commandment as cited by Jesus tells us to love God with all three parts of our being-spirit (heart), mind (soul), and body (strength). According to Jesus, the second commandment is like the first. We are to love our neighbor as ourself. The second commandment requires us to love our neighbor with all of our heart, our mind, and our strength.

Jesus was saying that the second commandment is so much like the first commandment that if we don't get the second commandment right, then we can't keep the first commandment. If we don't keep the first commandment, then we can't keep the second commandment.

"Therefore if thou bring thy gift to the altar, and there rememberest that thy brother hath ought against thee; leave there thy gift before the altar, and go thy way; first be reconciled to thy brother, and then come and offer thy gift" (Matt. 5:23-24).

What do you have as a gift worthy of God? Only you! He has everything else. So when you bring yourself before God to give Him your life, the first time and every time, then you must be in a righteous relationship with your brother.

The Lord's Prayer has an interesting footnote. Did you notice that after the

"Amen," there is this explanatory note: "For if you forgive men their trespasses, your heavenly Father will also forgive you; but if ye forgive not men their trespasses, neither will your Father forgive your trespasses" (Matt. 6:14-15).

The Bible is full of principles and practices as to how man should live with man. Perhaps three of the best chapters citing these relationships can be found in Ephesians 4, Romans 12, and 1 Corinthians 12.

"...And I pray God your whole spirit and soul and body be preserved blameless unto the coming of our Lord Jesus Christ" (1 Thess. 5:23).

Knowledge, Understanding, and Wisdom
Biblical Objectives for Learning
Why is Wisdom a Result of Understanding and Knowledge?

Finish this statement-"The fear of the Lord is the beginning of ______."

If you are like almost every Christian, you would have stated "wisdom." But Proverbs 1:7 states, "The fear of the Lord is the beginning of knowledge..."

Proverbs 2:5 states, "Then shalt thou understand the fear of the Lord..."

It is not until Proverbs 9:10 that we find specifically the expression, "The fear of the Lord is the beginning of wisdom." But let us finish that verse, "...and the knowledge of the holy is understanding."

Some translations do not pick up the subtleties of the use of these three words. Some Spanish translations actually use other words for "knowledge." Regardless of the precision with which the various translations are written, they still note these three words throughout the book of Proverbs as words interconnected, related, and even progressive.

Perhaps the following two passages of Scripture illustrate this point. (Note again, certain translations using other words besides "knowledge.")

"The Lord by wisdom hath founded the earth; by understanding hath he established the heavens. By his knowledge the depths are broken up and the clouds drop down the dew" (Prov. 3:19-20).

"Through wisdom is an house builded; and by understanding it is established; and by knowledge shall the chambers be filled with all precious and pleasant riches" (Prov. 24:3-4).

In both of these passages of Scripture the end result, the complete act is called wisdom. The Hebrews defined wisdom as "an act with understanding." The Greeks defined wisdom as "knowledge with understanding." The translator, or more accurately the paraphraser, of the Living Bible presented the Hebrew definition of wisdom even though he was paraphrasing from the Greek when he wrote, "If you want to know what God wants you to do, ask Him and He will gladly tell you, for He is always ready to give a bountiful supply of wisdom to all who ask Him. He will not resent it" (Jas. 1:5, LB). The King James Version reads, "If any of you hath wisdom, let him ask of God, that giveth to all men liberally, and upbraideth not; and it shall be given him" (Jas. 1:5, KJV).

If you had the knowledge of God's Word and could quote it from memory but never did it, would it be wisdom? Ideally wisdom, therefore, is something you know, understand, and do.

The passages of Scripture describing the founding of the earth and the building of a house began with wisdom but, in fact, was describing an accomplished activity and worked its way backwards. To start any new venture, one must begin with the raw ingredients (knowledge). Then one needs to know how to put them together (understanding) before the final result (wisdom) can be seen.

Technically and accurately speaking, the Bible is a book of the knowledge of wisdom, because it is not wisdom unless you do it.

The book of Proverbs uses these three words-knowledge, understanding, and wisdom-more than any other words to describe the essence of the entire book.

Knowledge is where the learner starts. It is the learner's responsibility. 2 Timothy 2:15 states, "Study to show thyself approved unto God, a workman that needeth not to be ashamed, rightly dividing the word of truth."

Knowledge is our responsibility. God will give us knowledge to make up for the deficiencies but not for laziness. Preparing ourselves, arming ourselves with knowledge, is man's job.

Now with a reservoir of information, Jesus told us how the Holy Spirit helps us. "But the Comforter, which is the Holy Ghost, whom the Father will send in My name, He shall teach you all things, and bring all things to your remembrance, whatsoever I have said unto you" (Jn. 14:27).

How can the Holy Spirit bring something to your remembrance if you didn't put it there? Knowledge that does not become understanding is usually forgotten. Most of what students learn in rote as unconnected facts will be forgotten unless it is understood and applied (wisdom).

Continually in the book of Proverbs, the writer reminds us to seek understanding. "Yea, if thou criest after knowledge, and liftest up thy voice for understanding…" (Prov. 2:3).

But what is understanding? Every teacher or pastor can recognize when understanding takes place. It carries a sudden physical response that signifies knowledge has now become understanding. "Oh, that's what that means!"

All 12 of the disciples knew, had the knowledge, that Jesus was the Son of God. He had told them. They all knew Him as Jesus. But there were a lot of Jewish people named "Jesus" (or more precisely, "Joshua"). Many families wanted their sons to grow up and become "The Savior of His People."

"Jesus" was a common name.

Jesus asked His disciples, "Whom do men say that I the Son of Man am?" (Matt. 16:13). They gave Him a variety of responses-John the Baptist, Elijah, Jeremiah, one of the prophets.

But Jesus' second question was not a knowledge question when He asked, "Whom do you say that I am?" (Matt. 16:15). Only Peter responded, perhaps the others could not respond, because the right answer was not "Jesus." "Peter said, 'Thou art the Christ, the Son of the Living God.' And Jesus answered and said, 'Blessed art thou, Simon Barjonah; for flesh and blood hath not revealed it unto thee, but my Father which is in heaven'" (Matt. 16:16-17). The disciples had the knowledge of Jesus but Peter had the knowledge and, by the revelation of God, the understanding as well.

Jesus went on to say (Matt. 16:18) that His Church would be built upon this revelation-the revelation that Jesus is the Christ, the Messiah, the Expected One, the Anointed One, the Son of God. It is so today as the Church is made up of stones (petros)-all of those who have had the revelation of the Rock (Petra) for the Church's foundation.

This discussion is not to make the case that knowledge isn't important, but to say that knowledge is not enough. There must also be understanding (revelation) and that is the work of God through the Holy Spirit to every believer.

This treatise must not be used exclusively for salvation or to be "born again," but for every aspect of becoming a mature, overcoming Christian.

After one has knowledge, then pray for understanding (wisdom). "**Wisdom** is the principle thing; therefore get **wisdom**; and with all thy getting, get **understanding**" (Prov. 4:7).

Understanding is the prelude to godly wisdom. An immature Christian may do (wisdom) the right thing by watching other godly people but will never evidence all of the fruit and blessings if understanding (revelation) is not also a part of the action. "Happy is the man that findeth wisdom, and the man that getteth understanding" (Prov. 3:13).

"When **wisdom** entereth into thine heart, and **knowledge** is pleasant unto thy soul; **Discretion** shall preserve thee, **understanding** shall keep thee..." (Prov. 2:10-11). Now enters the word discretion. Also you will find the word prudence. These words are words of strategy.

When you get wisdom, when you know what to do, then you also get strategy-when, where, how, and with whom. Jesus knew why He came and what He was to do. He had the wisdom of God, but now He needed strategy, which is the work of the Holy Spirit on a daily basis.

One can know the call of God which is answered by why and what-Why am I here? And what am I to do?

Paul said to walk worthy of the vocation (the work) which you have been called (Eph. 4:1). You have been called to a vocation. The call of God is both a spiritual and a vocational call.

Knowing why and what is not enough, as gratifying as that answer may be.

There are three, maybe four, very important days in your life: 1) the day you were born, 2) the day you were "born again," and 3) the day you discover why you were born. The fourth is the day you go to heaven.

Prudence and discretion must accompany wisdom. You may know what to do but miss the timing, the place, the people, the method. All of that strategy is given continually by the Holy Spirit Who is bringing to your remembrance knowledge, giving you revelation, and now leading you into all truth by telling you when, where, how, etc. Jesus depended daily on the Holy Spirit for strategy. So must we.

Knowledge, understanding, and wisdom, although essential to people of all ages, can be seen as emphasized by certain age groups. Children from the ages of infancy to 11 or 12 years of age ask predominantly questions of "what." What is this? What is that? What? What? This is the age of knowledge. They are like sponges and learn so many things quickly. They love information, to memorize, to do even routine things. They are great collectors and have an insatiable appetite for information.

Young people at the ages of 11 (for many girls) and 12 (for many boys) ask a different question "why." This happens with the onset of puberty about grade 6 and lasts for at least three to four years. This age group needs to explore, find answers, talk, investigate, and ask a lot of questions - including the questioning of authority, rules, etc. They want to know "why." The Holy Spirit is still the best revealer, teacher. Mature Christians need to work with this group. It is best not to assign first-year teachers or immature Christians or even those too near their age as leaders. Young youth leaders may relate to the group but can seldom provide the stability and guidance that is needed.

Young adults from 16 to 20 ask "when" and "where!" They are eager and impatient to get started without delay. They feel they have the knowledge and understanding and now want to prove themselves in action. Only a few more years of experience soon brings this group to respect wise adults who can also counsel with godly wisdom, discretion and prudence (strategy).

Knowledge, understanding, and wisdom reflect God's taxonomy for learning. If you want to become who God has called you to become, then you must enter the door of knowledge. It requires His advice and your work.

The door of understanding will be opened by the Holy Spirit and you may walk through. The door of wisdom belongs to God in His acts and His ways with prudence and discretion (strategy). God's wisdom is not like earthly wisdom (see Jas. 3:13-18).

PART III: PLANNING AND REAPING THE HARVEST (I CORINTHIANS 3:1-3)

If your reading was hurried through the spirit mind, and body series, then you will have missed a lot of the significance that God's Word wants to show us about becoming mature/overcoming Christians. Reread and ask the Holy Spirit to give you understanding (revelation) regarding each section. It is time for the Church to help all Christians be more mature and eat the "meat" of the Word and not just "milk" as babies.

Christian School Imperatives: Five Foundation Stones for Christian Education How can I Build on these Foundation Stones?

The Psalmist said, "If the foundations be destroyed, what can the righteous do?" (Ps.11: 3). Paul gave us the answer in his first letter to the Corinthians. "For no one can lay any foundation other than the one already laid, which is Jesus Christ" (1 Cor. 3:11).

Christ Centered: The first foundation stone of any activity or program of the church is that it must be "Christ-centered." To lay any other foundation stone would miss the point of everything being said in this treatise.

Without Jesus Christ as the revealed Son of God in one's life leaves only carnal or soulish knowledge, misdirected understanding, and earthly wisdom which is devilish (Jas. 3:13-18). Every child, every adult must be "born again" by having a God-given revelation of Jesus as the Christ, the Son of the Living God. With this revelation comes the mind of Christ. Now we must learn to use the mind of Christ as a renewed mind.

The chief goal of every church-sponsored and directed program, school, or activity must be the message of salvation and repentance. In order to be effective in leading and teaching others, all teachers and staff must also be "bornagain"-Christ-centered. To ask unregenerated minds to think or teach the things of Christ, His Word and His ways, is to expect an apple when squeezed to bring forth orange juice. You cannot give what you do not have. Non-Christians cannot teach Christian principles, precepts, or practices with understanding. They may have a knowledge of such things but not understanding.

A pastor from India came to me and said, "I want you to come to India and teach these foundational truths about becoming God's people. My teachers need to hear this Christian philosophy and education strategies."

I asked, "Pastor, how large are your schools?"
He said, "I have an average of 1000 students in each school."
"How many Christian teachers do you have?" I asked.
"Sixty," was his reply. "One for each school to teach a class in Bible."
What is the background of all your other teachers?" I asked.
"Hindu," he responded.
"Pastor," I said. "I have bad news for you. You have 60 Hindu schools that teach a class in Bible."
The Indian pastor's schools are typical missions schools. Some students get "born again" but are still taught by humanistic/new age teachers who constantly are feeding their students worldly, carnal, soulish knowledge and understanding.
A few years ago, I gave a commencement address at a Christian school in Central America. In the course of the address, I made the statement that a Christian school must have all "born again" Christian teachers. About six months later, I met the principal of the school at a Christian school conference for Central America. The principal told me that the day following my commencement address, eight of his teachers came en masse and resigned. They were greatly offended by my statement that all teachers must be "born again". The principal said that at first he was very angry with me. Where was he going to find replacements? But just six months later, he had a different testimony. God brought in "born again" replacements for every one of the worldly, soulish, carnal-minded teachers who left. The principal also said that after the eight resigned, he realized that these were the ones who were always opposing him. "Can two walk together, unless they be agreed?" (Amos 3:3).
"That the God of our Lord Jesus Christ, the Father of glory, may give unto you the spirit of wisdom and revelation in the knowledge of Him: the eyes of your understanding being enlightened; that ye may know what is the hope of His calling, and what the riches of the glory of His inheritance in the saints, and what is the exceeding greatness of His power to us ward who believe, according to the working of His mighty power, which He wrought in Christ, when He raised Him from the dead, and set Him at His own right hand in the heavenly places, far above all principality, and power, and might, and dominion, and every name that is named, not only in this world, but also in that which is to come: and hath put all things under His feet, and gave Him to be the head over all things to the church, which is His body, the fullness of Him that filleth all in all" (Eph. 1:17-23).
A Christian school's activities must include opportunities for all students to become "born again".
Bible-Based. The second foundation stone is the Word of God, the Bible.

In it is hidden the knowledge, understanding, and wisdom of the ages. The Bible contains the fundamental principles, precepts, and practices for every area of life.

Man has separated God's Word from His world-pretending that there is no relationship between the two and, even as was pointed out earlier in this treatise, the five greatest social/people impact areas of life-spiritual, educational, economics, communications, and political-are all addressed with principles, precepts, and practices throughout God's Word.

"For the word of God is quick, and powerful, and sharper than any two-edged sword, piercing even to the dividing asunder of soul and spirit, and of the joints and marrow, and is a discerner of the thoughts and intents of the heart" (Heb. 4:12).

The Bible must be taught as part of the regular course work for every grade level every year. An overall comprehensive strategy which includes a well-defined scope and sequence is essential.

The Bible must also become foundational to every class with teachers identifying biblical principles, practices, scriptures, and illustrations as they teach all subject areas. Making such notes of reference and guidance in the margin of daily lesson plans is a good idea in order to show relevancy with God's Word and to teach the mysteries of God with a renewed mind.

Holy Spirit-Controlled. The third foundation stone is the Holy Spirit. "For as many as are led by the Spirit of God, they are the sons of God" (Rom. 8:14).

The Holy Spirit is also referred to as the Spirit of truth. "...The spirit of truth; whom the world cannot receive, because it seeth him not, neither knoweth him, but ye know him; for he dwelleth with you and shall be in you" (Jn. 14:17). "Howbeit when he, the spirit of truth, is come, he will guide you into all truth: for he shall not speak of himself; but whatsoever he shall hear, that shall he speak: and he will shew you things to come" (Jn. 16:13)

In addition to being "born again", every teacher and child in the school/church should be Spirit-filled and Spirit-led. For the student who is filled and led by the Spirit of Truth, he has an advantage over students not filled with the Holy Spirit. Jesus said that the Holy Spirit would bring to our remembrance whatsoever we have learned or been taught and would lead us into all truth. What a tremendous "helper" the Spirit of Truth is to lead us into all truth if we will be led. "He who believes in me [Jesus]-who cleaves to and trusts in and relies on Me-as the Scripture has said, Out from his innermost being springs and rivers of living water shall flow (continuously). But He was speaking here of the Spirit, whom those who believed-trusted, had faith-in Him were afterwards to receive"(Jn. 7:38-39, AMP).

Individually Applied. Every person is important. Every "born again"

Christian is a part in the body of Christ-His church. All parts have different functions. Every person has different gifts, talents, and callings and should be respected and appreciated for their differences. Even though there is extreme diversity within the body of Christ, there is still the admonishment that all of the parts must be unified in purpose-diversity of function and unity of purpose.

The three chapters in the Bible that emphasize this principle of how the body of Christ, the Church, must function are Ephesians 4, Romans 12 and I Corinthians 12. These chapters stress the diversity of gifts, talents, abilities, and vocations that God gives to His people in order that the body as a whole might be complete. Paul even states in his letter to the Ephesians (chapter 4, verse 1) that we are to walk worthy of the vocation to which we have been called.

Every child, every person has different gifts, talents, abilities, and calling on his life. If we are going to truly be effective in our Christian school or other church-related programs, then we must recognize the need to help enhance, cultivate, and build upon these varying and differing functions. But all of this is for nothing if we do not also emphasize the importance of agreement or unity.

"Then we will no longer be infants, tossed back and forth by the waves, and blown here and there by every wind of teaching and by cunning and craftiness of men in their deceitful scheming. Instead, speaking the truth in love, we will in all things grow up into Him who is the Head, that is Christ. From Him the whole body, fitly joined and held together by every supporting ligament, grows and builds itself up in love, as each part does its work" (Eph. 4:14-16, NIV). Our goals should be to help each person learn and develop into mature Christians not only for their own sake but for the strength of the body of Christ.

Society Related. Christians have been charged to be in the world but not of the world (Jn. 17:14-16). Therefore, we must prepare ourselves to live in the world, but at the same time we are reminded that this world is not our home. We must not be influenced nor controlled by worldly thinking. "And this I pray, that your love may abound, get more and more in knowledge and in all judgment; that ye may approve things that are excellent; that ye may be sincere and without offense till the day of Christ; being filled with the fruits of righteousness, which are by Jesus Christ, unto the glory and praise of God" (Phil. 1:9-11).

Two of the skills that the Christian school and church need to develop in their students (disciples) today would be English and computer skills. English has become the international language and, because of that recognition, many churches are beginning programs in English as an evangelistic outreach.

People who can speak and write English have an advantage for positions in non-English speaking countries. The same is true for computer literacy.

In a South American country where a church had been persecuted for open witnessing and similar evangelistic programs, I advised them to begin computer classes. They followed the strategy suggested and have developed an outstanding program of evangelism and are growing the church. The church put up a sign outside so that people passing by could read it. They offered computer classes at a very reasonable rate.

When I visited the church, they showed me their classroom with 40 computers. Each class was for two hours per day, three days per week, for eight weeks. All the classes were full from 8:00 a.m. until 10:00 p.m. each night, six days per week. The class began each session with prayer, a short devotional, then each person practiced using biblical literature and stories to enter into the computer. At the end of each session, they printed their material and it became theirs to take home and review.

"How many of these people in today's class are from your church?" I asked the pastor.

"Only two in this group. The rest are from the street and community," the pastor responded.

"How many of these people are 'born again'?" I asked.

"Those students who have completed the course have all been 'born again' and all have come into this church," the pastor said. "This was the best evangelistic tool we have ever used to both evangelize and disciple at the same time. It really works!"

Every student who graduates from the Christian school should excel and possess the highest of academic, spiritual, physical, and social standards. There is no excuse for Christians not being the best in the world. After all, they have the mind of Christ and the Holy Spirit as the teacher of truth.

These five foundation stones are essential for every Christian school and program of the church-Christ-Centered, Bible-Based, Holy Spirit-Controlled, Individually-Applied, Society-Related.

Resurrection of a Dead Nation-A Biblical Strategy
How Does the Vision of "Dry Bones" Apply to Me...My Church...My Country?

The prophet Ezekiel was shown in a vision the deadness of the nations of Israel and Judah. This passage of scripture in Ezekiel chapter 37 gives a picture of a seemingly hopeless situation-not too dissimilar to the world's condition today or perhaps of your own country.

The vision showed a valley (always a low place of life symbolically in the scripture) which was full of bones-dry, very dry bones. The picture being revealed shows total hopelessness. God asked Ezekiel if these bones could live and, in a sense, God is asking each of us the same questions today. Ezekiel's response was, "Only You know, God!" But God wanted Ezekiel to see through eyes of faith a resurrected people. God said to Ezekiel, "Prophesy upon these bones, and say unto them, 'O ye dry bones, hear the word of the Lord…" (verse 4).

Two significant points of biblical strategy are noted here. First, it was man, not God, who was to speak to the bones. Secondly, the words spoken were to be God's words.

Today, God still is asking us to do it. When the disciples came to Jesus about the need to feed the 4000 or 5000 men, Jesus told them, "You feed them!" Today, many Christians resort to prayer and ask God to "do it", to "change things", when all along He has been saying for us to do it. We have the power, the authority, but fear and unbelief rob us of our willingness to be bold even in the face of such overwhelming need.

Additionally, God used His word to perform a miracle. From the first recorded words of creation, God used His word to perform His will. Jesus used the word to defend Himself from Satan during His time of persecution. "So shall my word be that goeth forth out of My mouth: it shall not return unto me void, but it shall accomplish that which I please, and it shall prosper in the things whereto I sent it" (Is. 55:11). The first fruit of God's word spoken by Ezekiel created structure but there was no life. Ezekiel had to speak again the words of the Lord in order to see life enter a dead body.

The third action taken by Ezekiel was to pick up two sticks and hold them together. They represented the houses of Judah and Israel. God wanted them to be one-united. It would only be through unity-agreement-that God's word would demonstrate its power. God looked down on the children of the world at the Tower of Babel and said, "They are of one mind; nothing shall be impossible to them" (Gen. 11:5-6). Jesus stated the principle of agreement (unity) this way, "Again I say unto you, 'That if two of you shall agree on earth as touching any thing that they shall ask, it shall be done for them of my Father which is in heaven" (Matt. 18:19).

Agreement starts with forgiveness. It did with God and man. It does with man to man. Matthew 18 is excellent in describing and illustrating these principles of power. Perhaps the visual given by Paul to the Ephesians illustrates this point of power best. "For whom [Christ] the whole body fitly joined together and compacted by that which every joint supplieth, according to the effectual working is the measure of every part, maketh increase of the body unto the edifying of itself in love" (Eph. 4:16).

The power of God is best demonstrated at the joint-the place where we come together. The joint causes the parts to increase their power and productivity. Unity increases individual power exponentially.

Scripturally, one godly person can put 1000 to flight and two can put 10,000 to flight. (Deut. 32:30; Ps. 91:7). If one is equal to a thousand and two is equal to ten thousand, then three must be 100,000, and four 1,000,000, etc. God uses higher math and multiplies after His initial steps of addition. (Reference the growing of the church in the book of Acts where addition soon changed to multiplication.)

God reminded Ezekiel that if he would do as commanded-structure, life, unity-that He (God) would "make a covenant of peace with them; and it shall be an everlasting covenant with them; and I will plant them, and multiply them, and will set my sanctuary in the midst of them forevermore. My tabernacle also shall be with them: yea, I will be their God and they shall be my people" (Eze. 37:26,27). The conditions of the world are impossible for man but not for God or through His people when God's Word and power flow through them in unity.

Preaching, Teaching, and Healing- Jesus' Practices and Priorities How Can I Use These Practices in My Life?

"And Jesus went about all the cities and villages, teaching, in their synagogues, and **preaching** the gospel of the kingdom, and **healing** every sickness and every disease among the people" (Matt. 9:35).

Jesus did three things-teaching, preaching, and healing. These strategic practices would be incomplete if praying was not also acknowledged. Of these four practices, teaching undoubtedly consumed most of His time as He was known as Jesus the Teacher. Perhaps we can get some glimpse into His strategy when the disciples asked why Jesus taught in parables. (Matt. 13:10) "He answered and said unto them, 'Because it is given unto you to know the mysteries of the Kingdom of heaven, but to them it is not given'"(Matt. 13:11).

Jesus goes on to say that the disciples are to understand the meaning of the parable-not just the story. In may ways, this illustration parallels what the psalmist said about Moses and the children of Israel. "He [God] made known His ways unto Moses, His acts unto the children of Israel" (Ps. 103:7).

Preaching is proclamation, motivation, and bringing people to a point of decision. Teaching is for explanation, insight, and bringing people to a point of application. Teaching takes longer. After Jesus taught the parables, the object lessons, to the masses of people, the disciples undoubtedly were to follow up to help the people live out the parable. Certainly we benefit from the parable in that fashion today. And wherever Jesus was preaching, He was healing and wherever Jesus was teaching, He was healing.

Conferences, Models, and Leadership Training
A Strategy for Harvest
What is My Call, My Job in the Harvest?

The basic activity strategy of Jesus of preaching, teaching, and healing is the same basic activity strategy recommended today.

The conference (seminar) is the platform for preaching. Its primary purpose is to introduce basic truths, principles, precepts, and practices foundational to God's Word. It is designed to inspire, motivate, and bring people to a point of decision-to start Christian schools, Bible schools, Christian universities, and other such discipleship programs and activities in the church.

The model provides the essence of teaching. Jesus had a model-He said it was His Father. Paul had a model-he said it was Jesus. Timothy had a model-he said it was Paul. We need model Christian schools, model Bible schools, model Christian universities, model curriculum, model training programs, model materials.

Leadership training is first a healing process. All members of the body of Christ are leaders in their areas of giftedness and calling. All have failed and fallen short of the glory of God. All need some time of healing if they are ever going to become "healed helpers." Many people go to Bible schools today under the guise of preparing for the ministry when, in fact, they are there for personal healing.

These three strategies were not only Jesus' strategies, they have also been adopted as the three basic strategies that TELED International uses to direct its activities of discipleship around the world. Perhaps first you should know that TELED International is a coined word from two Latin words, **tele** and **educo**, or literally "at a distance" and "to instruct or teach". For Christians, it uses two of the action words of the Great Commission-Go and Teach-all nations. The ministry of TELED International is first to establish conferences and seminars in a nation. Secondly, model schools are appointed in order to help others. Thirdly, individuals are identified who have a heart to resurrect their nation and intensive training, materials, and even advanced degrees are sought and established in such individuals.

Today, this vision is actively functioning in over 20 nations of the world and another 30 are in the beginning stages of participation. Soon this three-pronged strategy will sweep all around the globe.

Now the most active areas on the world for TELED are the United States, Latin America, and Africa. As nations are ready to participate, more will be added.

At least one national Christian school conference should be held each year in each country. The model school(s) should then conduct at least two inservice staff development seminars each year and invite surrounding Christian schools and ministries working to start schools.

From the unity developed at the national conference, a Christian school association must form in order to broaden participation and strengthen the members through agreement by working together. Such a working group will eventually lead to the establishment and development of a national accrediting body. Accreditation will assure both parents and government of the quality of the school but, even more, it will help the school continue its paths of development in excellence in Christ.

Only 65 model schools are needed to cover all of Latin America, and 75 model schools for Africa-700 for the whole world. Those model schools are chosen because the pastor and school have a vision to help their nation. Such an activity is very worthwhile as the model school provides a tangible place where others can come and learn and see.

As of this writing, over one third of the model schools are in place in Latin America and the remainder will be appointed over the next five years. It is hoped that by the year 2000 all the model schools for Latin America will be in place, helping to raise up thousands of other schools.

Already one model school in Africa has started 92 other schools. One Christian school in Mexico is working to establish 18 new Christian schools this year. Leadership training programs are already being developed for teachers for the Christian school as well as masters and doctoral degrees for school and church leaders. This vision is already happening with over 1883 new Christian schools being pledged to develop in 22 nations of Africa. Hundreds of Christian schools are developing in Latin America, Asia, and even Europe and Eastern Europe.

"If the foundations be destroyed, what can the righteous do?"(Ps. 11:3). We can re-lay the foundation in Jesus Christ.

As we look on the fields white with harvest, there are some areas that still need seed, still need tilling, still need planting. Christ's return is not so much predicated on the evil and hopelessness of the day as to "...and this gospel of the Kingdom shall be preached in all the world for a witness unto all nations and then shall the end come" (Matt. 24:1-4).

Jesus is coming for a prepared Church, a bride properly adorned. The foundational truths in this treatise would help guide the Church in its response of preparation.

"...His [Jesus'] disciples came unto Him, saying 'Declare unto us the parable of the tares of the field.' He answered and said unto them, 'He that soweth the good seed is the Son of man; the field is the world; the good seed are the children of the Kingdom; but the tares are the children of the wicked one: the enemy that sowed then is the devil; the harvest is the end of the world; and the reapers are the angels. As therefore the tares are gathered and burned in the fire; so shall it be in the end of this world. The Son of man shall send forth His angels, and they shall gather out of His Kingdom all things that offend, and them which do iniquity; and shall cast them into a furnace of fire; there shall be wailing and gnashing of teeth. Then shall the righteous shine forth as the sun in the Kingdom of their Father. Who hath ears to hear, let him hear" (Matt. 13:36-43).

CHAPTER 16

THE ROAD TO COMMUNITY TRANSFORMATION

George Otis, Jr.

George Otis, Jr. is the founder and president of The Sentinel Group, a multifaceted Christian research and information agency headquartered in Lynnwood, Washington. In the 1980s, his research expertise in restricted-access lands led to his selection as a Senior Associate with the Lausanne Committee for World Evangelization. More recently, Mr. Otis was appointed as co-coordinator of the A.D. 2000 & Beyond Movement's United Prayer Track, a position that includes leadership responsibilities for the Track's Spiritual Mapping Division. He also serves as an advisor to Women's Aglow International and the Lydia Prayer Fellowship.

Mr. Otis has authored several books over the years including The Twilight Labyrinth, The Last of the Giants and Strongholds of the 10/40 Window. His ministry calling has taken him to nearly 100 nations. Mr. Otis lives near Seattle, Washington, with his wife Lisa and their four children.

On a Personal Note...

I have a special appreciation for George and Lisa Otis. They are an exemplary couple in the ministry. George has unique qualities but I especially admire the ability he has to intellectually stimulate others. Each conversation with George, each of his messages, and certainly his books are a tremendous source of information and revelation. Yet his presentation is always marked with the total absence of pride.

George and Lisa are a couple who exhibit integrity and love-gifts that are certainly needed in the ministry to which God has called them.

When George inspired the body of Christ to pray against strongholds in the 10/40 Window, the destiny of these nations was eternally affected. He coined the term "spiritual mapping." I have no doubt that his teachings about community transformation will truly be a landmark in the history of the Church.

Please read this chapter over and over again. It will change your life.

Thank you, George.

Harold Caballeros

Transformed communities do not materialize spontaneously. If they did we might legitimately wonder why an omnipotent and ostensibly loving God did not turn the trick more often. We would also be left to ponder our own value as intercessors.

Fortunately such thoughts can be banished immediately. This is because community transformation is not an arbitrary event but rather the product of a cause and effect process.

My certainty in this matter derives, first and foremost, from the teachings of Scripture. God's Word makes clear that divine revelation and power are called forth by sanctified hearts, by right relationships, and by united, fervent and selfless intercession (see II Chronicles 7:14; Jeremiah 29:13; John 15:7; James 5:16; I John 3:21-22 and 5:14). Colorado Springs pastor Dutch Sheets adds that in the Old Testament era the fire of God was summoned by the presence of an appropriate altar and an acceptable sacrifice (Exodus 24; Joshua 8:30-31; Judges 6:17-21; I Chronicles 21:25-26; Ezekiel 43:18-27). To meet this standard it was sometimes necessary to rebuild broken altars and/or tear down false ones (Judges 6:25-26; I Kings 18:30-38; II Kings 23:3-15; Ezra 3:1-6).

In other words, there are definitive steps that we can and should take to position our communities for a visitation of the Holy Spirit. And if the above passages are not reason enough to believe this, you might want to consider recent evidence that shows God's people are acting on this proposition with great success. I know this because I have spent the last several years analyzing more than a dozen newly transformed communities.

IDENTIFYING COMMON THREADS

Transformation case studies are best considered collectively. A solitary story, no matter how remarkable or inspiring it may be, inevitably comes with a nagging question: Is it reproducible? You are never quite sure.

Bump into this same story ten or twelve times, however, and your confidence will rise. You now have an established pattern, and patterns are compelling. Laden with reproducible principles, they transform inspirational stories into potent models.

My own investigation into the factors responsible for transformed communities has yielded several major "hits". These include, but are not limited to, the following five stimuli:

Persevering leadership (Nehemiah 6:1-16);

Fervent, united prayer (Jonah 3:5-10);

Social reconciliation (Matthew 5:23-24; 18:15-20);

Public power encounters (Acts 9:32-35);

Diagnostic research/spiritual mapping (Joshua 18:8-10);

Although each of these factors recurs often enough to be considered common, two of them-persevering leadership and united prayer-are present in all of our transformation case studies. This observation suggests a possible distinction between core factors and contextual factors. Core factors, given their ubiquity, appear to initiate (or at least signal) divine involvement. Community transformation simply does not occur unless they are present. Contextual factors, on the other hand, are measures commended by God on the basis of local history, habits, and ideology.[18] They are the unique and added touch that turns potential into victory.

With this distinction in mind, I want to take a closer look at the two core factors on our list. If they indeed play a central role in community transformation, it seems prudent to become better acquainted with them.

Persevering Leadership

Determined leaders figure prominently in the Scriptural record. Noah spent decades constructing a massive ark while his neighbors mocked him as an eccentric fool. Nehemiah rebuilt the walls of Jerusalem in the face of persistent threats from Sanballat. Jesus ignored protestations from well-meaning friends in order to lay down His life at Calvary.

It should therefore come as no surprise that catalytic leaders associated with recent community transformations have also battled through strong opposition. Exhibiting a characteristic I call determined activism, these spiritual change agents have refused to accept anything less than God's maximum-even when the pressure has come from family members and ministry colleagues.

When things got rough for Robert Kayanja in Kampala, Uganda, his own parents were among those urging him to leave. "God wants to save these people," they said, "but he doesn't want you to die in the process." Christian activists ministering in the violent city of Cali, Colombia have heard much the same thing. When pastor Julio Caesar Ruibal was gunned down in December 1995, well-meaning friends urged his widow to leave town before the same fate befell her. Ignoring this counsel (and persistent death threats), she became a rallying point for hundreds of city pastors.

Other warnings have been linked to perceptions about unresponsive attitudes and appropriate ministry venues. When Thomas Muthee announced that he was planting a church in Kiambu, Kenya, his ministerial colleagues could only ask, "How will you manage?" One area pastor flatly declared, "The people here don't get saved. We preach, but they don't respond." Not persuaded by this claim, Thomas went on to found the largest church in

Kiambu's history.

Whether we view these determined activists as instruments of divine sovereignty or as magnets for divine intervention, their role is obviously critical to the process of community transformation. In every case their single-minded faith-demonstrated by importunate prayer and a steadfast commitment to the community-led to dramatic results. And while this may strike us as extraordinary, it is has long been the promise and pattern of Scripture.[19]

United Prayer

The second core factor in community transformation is fervent, united prayer. In each of our featured case studies, breakthroughs occurred when intercessors addressed specific concerns in common cause. Many of these group efforts took on their own unique identities. In Cali, Colombia, 60,000 intercessors held all-night vigilias in the Pascual Guerrero soccer stadium while others circled the city in mobile prayer caravans. In a daily practice they called the Wailing Wall, prayer warriors in the "Beirut of Kampala" cried out to God while holding hands around their church property. In Kiambu, Kenya believers petitioned God from a store basement they dubbed the Prayer Cave. Their stunning success led to subsequent intercessory campaigns like *Morning Glory and Operation Prayer Storm*.[20]

In December 1995 Pakistani evangelist Javed Albert established a routine he calls tarry nights to counter powerful demonic influences associated with shrine pilgrimages and witchcraft activity[21] These prayer and praise vigils begin at 9:00 PM on Thursday and Saturday evenings and continue until dawn. Because participants stand through the entire affair, they are also called standers meetings. The program, which began at Albert's modest church compound in Faisalabad, has since spread to twenty-five cities and 4,000 people.

United prayer is a declaration to the heavenlies that a community of believers is prepared for divine partnership. When this welcoming intercession is joined by knowledge it becomes focused-leading to and sustaining the kind of fervent prayer that produces results.

THREE STAGES OF PROGRESS

Recent case studies suggest that the road to community transformation passes through three distinct and measurable stages. These include:

1. Spiritual beachheads, an initial phase when revived believers enter into united prayer;

2. Spiritual breakthrough, a subsequent interval characterized by rapid and substantial church growth;

3. Spiritual transformation, a climactic season attended by dramatic socio-political renewal.

A fourth stage called *spiritual maintenance* could easily be added to this list. It is entered whenever liberated communities turn their attention to the business of preserving hard-won victories. For Christian leaders this means continuing to champion the things that attract God's presence: namely unity, prayer, humility and holiness. For born-again politicians, journalists, businessmen and educators it means perpetuating Kingdom values through the institutions they serve.

The ideal is that spiritual transformation remains a permanent condition. Unfortunately, history shows that the blossom of revival (to use a loose definition of the term) lasts an average of 36 months. Exceptions exist-the Argentine revival has lingered more than fifteen years-but these are few and far between.

My immediate goal, however, is not to discuss the maintenance of transformed communities (this discourse will come in due time), but rather to examine the process of achieving them. As all true champions have learned, you can only maintain what you have first attained.

We will begin our journey by investigating the role of spiritual beachheads. And do pay attention! More high hopes have been dashed here than any other place on the road to community transformation. It is during this early stage that you must build the spiritual momentum necessary to carry you over the mountains of apathy, pride and unbelief.

ESTABLISHING SPIRITUAL BEACHHEADS

Beachheads are small plots of ground (often a beach) that serve as staging areas for invading military forces. Because of their strategic potential, defending armies will fight vigorously to prevent them from becoming established. As a consequence, most beachheads are secured at high cost.

Beachheads can also be established in the spiritual dimension. Like their counterparts in the material world, they serve as staging areas in which intercessors and evangelists can amass sufficient strength to launch breakthrough assaults on enemy strongholds.

While beachheads can quickly swell with men and material, their initial occupants are typically few. In some cases spiritual beachheads have been established by a mere handful of intercessors. The transformation of Hemet, California began with twelve men praying through the night in a mountain cabin. Robert Kayanja's church planting effort in the "Beirut of Kampala" started with five prayer warriors. Thomas Muthee established the spiritual beachhead in Kiambu, Kenya with but a single partner-his wife Margaret. Although this modest level of participation appears to be incompatible with the primary characteristic of spiritual beachheads-namely united prayer-three things must be kept in mind. First, the population of beachheads tends to escalate with time. Breakthrough drives are rarely launched before sufficient troops have accumulated. Second, in some cases even a modest group of intercessors can represent a high percentage of the church. This is especially true in frontier or under-churched areas. Third, united prayer has more to do with heart attitudes than mass movements. As Jesus reminded his disciples in Matthew 18:19-20, God's presence and power is manifest when just two or three believers agree in prayer. (See also Ecclesiastes 9:14-15 NIV.)

If numbers are not essential to successful intercessory beachheads, spiritual passion is. Believers who wish to position their community for spiritual breakthroughs must pour their heart and soul into the effort. Unless the church is consumed with a burning desire for divine visitation, united prayer will become merely another project.

As I have taught seminars on this subject throughout the world, people often ask me to provide examples of genuine spiritual beachheads. Although they are inspired by stories of evangelistic breakthroughs and transformed communities, the results-oriented emphasis of these accounts sometimes obscures important formative details.

The good news is that contemporary spiritual beachheads abound-just don't expect uniformity. Depending on their developmental status, they can appear quite different.

Newly formed initiatives are typically small, unpublicized affairs in which a handful of dedicated intercessors seek to stimulate a renewed hunger for unity, holiness, and prayer-especially among community pastors. The stakes here are enormous. Without an increased appetite for the things that attract the presence of the Holy Spirit, evangelistic breakthroughs-let alone community transformation-will simply not occur.

Successful beachhead builders are content in their role as supporting actors. They have no craving for the limelight. This characteristic, however, should not be misinterpreted as indifference. Foundational intercessors are also passionate about doing whatever it takes to prepare their communities for divine visitation. Their unceasing petition is that God will replace the Church's bird-like appetite for prayer and unity with a ravenous hunger.

Latter-stage beachheads by contrast are nearly always characterized by intense groundswells of corporate repentance, social reconciliation, and united prayer. In many instances these developments are sustained by intelligence acquired through cooperative spiritual mapping campaigns.

Given the enormous pent-up energy displayed during latter-stage beachheads, observers have likened this season to a shuddering rocket just prior to launch. Others refer to these exciting days as the "hard labor" that necessarily precedes the birth of a new era.

The bad news is that very few spiritual beachheads ever last long enough to realize their potential as breeding grounds for revival. Most start with good intentions and then fizzle out.

Among the more common reasons for this attrition are weak leadership and the tendency to make unity an end in itself. Pastors gather for prayer but their rendezvous are often lacking in passion. This is because the emphasis is placed on corporate assembly rather than corporate vision. Trying to attract the widest possible cross-section of participants, they create an environment in which personal agendas proliferate like mushrooms. In the end, unity is trumped by cordiality. Unable to achieve a common vision, they settle for a common place.

Happily, there are exceptions to this trend. In Oklahoma City, for example, over half of the community's spiritual leaders gather monthly to petition God for a spiritual breakthrough. A principle catalyst for this focused prayer and fasting was the April 1995 bombing of the Murrah Federal Building which claimed 168 lives. In the aftermath of this tragic event the intercessory prayer force in the city jumped from 9 to more than 140 pastors and ministry leaders.

Another important development occurred in September 1996. As the leaders gathered one day for prayer, God revealed to them that their newfound "unity" was still superficial. There was almost no Native American participation-despite the fact Oklahoma hosts more than 60 tribes and the second largest Indian population in the US. Deeply convicted, one Anglo believer with deep roots in this state of "soil, oil, and toil" repented publicly for the way his ancestors, both in and out of government, had swallowed up land set aside for displaced Native Americans.

The consequences of this Spirit-led action were quick in coming. Welcomed and empowered by this public gesture, Native American attendance at the monthly prayer meetings tripled. Today their voices are heard alongside 1,200 other intercessors that have covenanted to pray for a spiritual breakthrough in Oklahoma City.

While reconciliation between believers and between the church and the community is an important catalyst for evangelistic breakthroughs, the history of revival-a term which has been defined so loosely at various times to apply both to spiritual beachheads and spiritual breakthroughs-reveals that general unity is not as critical. Since believers of differing backgrounds and persuasions can and do come together in intercessory common cause over the issues of revival and evangelistic breakthroughs (see Acts 1:14 KJV), unity and united prayer are not necessarily synonymous. In a recent article entitled "Prayer: God's Catalyst for Revival," Robert Bakke wrote:

[In the 18th century] Count Nicholas Von Zinzendorf gathered an incredibly diverse group of Christians (Catholics, Lutherans, Calvinists, etc.) from across Europe. He was able to forge and sustain their union as a single movement (the Moravians) only when he called his community to a lifestyle of united praying.[22]

It should be pointed out, however, that united prayer is not always unanimous prayer. A spiritual critical mass can be achieved even if some members of the community choose not to participate. This was certainly the case in Charles Finney's day. When the great evangelist launched his ministry in New England over a century ago, many conservative clergy opposed his efforts. Despite this hesitancy, enough intercession was mobilized to usher in the most dramatic season of community transformation in American history.

ACHIEVING SPIRITUAL BREAKTHROUGHS

While united prayer is a potent catalyst for revival, community-wide evangelistic breakthroughs require that intercession be fervent and sustained as well. Like many things that start well, petitions that lose their focus or fervor soon become pipe dreams.

This is not to say that fervent prayer is always articulate. God is a heart reader, not a lip reader (see II Chronicles 30:18-20; Matthew 6:5-8). When I petitioned God for the life of my two-year-old daughter, who, in 1996, nearly drowned in a swimming pool accident, I did not pause to consider my words. In fact, there was nothing eloquent about my cries and groaning.

At the same time, my prayer was fervent. And it was fervent because I was consumed with the details of the case. As I looked down on my daughter's lifeless face, I recognized every tiny crease. I was familiar with her budding gifts and idiosyncrasies. I could recall each word spoken over her when she was still in the womb. In short, I prayed hard for this little girl because I knew her (and the situation at hand) intimately.

Community intercession is not much different. To pray fervently for a neighborhood we must first familiarize ourselves with its history and features. And since reality is often painted in shades of gray, this requires us to linger in spaces both dark and light. It is not enough to merely acknowledge the community; we must become acquainted with it.

And perseverance is no less important than fervor. History shows that spiritual breakthroughs are often delayed reactions, their spectacular fireworks the result of an intercessory match struck months, or even years, earlier. The challenge is to keep the fuse burning to the point of ignition. Two factors that have proven particularly effective in sustaining fervent corporate intercession are progressive revelation and positive results.

In the first instance, people are motivated by new details about the case at hand. The psychology is the same as that which pulls readers through a good mystery novel or hobbyists through a challenging puzzle. In both situations, participants are rewarded with a sense of momentum toward an ultimate solution. Incremental disclosure is not only tolerated. It is enjoyable.

This was certainly the experience of a spiritual mapping team operating out of the El Shaddai Church in Guatemala City during the early 1990s. Their mission was to identify obstacles to revival in their community. To accomplish this, team members were divided into three working groups that investigated respective historical, physical, and spiritual factors.

The process began when God led the historical team to a Mayan archaeological site. As they reviewed the weathered remains, it suddenly became clear that their spiritual challenges were part of an ancient continuum of idolatry and witchcraft. At this precise moment, the physical factors team (which had been operating independently) located a vacant house adjacent to the ruins where occult rituals were being practiced. A third team comprised of intercessors received a revelation that the territorial spirit over that place was linked to a human co-conspirator whose lifestyle included idolatrous and occult practices.

The next series of developments, which pastor Harold Caballeros describes as "truly exciting," began when the Lord indicated His intention to disclose the man's identity in the city newspaper-even going so far as to reveal the date and page on which the information would appear. When the team finally turned to the appropriate page they were stunned to find not only the name of the suspect, but a photo matching a precise physical description the Holy Spirit had provided earlier. "To cap it off," writes Caballeros, "we discovered that this man was also the owner of the vacant house where the occult rituals were taking place, right across the street from the archaeological site!"[23]

Where believers are united in their desire to see a community transformed by the power of God, spiritual mapping can provide the kind of revelatory focus that sustains fervent and effectual prayer. When this intelligence is carried into spiritual warfare, God is released to provide an "open door" for ministry (see Colossians 4:2-4).[24] Evangelistic breakthroughs and church growth often follow.

Answers to prayer offer equally potent motivation for corporate intercessors. Like progressive revelation, timely results encourage pray-ers to stick with their assignments. Besides the pleasure associated with seeing desired changes take root in broken communities, there is an exhilaration that comes from knowing our words have moved the Almighty.

To find an example of results sustaining fervent intercession we need look no further than Cali, Colombia. Forty-eight hours after that city's first all-night prayer vigil the local daily, El Pais, reported a notable decrease in homicides. Corruption also took a major hit when, over the next four months, nine hundred cartel-linked officers were fired from the metropolitan police force. "When we saw these things happening," one participant told me, "we had a strong sense that the powers of darkness were headed for a significant defeat."[25]

In June 1995, this sense of anticipation was heightened when several intercessors reported dreams in which angelic forces apprehended leaders of the Cali drug cartel. Six weeks later the Colombian government declared all-out war against the drug lords. By August, federal authorities had captured all seven targeted cartel leaders-Juan Carlos Armínez, Phanor Arizabalata, Julian Murcillo, Henry Loaiza, Jose Santacruz Londono, and Gilberto and Miguel Rodriguez.

Emboldened by this success, Cali's Christian community decided to fuel their all-night prayer rallies, now 60,000 strong, by launching spiritual mapping campaigns in each of the city's 22 administrative sections. The compiled results soon gave the church an unprecedented picture of the powers working in the city. "With this knowledge," one veteran missionary explained, "our unified intercession became truly focused. Praying in specific terms, we began to see a dramatic loosening of the Enemy's stranglehold on our community and nation."[26]

While these abbreviated examples do not detail the community-wide church growth that resulted in Cali and Guatemala City, it is this level of expansion that defines them as authentic spiritual breakthroughs. Growth that is confined to individual churches, while generally desirable, is not the same thing. This is because there are any number of reasons short of divine visitation that might explain proliferating numbers (including charismatic leadership, quality management, and appealing programs). Genuine evangelistic breakthroughs, on the other hand, tend to spread spontaneously across geographic, ethnic, and denominational boundaries.

FROM BREAKTHROUGH TO TRANSFORMATION

Given the heady atmosphere that accompanies spiritual breakthroughs, some Christians misinterpret these seasons as the climax of divine activity and intention. This is an understandable, if unfortunate, error. For while spiritual breakthroughs are by their very definition advanced achievements, they are by no means the end of God's ambitions for a community.

If intercessors continue to press in during the spiritual breakthrough phase, a point of critical mass will eventually be reached where community transformation occurs. At this level the social, political, and economic fabric of the entire community begins to metamorphose. As an ever-increasing percentage of the population comes under the Lordship of Christ, the sin-wrought citadels of corruption, poverty, violence, prejudice, and oppression are transformed into ghost towns. Confirmation of this new heavenly order comes not from Christian triumphalists but from the evening newscasts and banner headlines of the secular media.

This is not to suggest that transformed communities are perfect communities-at least not in a millennial sense. Even sympathetic observers will have little trouble locating blemishes. Violence, immorality, and apathy are ubiquitous in our world, and this includes cities that have been visited by Divine Grace. Spiritual transformation is not a total absence of sin but rather a fresh trajectory with acknowledged fruit. Communities that have been so touched should be measured not by what they still lack, but by what they once were.

Asia has arguably experienced more divine visitations than any other region in recent history. This has led to phenomenal church growth in various parts of China, South Korea, India, Bangladesh, Nepal, Indonesia, and the Philippines. Less encouraging is the fact that the continent has only one documentable case of community transformation-the province of Nagaland in eastern India (three other cases are currently under investigation). Noting the sharp drop-off between breakthrough and transformation one cannot help but wonder about the factors responsible for this attrition.

Two reasons stand out. First, as we mentioned earlier, there is a tendency for Christians to misinterpret breakthroughs as the climax of divine activity. If people are getting saved and our churches are growing, what more could we ask for? How could these blessed and exciting developments be anything other than God's maximum intent?

The second reason is closely related to the first. Community transformation fails to occur because local inhabitants do not perceive a need for change. Affluent societies in particular tend to be self-sufficient and self-satisfied-qualities that make them poor candidates for divine intervention. They are the collective embodiment of Jesus' teaching about it being easier for a camel to pass through the eye of a needle than for a rich man to enter the kingdom of God (Matthew 19:23-24). While the obstacle of affluence (or security) can be overcome, history has shown this to be a rare occurrence.

Of the case studies consulted for this chapter, it is noteworthy that only one-Hemet, California-is located within the Western world, and even it is faced with significant maintenance challenges. While Asia has long been viewed as distinct from the West, the region's economic growth (recent downturns notwithstanding) has blurred this distinction. Places like Singapore, Malaysia, Japan, and Taiwan are now awash in the same abundance and political stability that one finds in Europe and North America. Unfortunately, they have also begun to adopt the self-satisfaction that so often accompanies these blessings.

This problem is compounded in churches with large memberships. When the pastors of these congregations survey their ministry they see little that would suggest a need for change. Competent staff are busy running well-conceived programs and the sanctuary is filled every Sunday with a sea of eager faces. While the status quo is not perfect, neither is it a rationale for extreme measures. Change, if and when it is needed, is best sought in manageable increments.

The danger in this perspective lies in its introversion. Because their sphere of influence is large, the leaders of well-heeled mega-churches tend to view their community from inside that circle. They see other churches (or circles) in the community not as partners in a collective vision but as competitors for market share. There are exceptions, of course, but not many. The mirror of history reveals that the grander a church becomes the more likely it is to fall victim to the Laodicean Syndrome. And one of the primary symptoms of this complex is a subconscious shift from kingdom mentality to empire mentality.

While many churches today are preoccupied with growing their circle, God's focus is on the area between the circles. He worries not about the one sheep that is found, but the ninety-nine that are lost. He wants to break out of our churches and into area boardrooms and courtrooms. In short, He wants to introduce His kingdom into every area of society.

Some time ago I took a wrong turn on my way to Sunday church services and found myself on unfamiliar streets. This caused me to pay attention to my surroundings in a way I would not have otherwise. The sights disturbed me. A pair of homeless drunks staggering down the sidewalk; a video arcade filled with troubled teens; and hordes of preoccupied antique shoppers.

When I finally pulled in the church parking lot my senses were on full alert. It was then that I noticed something else that had escaped me on previous Sundays. A simple sign announcing "Celebration Services" at 9:00 and 11:00 AM. On this morning, however, I did not feel like celebrating. Whatever blessings I might count clearly did not extend to the streets of my community.

Most of us want to see things change in our communities. Unfortunately, few of us ever have. We do not seem to know how to get where we want to go. (Theories on community transformation have always been more abundant than successful case studies.)

Excerpted from Spiritual Mapping Field Guide by George Otis, Jr., Ventura, CA, Regal Books, 1997. Used by permission of Regal Books and the author.

CHAPTER

17

ALMOLONGA - THE MIRACLE CITY

Mell Winger

Dr. Mell Winger is the director of the Bible Institute at El Shaddai Church in Guatemala City, Guatemala. The institute trains leaders to plant churches throughout Latin America. He and his wife, Paula, and their three children are missionaries from Springs Harvest Fellowship in Colorado Springs, Colorado. Prior to ministering in Guatemala, Dr. Winger was Vice-President of Church Ministries and the International Director of Prayer for Every Home for Christ, a missions organization with offices in more than 100 nations. He was also a pastor in the USA for 11 years.

Dr. Winger received his doctorate in ministry from Fuller Theological Seminary in 1997.

On a Personal Note…

In October 1994, Dr. Mell Winger came to Guatemala to teach a prayer seminar. The impact of his ministry greatly blessed Guatemala, and God used that trip to plant in Mell a seed of love for the nation of Guatemala.

Toward the end of 1997, God guided the Winger family to move to Guatemala to serve Him as fulltime missionaries. We have witnessed the effort the whole family has made to adapt to a new culture, new language, and the Latin way of doing things.

Since the beginning, Mell has been a blessing to us, not only because of the gift of God in his life, but also because of his personality and character that continually reflect Jesus.

Mell and his wife, Paula, have made an extraordinary contribution to this book. Mell fell in love with Almolonga when he went there to investigate what God had done. He has written about it for the magazines Charisma and Vida Cristiana, and now brings us this special chapter.

I had hoped that this chapter covering Almolonga would be written from a North American (Western) perspective by someone whose first language is English. My desire couldn't have yielded better fruit. Mell has done an excellent job. I pray to God that this testimony inspires great faith in you and blesses you as much as it has me.

Harold Caballeros

Before and after: two simple words frequently used to describe a city in western Guatemala named Almolonga. The locals consistently refer to their city in terms of two eras: before the power of God came in the mid-1970s, and after, when it is reported that 90% of the 18,000 residents became born-again Christians. The way the people of Almolonga say "before" is reminiscent of how others might say, "in the dark ages..."

After. The word signals a new epoch for the city, marked by family harmony, prosperity and peace in the Holy Spirit. The contrast is stark and real to these people who remember how, just 25 years ago, demons, fear, poverty, disease, idolatry, and alcohol dominated their region and their families.

Some call Almolonga the "Miracle City" because of the radical transformations in many dimensions of this ethnically Quiché society (descendants of the Mayans). Some Christian leaders say Almolonga is the best example they've seen of how intercession, spiritual warfare, and evangelism can transform a community.

Driving into Almolonga, one is immediately struck by the brilliant green hues of the fertile fields spreading throughout this magnificent valley. Even before the onset of the rainy season, when much of the Guatemalan landscape is still dry, Almolonga remains vibrant and lush. Hence, Almolonga is nicknamed "America's Vegetable Garden".

But it wasn't always so. About 25 years ago, the Church was small and weak, the fields were undeveloped and the city was characterized by an alcohol-induced lethargy—the fruit of serving an idol named Maximon. This perverse idol is associated with the vices of smoking, drinking liquor, and immorality.

Maximon is a 3-foot idol consisting of a clay mask and a wood and cloth body. He receives the kisses of the faithful who kneel before him. Placing at his feet bottles of liquor purchased with their meager earnings, they hope against hope that their offering will bring blessing and healing. The priest offers lit cigars to the idol, and taking a mouthful of the liquor offering, spews it over the devotees. The followers leave expecting a blessing, perhaps receiving a demonic display of power, but nonetheless slipping deeper and deeper into an abyss of oppression.

Sadly, his influence is so strong that he is considered the patron saint and protector of many Guatemalan mountain villages. In addition to serving Maximon, many of the residents of Almolonga once sought the blessing of other idols as well. Pastor Genero Riscajché, one of the pastors at Almolonga's largest church, Mission Evangelical Monte Calvario, notes, "Before, this was a very idolatrous town. There were many different types of idols. Many worshipped the silver image of Almolonga's patron saint, San Pedro."

But in 1974-75 the Kingdom of God dramatically started clashing with

Maximon and the ruling powers of darkness controlling Almolonga. Following the pattern of historic revivals, God first began this community transformation in the heart of one of His consecrated servants. Mariano Riscajché (no relation to Genero), now the pastor of El Calvario Church, was a typical young man of Almolonga who sought the protection and blessing of idols before he encountered the living God.

At his conversion, Pastor Mariano heard the Lord say, " I have elected you to serve Me." He said it was like waking from a dream; his understanding was opened and the promises of the Bible became real. Pastor Mariano's burning desire was to see people come to Christ and find freedom. Then, one by one, his own family was saved.

A new season of power encounters with Maximon began shortly after Pastor Mariano's surrender to Christ. Mariano and other pastors in town, such as Guillermo Satey, founding and senior pastor of Mission Evangelical Monte Calvario, saw more than 400 people delivered from demons. When believers asked a demon to identify itself, "Maximon" was sometimes uttered by the oppressed one. This mass deliverance was similar to the book of Acts where people burned their possessions that linked them to a past consumed by witchcraft and idolatry. "...Those who practiced magic brought their books together and began burning them..." (Acts 19:19, NASB). The eviction of these demons not only brought freedom to individuals, but the spiritual oppression over the city began to lift as well.

The early days of spiritual warfare were extremely intense. Those being set free were sometimes thrown across the room, and at times coughed up blood. The Church continued steadfast in intercession, spiritual warfare, and evangelism as the Name of Jesus was demonstrated to be the dominant force in this battle. Pastor Mariano asserts that the enemy had to be confronted directly and boldly.

One of those set free from demonic control was a powerful priest of Maximon named José Albino Tazej. Many people in Almolonga sought him out to heal their illnesses, foresee their future, and to bless their businesses. But one night, José, near death after a month-long drinking binge, cried out to God to save him. At 11:00 PM, José woke his family to share the glorious news of his new-found freedom in Christ. In repentance, the family burned all of their idols and witchcraft paraphernalia. The following day, José went to the mountains to fast and seek the Lord.

Witnessing this well-known slave to witchcraft come to Christ intensified the Church's intercession for God to transform not only individuals like José, but their whole community as well.

Before his conversion José would abandon the family for eight to ten days at a time to drink and conduct witchcraft activities for Maximon. He often left his family without any money for food. As his dedication to Maximon grew, so did his addiction to alcohol.

José's oldest daughter, Francisca, grimaces and lowers her voice as she recounts the memory of herself and the other children kneeling before Maximon, burning candles and bringing their offerings. But quickly she diverts the subject to "after we surrendered to Jesus" and joyfully asserts that God changed everything 24 years ago. She proudly inserts, "We were some of the first converts during the mid 70s."

"Before we received Christ, we didn't have any money, little food, or a decent house, and only clothes discarded by others," she continues. "My father started seeking God and fasting. He began a business and started working diligently. Now, God has given us a house, a small store, and a calm, hard-working, godly father."

Francisca recounts, "The church accepted us and didn't leave us in the middle. They loved us and visited us, and really struggled with us as we became established in Christ." This care for new converts is one of the key ways God has used to maintain and deepen the effects of this revival.

As his grip started loosening, the evil one instigated a persecution against the Church. Some merchants would not even sell food to believers recently set free from the old ways. Enemies of the Gospel would go into church and do witchcraft to disrupt the services. The believers suffered under this backlash for years, but one particular incident stands out in Pastor Mariano's memory. Six men attacked him, tying his hands behind his back. They knocked his front teeth out, then one man shoved a gun in his mouth. Pastor Mariano prayed for God to cover him, and as the Lord's presence descended he heard the "click... click... click" of the gun, unable to fire. Bewildered by this divine intervention, his attackers ran away.

Pastor Genero, a native of Almolonga, describes the early resistance to the Gospel as follows: "If a person from outside Almolonga came to someone's home to share the Gospel, people would kick them out of their house with sticks, stones, and even shovels. It was terrible! They didn't view the Gospel as Good News, but as something offensive. Unbelievers circulated rumors about the Church and accused the Christians of being lazy." Some of the unbelievers threw stones at houses where the church met for prayer. Pastor Genero notes, "Many of those who threw stones are now leaders in the church. Things have now changed, for even the non-Christians respect the Gospel."

As one who has pastored a little over one year in Almolonga, Pastor Joel Pérez agrees and says, "Even unbelievers in Almolonga recognize the marvelous work of God. These few unbelievers acknowledge that the advances in their society and agriculture are due to the Gospel. They do not resist the Church now, as we heard about in the early days. More than once, I have been eating in a restaurant and someone has said, 'You are a pastor, aren't you? I'm not a Christian, but let me buy your lunch.'"

Since the power of God started transforming the community, crime has taken a definite downturn. Donato Santiago, chief of police, can sometimes be spotted resting in the shade during market days. Armed with a whistle, this tranquil brother has seen it all during his 23 years as a policeman in Almolonga. "We used to average 20 to 30 people in jail each month," he recounts. "Crowds would gather just to watch the drunks fight. It seemed like I had no rest. I was often awakened in the middle of the night to stop family violence. Before, we had four jails and that was insufficient to adequately house all of our prisoners," Donato recalls. "Things were so bad we enlisted around a dozen citizens at night to help the officers patrol the streets. But now things are different! The people have changed their attitudes. Crime has risen in many places over the past 20 years, but not here in Almolonga."

What accounts for this dramatic change in the townspeople? Donato is quick to respond, "The Word of God! Once people were converted they changed their customs and left behind drinking. They gained respect in the community. Day by day the rest followed and joined the church because of the changes they saw in the lives of Christians. People living with a deep respect for God accounts for the changed attitudes. Crime and drinking are now viewed by the people as a waste of time and a waste of money."

The last jail closed in 1989! Now remodeled and called "The Hall of Honor," it's a place for celebrating weddings, receptions, and community events.

In addition to the drop in the crime rate, great societal changes can also be observed by the absence of prostitutes and the number of bars turned into small stores with new names like "Little Jerusalem" and "Jehovah Jireh." Before, there was a house of prostitution and people often waited in line to get into the packed bars. "There was even a custom in which we threw a party and gave alcohol (in small portions) to the little ones," says Pastor Genero. In the 1970s, 34 cantinas did a brisk business in Almolonga; today there are only three. After the bars started shutting down, a new one opened but the owner closed the doors when he met the Lord three months later. He now plays in a Christian band called "Combo Israel."

God's mercy over Almolonga is evidenced in many ways, but one often-repeated display of grace is the incredible number of miracles. Many have come to Christ through signs and wonders. Teresa and her family found new life in Christ after she received a last-chance miracle. In 1984, the incision from her poorly performed Cesarean section became infected. This gangrenous state progressed to the point where she couldn't eat; drinking was extremely difficult.

Teresa continued to weaken. Different doctors each said that she was in a very dangerous state. Valeriano, her husband, remembers the days of just hopelessly waiting for her to die. She died about 10:00 PM one night. Her husband checked for a pulse and placed a mirror beneath her nostrils to see if she was breathing, but there were no signs of life. For three hours she lay motionless. Grief stricken, at 1:00 AM Valeriano went to look for Pastor Mariano to make funeral preparations. As Pastor Mariano and Valeriano were walking back to the house, Pastor Mariano heard the unmistakable voice of the Lord saying, "Do not prepare for the funeral; pray for her. I will lift her up."

Pastor Mariano recalls coming into the home seeing distraught people frantically running back and forth. He grabbed Valeriano and they began to pray for God's miraculous intervention. After 10 minutes, Teresa suddenly began stirring. Her color returned and she sat up on the bed! Valeriano was astounded at this display of God's power. Pastor Mariano began to preach the Gospel to all the neighbors and family who had gathered at the home that night. And in the days that followed, many believed.

Teresa's strength was restored day by day. In deep gratitude, she and Valeriano also gave their lives to Christ. Now people come to their home to receive prayer for healing. Remembering her miracle inspires faith when Teresa prays for others; she has witnessed many miracles as a result. Valeriano now preaches the Gospel and testifies of a miracle working Heavenly Father. He joyfully says, "God is the only one Who is on our side and only He can do these miracles."

Just as Valeriano and Teresa's family opened their hearts to the Gospel after this powerful miracle, in many cases the revival has spread through family units. Pastor Mariano articulates a truth held dear in Almolonga when he says, "True success is when your whole family comes to the Lord." Therefore, believers seriously fast and pray to bring their family into God's family.

Although the women still weave and wear the beautiful indigenous dresses and carry heavy loads upon their heads (like Quiché women have for hundreds of years), they walk in a new dignity-a result of the redemption of the family. Prior to God's inbreaking, Pastor Genero recalls, "The majority of men drank and the homes were disorderly. Neglect and physical abuse were rampant. It was common for men to hit their wives, sometimes even with sticks."

"The family system before was at the bottom," comments Pastor Francisco Garcia of Iglesia de Dios de la Profecia Universal. Women were largely viewed simply as servants. Pastor Genero comments, "Before, the custom was that only the men would study. We believed that schools were not for women. Since the Gospel came, we teach that both sexes have the same opportunities. Today we see some women who are professionals."

Ramon Cotzoy's wife recalls the earlier days. "My husband would sometimes treat me harshly and try to throw me out of the house. Things have changed. Now he is a humble man of God."

Ramon admits that he neglected and mistreated his family prior to surrendering to Christ. Now he ministers to men in the community and exhorts them to stop drinking and start loving their families. Ramon observes, "Because the unbelievers see the peaceful example of how the Christian men are living with their families, they are treating their wives better now."

"Today there is more communication within families and very little abuse in Almolonga. In the church, we teach a lot on biblical family orientation," says Pastor Genero. "Couples solve their problems through dialog and communication."

This renewal of family harmony has opened the way for the Spirit of God to span the generations and impact all age groups, including the youth and children. The youth do not view Christianity as simply something for the older people. There is a new thrust of youth-motivated home groups with the focus to bring the remaining unsaved youth in the city to Christ. Pastor Joel observes, "The youth are getting hold of God. In different churches some of the youth groups even go on special fasting retreats."

Chief of Police Santiago says, "The parents are taking better care of their children now." Santiago explains why there aren't teens loitering around town. "The youth work hard to buy farm trucks. This atmosphere of diligent work is the best atmosphere to grow up in."

Seeing the youth and children cheerfully working alongside their parents in the fields and marketplace evokes a smile in visitors to Almolonga. Pastor Mariano's father, one of the oldest men in the city, observes, "Everyone in Almolonga works. Even the 12-15-year olds fill a truck with vegetables to sell. They throw themselves into God and into their work."

This work ethic has produced an economic renewal, an incredible dimension of community transformation throughout Almolonga. There is no evidence of the unemployment, the beggars, the drunkards asleep in alleyways, or the loiterers that so often characterize similar places. In other cities around this region people often appear exhausted with life. Not so in Almolonga.

The people's diligence and tenacity have seen this valley come alive with multiple harvests each year. Celery, leeks, cauliflower, turnips, cabbage, potatoes, carrots, radishes, and watercress thrive under the skillful care of Almolonga's farmers. These vegetables are often incredibly larger than the size of those grown in the surrounding villages. Pastor Joel attributes this agricultural blessing to the Lord of Glory. He mentioned a time when agronomists from the U.S.A. visited Almolonga to test their scientific principles to produce better crops. The result? Pastor Joel says, "The wisdom God gave the farmers of Almolonga produced more than the scientific methods yielded."

A subterranean stream provides a constant source of water for the farms. These lucrative products have elevated the lifestyles of many of the believers. Pastor Mariano's father was one of the former bar owners who now runs a *tienda* (small store) and raises vegetables. He reports that the greatest changes in commerce came in the 80s because the farmers not only quit spending their money on liquor, but they began to incorporate principles from God's Word, saving and investing their profits. Before the farmers would farm just enough to support their drinking habit; they had no vision beyond that.

Then God started giving the farmers understanding. They began to plan ahead and invest in topsoil and fertilizers. Some farmers have even paid cash for Mercedes trucks, emblazoning them with names like *Regalito de Dios* ("Little Gift from God"). Many farmers have now hired others to work their fields. They are even developing farms in the surrounding communities as they shift from being farmers to businessmen. Mariano's father marvels, "We never dreamed of selling our produce outside of Guatemala, but now we export to other nations."

Since this relatively small town has so many growing churches, a question often arises concerning the relationship between the pastors. Pastor Joel describes the fellowship among pastors as "a tight fraternity of ministers." He further notes, "We have an agenda of prayer and fasting. We go outside the city to a hill to pray and earnestly seek the Lord...When we have little things come up or if the enemy tries to interrupt our unity, we quickly restore it through seeking the Lord for more souls to come into the Kingdom."

Pastor Genero says, "Presently we are strengthening our fellowship. Years ago there was an association of pastors, but it faded out because of individuality. This year we have restored the pastoral association again." Two Christian radio stations service Almolonga. Pastor Joel reports that these stations enhance unity by allowing air time for all the evangelical pastors to use for a token price.

Reaching 90% of the city with the Gospel doesn't satisfy the pastors' evangelistic zeal. Pastor Francisco emphatically asserts, "We are applying God's guidance for the churches to keep growing. We have the goal to reach the whole town!"

Pastor Mariano believes God is giving the Church insight into the strategies to deepen and extend this community impact into future generations. His heart breaks when he hears about powerful revivals which were not passed along to the next generation. To maintain the results already reached in Almolonga, Pastor Mariano's strategy encompasses a fivefold focus: living in the *fear of the Lord,* maintaining intense prayer and fasting, building Christian schools, caring for new converts, and establishing strong families. Firstly, he urges his flock to, "always live under the direction of the Holy Spirit. Live your life in the fear of the Lord as a good testimony. When we truly live the Christian life, demonic principalities are more easily overthrown."

Secondly, to maintain the results won through intercession and spiritual warfare, the Church must continue steadfast in *prayer and fasting.* Long past the breakthroughs in the 70s, many believers in Almolonga continue weekly disciplines of prayer and fasting. At El Calvario Church, people are held accountable to participate in prayer and fasting.

Thirdly, Pastor Mariano is taking steps to *build a Christian school,* which he believes is critical to sustain the revival. He says that the children not only need an education, but a Christ-centered education taught by Christian teachers. "Education without Christian teachers can set up a counterattack from Satan by introducing traditions outside of Christianity. Then all that we have reached [in the revival] can crumble."

A fourth ingredient to maintain revival is an intentional plan to *care for the new Christians.* Someone from the church personally visits the new believers. They hold special discipleship meetings focusing on basic Bible doctrines. Deliverance and a clear break with their past life are important. "We inspire them toward diligent hard work, debt reduction and to live in the fear of God. New believers are instructed to prepare themselves for baptism. Fasting is one of the first spiritual disciplines taught to the new Christian," reports Pastor Mariano.

The fifth and final major focus to sustain the revival's impact is *establishing strong families.* Christians are instructed to only marry fellow believers. One countercultural measure El Calvario introduced in the late 1970s was the concept of letting people decide for themselves whom they would marry. Today, parents are consulted and there is a process of obtaining parental blessing and approval in mate selection, but the decision rests with the couple. Before, the parents would determine whom their children would marry. A courtship period was also unheard of in their culture; now they recommend a 6-month to a year courtship during which the couple gets to know each other. This has increased marital harmony within the Christianity community. Consequently, other churches in the community also follow similar plans.

Testimonies of individuals being changed relationally, spiritually, and financially by God's power are common in Christianity. But the amazing distinctive of Almolonga is that Christians there tell their testimony not simply as

individuals, but collectively, as families and as a people.
Visiting a service at El Calvario Church is a little taste of Heaven. The church building is one of Guatemala's largest and most beautiful. This debt-free sanctuary (seating 1200+) is the gathering place of exuberant worshippers. Their release of emotions toward the Son of God is noteworthy because culturally these people are generally stoic and very reserved in expressing their emotions. To watch this passion for Jesus, especially among the youth and children, it is hard to imagine that only a generation back, their families were in bondage to alcohol, idols, and demons. Perhaps that legacy of suffering explains the great abandon with which they worship Jesus: these people *know* they have something to celebrate!

CHAPTER 18

A COSMIC FRAMEWORK FOR SPIRITUAL WARFARE

José L. Gonzáles

José L. González is the President of Semilla, Inc. a ministry serving key and emerging Latin American Christian Leaders who are committed to transforming their society by the Word of God. He is Adjunct Professor of Latin American issues at the Robertson School of Government of Regent University, a Christian graduate university in Virginia Beach, Virginia. He lectures and consults on cultural, government and leadership development issues throughout Latin America.

On a Personal Note...

In 1995 I was trying to establish the link between "the powers" and "the culture" of a territory. It started to become obvious to me that the receptivity or resistance of a society to the Gospel was related, not only to the powers in the heavenlies, but also to the residents' way of thinking.

The ideas, concepts, and arguments make up what we call the "culture or idiosyncrasy" of the place. My intention was to demonstrate that the culture is a result of the influence of the "unseen powers."

I had met José González a few years ago, but just in time I received two of his articles. He wrote about the soul of Latin America. This really inspired me and I invited him to the Interamerican Consultation on Spiritual Warfare that was held that year. José's participation was a blessing and our friendship hasn't stopped growing since.

God's call over José's life is very special. Like many other Latin Americans, he lives in the United States but his heart remains in our countries. He is a modern-day Joseph who dreams that believers will have positions of great influence (like Daniel and Joseph and other biblical characters). In other words, some Christians are called to places of leadership and government.

The subject of believers being involved in politics has been a very controversial one. We wanted to include José's point of view in this book, believing that community transformation will certainly need qualified leaders. These believers who accept God's challenge will need to be well prepared spiritually, emotionally, and intellectually to serve Him in every facet of society.

Harold Caballeros

In the last two decades of the 20th Century, certain global trends are emerging which deserve attention and discernment by prophetic leaders, captains of prayer and intercessors. Three significant trends are:

After a century and a half of unpopularity, religion is becoming fashionable in the advanced world, not in its traditional Christian garb, but as a sort of do-it-yourself "new age" spirituality[27]

For their part, the gathering forces of global unity seem animated by a new collective faith, an emerging religious paradigm enshrining a humanist idea of "peace," "freedom" and of "tolerance"[28] without a personal God or personal accountability.

In dozens of Muslim and Communist-dominated nations, outright repression and persecution of Christians has been increasing.[29]

All of these forces share a negative attitude toward Christianity that ranges from antipathy to open enmity. Not surprisingly, in the United States, as Christian principles, which nursed this nation, are increasingly discarded from the public arena, believers organize politically to protect what remains. And as the number of Christians reaches critical mass in many societies, some believers begin to prepare and take steps toward positions of political and civil authority.

Whatever their personal merits, preparation or tactics, it is clear that the Holy Spirit is saying to large numbers of His people something different about government and politics than what the Church has grown accustomed to hearing and doing from an isolated posture over the last century. The result is that hundreds of Christians are involved in parliaments and state governments and dozens of political parties of Christian inspiration have emerged since 1980.

What do all these things mean? And how should we then pray and act?

We know, of course, that God is directing history toward its appointed end. But is it possible to connect these separate phenomena, to read them as "signs of the times?" Do they say something to Christian leaders called to spiritual warfare and intercession? The answer, I believe, is yes. These events belong to that stage in the divine timeline immediately before the Second Coming of Christ.

On the one hand, the isolation, unpopularity and widespread persecution of Christians, has been prophesied in every generation (John 16:33), but it will take on apocalyptic proportions at the end (Rev. 13:7). Also, an unholy alliance of a global government, world church and world economic system is also predicted in Scripture (Rev. 13:2-4,12,16,17).

On the other hand, we know that one day the earth will be filled with the knowledge of the glory of the Lord (Hab. 2:14); we also know that Christians will rule and reign with Christ forever (Rev. 22:5). Isn't it, therefore, predictable that at some point in history the Holy Spirit will motivate God's people to prepare to occupy positions of influence and authority in their nations?

Like Jesus' disciples some Christians may ask: "When shall these things be? and what shall be the sign of Thy coming, and of the end of the world?" (Matt. 24:3).

Jesus' answer resounds throughout the ages: "It is not given to you to know the times that the Father has reserved to Himself." The precise timing (day and hour) of the Son's coming no man knows, because the Father has reserved these to Himself (Matt. 25:13). But, the changing seasons of God, manifested in the things He both does and permits, these we should observe and through prayer and counsel, discern their meaning. He sent us the Holy Spirit to guide us into all truth, and rebuked the Pharisees for failing to discern the times in their day (Matt. 16:3).

Many today would probably agree that these signs tell us that the fulfillment of God's end-time promises is not very far off. They confirm the inner witness of many Christians, that the Holy Spirit is saying to the Church not only to "be ready" (a way of life), but also "to prepare" (to take specific action steps) for the coming of the Lord. Events like these convince us that these are the "last days" of which the Scripture spoke from Genesis to Revelation (Gen. 49:1; Isa. 2:2; Mic. 4:1; Acts 2:17; 2 Tim. 3:1; 2 Pet. 3:3; Jas. 5:3).

I am not announcing that Jesus is coming tonight (although the Bride is always ready and eager, for Him!), nor predicting any particular day, month or year. I am saying that we are at a point in the timeline of history in which the events of the end begin to shape the events of today.

This brings new nuances to Christology: While as individuals we continue to grow with Isaiah's Suffering Servant as our model, as a Body, we are increasingly responding to the coming King of kings. These two different roles of Christ are not in contradiction, but they may cause tension between servants being transformed into the one and servants being called to the other.

This is in part what it means to "know the times." It is to discern the different roles of the Body, and to be able to adapt and flow with them, regardless of our personal calling and function. Also, we must be in tune with what the Holy Spirit is broadly saying. Those who expected Jesus in His time to take the throne of Israel were out of sync with God's timetable. The same will be true soon of those Christian leaders who refuse to admit that God is preparing His people to occupy the thrones of the earth.

Because these are the last days, we are receiving fresh end-time understandings, and very likely the illumination of last things (*apocalypse*) will grow steadily in the church from now on.[30] The Spirit shall give the Bride such illumination of the Scriptures and other instructions as she needs at each particular time and place (Mark 13:11; John 16:13).

For the end-time Church to be fully equipped there will need to be a more explicit understanding of the battlefield in which it is called upon to fight. It is a multidimensional battlefield, with spiritual and physical realms, operating simultaneously on the temporal and the eternal planes, utilizing weapons and confronting enemies which are not carnal (empowered by merely human means), but mighty (empowered by the Almighty) and fighting (not only) flesh and blood but (also) invisible powers and principalities (fallen angels).

Intercessors and prayer warriors are of necessity more versed in such things than the remaining of the army, because they need that spiritual technology to fulfill their call. Far from instructing them, this chapter attempts to organize a number of ideas that are commonplace among them, so as to facilitate discussion and discernment by the elders of today's Church.

The Value of a Cosmic Framework

In his classical work on the Middle Ages, The *Discarded Image*, C.S. Lewis speaks of medieval man as an "organizer, a codifier, a builder of systems," and labels the mental idea of the universe prevalent in medieval society, "the Model." I believe that the contemporary Church needs to regain its understanding of the cosmic framework implicit in the Bible to better understand our times, the past and the coming end-time events. A healthy preoccupation with such things is a natural component of learned Christianity. The Church lost interest in that cosmic framework after the Middle Ages, when it jettisoned so much of its own history which had been tarnished by the adversaries of God with the brush of "Dark Ages."[31]

Perhaps there was a time in which over-fascination with the mystical dimension needed to be counterbalanced. The pendulum has swung too far, so that in today's scientific culture, the Church is afraid of speaking about the relationship between the natural and the supernatural.

Restoring a discussion of the supernatural, has the potential to illuminate and perhaps even heal some of the intellectual schizophrenia that the contemporary Body of Christ suffers, helping us to reconcile seemingly disparate topics as predestination to free will, supernatural and scientifically informed faith, separation from the world and political activism, dominion and martyrdom. An understanding of history from an eternal perspective, such as the cosmic framework allows, will certainly attract prophetic prayer to areas and issues where it is critically needed.

These gleanings are born of the Scriptures, not approached with the rigor of a theologian, but with the need of a Christian layman active in today's world. I have tried to understand and to explain the mystical relationship between the natural and the supernatural in practical, everyday terms. Using the Bible as our ultimate authority, although informed by the testimony of nature, history, tradition, science, consensus, intellect and experience, we arrived at the following sketch of a cosmic framework. It is a simple approximation, which is why I felt free to use a metaphor such as a mathematical formula.

If any error or contradiction to Scriptures are found by any reader, I ask that they follow first of all their conscience and the authoritative teaching of their church on that matter. I also implore them to contact the author explaining their scriptural objection[32]. I will prayerfully consider the objection, share it with other elders, and we will endeavor both to respond to the reader and to publish whatever correction may be called for, in any future edition of this chapter.

So, we submit these preliminary findings with humility to the elders of today's Church so that they can discern them, and correct them, on the basis of the witness of the Spirit and the balance of Scripture. In the multitude of counselors, there is safety (Prov. 11:14). If this effort glorifies God and helps the reader to "see" how a few scriptures "fit" into His grand plan, it will have served its purposes gloriously.

A Cosmic Framework of Reality from a Biblical Perspective

The Bible opens with the words "In the beginning." But what was it that "began" at that time? I would like to submit that what "began" then was "time" itself. God certainly did not begin then; God is eternally existent; He does not have a beginning or an end. So, when in the course of endless eternity, God established a "beginning," it was as if in the middle of a mathematical formula, we opened a parenthesis. That opening presupposes a closing of the parenthesis; when it comes to time, "the beginning" anticipates "the end."

What did God create "in the beginning"? "The heavens and the earth." Here the idea is a differentiation between two realms, one purely spiritual, eternal, invisible, and the other (although immersed in the first one) material, temporal, visible. The physical world, "earth" contains the idea of "cosmos" which would include the heavens, the earth and the waters under the earth (Ex. 20:4).

And who was the Creator? The Bible reveals that the Word, was the craftsman of creation (John 1:3). He is before all things and by Him all things consist (Col. 1:17); in other words, He holds them together by the word of

His power (Heb. 1:3). He is not only the beginning, but also the end of all things: in time, in space and in essence (Rev. 1:8,11; 21:6; 22:13). He is the one who is, and was, and is to come.

The following illustration shows the parenthesis and some of its basic components: time, space, matter and energy. Outside the parenthesis and penetrating and suffusing its contents, are eternity, infinity, the purely spiritual world, and its own power.

In the beginning **In the end**

(time space matter energy)

(open parenthesis) *(closed parenthesis)*

Thus viewed:

Time	*is a subset of and subordinate to*	*eternity*
The physical realm	*is a subset of and subordinate to*	*the spiritual realm*
Physical matter	*is a subset of and subordinate to*	*spiritual substance*
Physical energy	*is a subset of and subordinate to*	*spiritual power*

What is the relationship of that which is outside to that which is inside the parenthesis? The elements outside condition influence and rule those inside. The spiritual, eternal, infinite realm contains, penetrates, includes the physical, temporal, limited realm. Spiritual reality includes material reality, but transcends it. Material reality applies only inside the parenthesis, whereas spiritual reality occurs both inside and outside the parenthesis. Of course, the material is subordinate to the spiritual. That is why in his resurrected body Jesus could walk through a wall: spiritual reality is more "real" than the physical, which is like a representation of the spiritual (Heb. 8:5). The "real" (spiritual) Ark of the Covenant, of which the physical was a mere representation, appeared in heaven and the heavenly Jerusalem will replace the merely earthly one (Rev. 3:12; 11:19; 21:2,10; Heb. 12:22).

Also inside of the parenthesis we would find "time." Time allows us to arrange all events in a sequential order, with a beginning and an end, a "timeline." Each of the elements in a timeline is related to the preceding and the succeeding elements, and also to those events and elements which modify the parenthesis, outside of it. Time and eternity interact, just as in mathematics the elements outside of a parenthesis modify and interact with the elements within it. The "cosmic timeline" also allows us to forecast approximately what comes next.

This very simple framework allows us to understand that all spiritual battles must be fought in two dimensions simultaneously: the spiritual, which is eternal and invisible and the physical, which is temporal and visible. These dimensions are interdependent, with the spiritual ruling over the physical. The best example of a battle fought in two realms simultaneously is found in Exodus 17, during the battle of Rephidim, in which Moses "fights" on top of a mount with his arms raised (symbol of invocation to God) while Joshua fights in the valley. Each time that Moses' arms tire and fall down, the battle goes against Joshua, but when Moses' arms are up, Joshua wins the battle below. In other words, as God is praised and invoked, He fights the battle; when He is ignored, man loses the battle against spiritually superior forces. The solution was for Aaron and Hur to join Moses on the mountaintop, letting him rest by sitting on a rock, while holding up his arms.

Since the battle is simultaneously in the spiritual (eternal) realm and in the physical (temporal) realm, God always pairs up prayer warriors with "war partners." While one concentrates on prayer (spiritual action), the other will concentrate on activity (physical action). An intercessor who is not committed to another activist Christian is like a Quarter Master who refuses to supply his fellow soldiers. Conversely, an activist or Christian leader who is not communicating assiduously with his intercessors is like a soldier who goes to battle and cuts himself off from his supply lines. The prayerlessness of the contemporary Church for "those in authority" is appalling, in light of this principle (I Tim. 2:1-4). Should we be surprised at the weakness of our leaders, and the ineffectiveness of their efforts? And lack of prayer can hinder the work of the Gospel (I Thess. 2:18).

The War is for the Thrones

The cosmic framework can help us to understand theologically some of the current global events. The Scripture describes the tribe of Issachar as men who knew the times, and what Israel should do (I Chron. 12:32). Spiritual warriors, and those whom God equips with prophetic vision, belong to today's "tribe of Issachar."

Two worldwide trends, quite distinguishable today, are more easily interpreted in light of the cosmic framework and the Kingdom timeline it implies. As previously mentioned, these trends are: the increasing persecution of Christians, and the growing involvement of Christians in politics.

Persecution has always existed, but never as in the 20th century. Also, the convergence of a one world government, church and economic system, increasingly intolerant of Christian "fundamentalism" (our insistence on One Way, Truth and Life), portends worldwide restrictions, pressure and eventually persecution on a worldwide scale.

Why have believers been persecuted since the time of Abel? Persecution results when those in power feel threatened by a group, either as potential competitors for power or because they are a serious obstacle standing in the way of the complete domination of a people. Are Christians competing for power? Are we hindering a plan of world domination? The answer is "Yes."

Christians were persecuted by civil authorities, from the beginning because they (and us) unequivocally declare Christ's lordship over all, His right to govern all, in heaven and on earth. What got them into trouble was their refusal to obey men rather than God and their insistence that "There is another king, one Jesus" (Acts 5:29; 17:7).

Just because Jesus did not come the first time to sit on the throne of Israel, the "Gospel" He preached was not "apolitical." In an empire made up of slave nations, to announce that He had come to set the captives free, to open the doors of the prisons to them that are bound, and to set men "free indeed" were hardly apolitical statements. Of course, Jesus did not at that time take the throne, but He certainly laid claim to it. Besides, in New Testament times, the word *evangelion* (good news) was used to refer to the edict of a new ruler, announcing his new rule. Caesars would issue their *evangelion,* so for Christ to label his message the "*evangelion of the Kingdom*" was profoundly threatening to governmental leaders.

The Apostle Paul was hardly politically naive; he used his Roman rights, and more than once astutely used the politics of his enemies to set them at war with one another. Nor did he ignore the politicians of his time: the Book of Acts records 17 instances in which he specifically addressed the civil rulers. So the idea of an "apolitical" Christianity is at odds with the New Testament and with the historic posture of the Church.

The war for the thrones is very old. In heaven Satan disputed the throne of God and was cast down to earth (Isa. 14:12-14). On earth God gave Adam dominion over the work of His hands, but Adam gave it to Satan, including the power to give the thrones to whomever He wants (Luke 4:6). However, Jesus wrestled that power from him, receiving all power in heaven and in earth (Matt. 28:18).

Eternally speaking, the matter of the thrones is settled: Jesus has the name that is above every name, and it is already decreed that every knee shall bow and every tongue confess His lordship. But temporally speaking, He sent us to disciple all nations in His name.

Historically the Church has always been interested in who occupies the thrones of the earth. Often that interest has been mixed with carnal motives, such as during Constantine's time, Charlemagne's Holy Roman Empire, in the Crusades, the Inquisition, or John Calvin's political rule of Geneva. During the 20th century the Church did not focus much on the thrones of the earth, because the spreading of the Gospel was more important. But as Christians grow in numbers and maturity in any society, and they begin to disciple their nations, the thrones (authorities, influences) over their people become more and more strategic targets.

These "thrones" are not only the civil and political authorities, but also any authorities that influence men: economic, religious, academic, cultural, as well as political.[33] They are thrones because they are positions of authority and influence. And our cosmic framework helps us to understand that although they may be physical, visible, authorities, they are animated, inspired, by spiritual, invisible forces (Eph. 6:12; Jer. 13:18; Isa. 14:16). That is true of both good and bad authorities: Michael, the prince of God's people, teamed up with Gabriel to help the prophet Daniel (Dan. 10:13,21). This is why spiritual warfare must be fought simultaneously in the natural and in the spiritual realms.

The cosmic framework described here can help to understand the increasing involvement of Christians in government as part of God's grand strategy for the end times. It can also illuminate other important issues such as the legitimate uses of power, the lawful means for attaining and exercising it, the multi-dimensional nature of the Christian civil witness, what may be the immediate, intermediate and ultimate aims of Christian political involvement, the acrid controversy over "Christian nations," the steps and means to "Christianize" human society, etc.

Most important, it can help to clarify what the role of the Body, as a whole, and organ by organ, is, ought to be, and ought not to be, in the sphere of civil authority. The Apostle Paul's caution is applicable here: "If the foot shall say, Because I am not the hand, I am not of body; is it therefore not of the body?" (1 Cor. 12:15).

Those to whom God shows what hour this is, must respond accordingly. Pastors and prophets over nations cannot ignore the fact that the Holy Spirit is leading thousands of Christians into government, and tens of thousands of those involved in government unto Christ.

Who will pastor these politicians? Who are the Deborahs of today's Baraks, the Samuels of our Sauls, the Nathans of our Davids, the Ezras of our Nehemiahs? More pointedly for spiritual warriors, who will be the Moses, Aarons and Hurs to the Joshuas of today's battles in the political arena?

Some Applications to Spiritual Warfare

Prayer is a temporal action with eternal repercussions. It is a partnership with God in which He initiates, we participate and He responds, in accordance with a preordained plan. The cosmic framework serves as a background for the commonplace experience of every Christian who prays. The process of prayer is as follows:

1. Prayer begins in the eternal mind of God.
2. It is inserted by the Holy Spirit into history (by communicating it to us, members of His Body, in a given time and space).
3. It is acted upon by God in accordance with His preordained plan.
4. It is implemented by God's power and in His mysterious ways (and times).
5. It is cause for rejoicing in the Church, for God has "answered prayer."

Not every spiritual victory is manifested immediately in the physical, temporal realm. Every work of God requires faith on our part, who believe without seeing. This is what happened at the Cross. The spiritual victory was attained, totally and forever, by Jesus Christ, who declared His mission on earth "finished." For His victory He was raised from the dead and ascended to heaven to sit at the right hand of the Father. Yet on earth, within the framework of time and space, His Body continues to battle, under His direction, "from generation to generation" (Ex. 17:16), while Jesus waits for His enemies to be made into his footstool (Ps. 110:1).

God's victories do not necessarily look to natural man as victories. The spectacle of the Cross was disheartening to the disciples until God revealed to them through the Resurrection that what appeared like a final defeat was actually Jesus' victory. Christians should be prepared to endure persecution and suffer opposition and defeat at the hand of their enemies without falling into the temptation of "judging by the seeing of the eyes." There are many different kinds of faith victories. Hebrews 11 lists a veritable "Hall of Fame" of the heroes of the faith, showing clearly that not all attained physical victory. Three categories of heroes are listed, each with a different visible, temporary outcome, yet all assured of eternal victory.[34]

Spiritual warfare and prayer are part of our intimate relationship with the Lord. "Since the foundation of the world" God has prepared works for us to do, but it is only through Jesus Christ that we can do them. Jesus said, "I can do nothing of myself" (John 5:30). Yet He reserved for us other works for us to do with Him, "greater works than these you will do (in the temporal, physical realm), because I go to the Father" (to accomplish them in the spiritual, eternal realm; John 14:12). In the midst of all of our spiritual warfare battles in the natural and spiritual realms, we can take great courage that our Lord has said, "Lo... I am with you always, even unto the end" (Matt. 28:20).

To truly disciple a nation and to see our communities transformed by the Gospel it is critical that the Church mobilize leaders into positions of influence throughout society. Nevertheless, for believers to proceed into political arenas without adequate prayer covering is anemic at best.

On the other hand, there will be only a partial impact if the Church simply prays for a nation and yet refuses to release and encourage Christians to occupy positions where righteous decisions can truly make a difference in their society.

An authentic uniting of the authority of prayer and the mobilization of leaders into positions in society allows for reformation. We should encourage all believers (who are called to do so) to step past isolation and become "salt" and "light" in dark places.

The battle is for the thrones. If the spiritual realm is controlling what we see physically in governments, why not focus our prayers toward the defeat of wicked spiritual forces? However, we must not stop there. Then we must prepare to assume positions of influence so that when the Lord calls us to them, we may govern wisely according to the Word of God. When we combine the spiritual power of intercession with a corresponding physical action of righteous civic and political involvement, we can experience the blessing of what Scripture says; "Righteousness exalts a nation" (Prov. 14:34).

"...The kingdoms of this world are become the kingdoms of our Lord, and of his Christ, and he shall reign forever and ever" (Rev. 11:15).

CONCLUSION
by Harold Caballeros

The word "synergy" has been in style in the 90s. Synergy refers to the concept that separate elements, when combined, have a greater effect or result than the simple addition of each element. I believe this accurately describes a book like *The Transforming Power of Revival.* Each chapter has real value. But the combination of all of them creates a unique spiritual impact within us. These words are a challenge from the Holy Spirit.

The Church needs to receive prophetic direction and vision (Prov. 29:18). How wonderful that God, glorifying His creativity, uses such a diverse group of ministers, representing different continents, cultures and backgrounds, to bless us with a series of prophetic strategies. These strategies will renew our minds and give us an opportunity to catapult the Church toward an authentic spiritual revolution.

If we wish with all our hearts to see the Great Commission fulfilled, if we want to witness God's impact upon our nations, if we want to be the "salt of the earth" and "the light of the world," then this book becomes potentially a great weapon in the hands of the Church.

It seems to me that it answers the most common questions that arise in relation to the prayer movement, such as: What? Why? How? Where are we headed?

All believers agree on the necessity of prayer. Nevertheless, only lately has the theme intensified. Why? Because prayer always existed as a type of shadow, a mist, and a belief that prayer was answered only "sometimes." The prayer movement has contributed to erasing the fog and the shadow. The Church has been assured that God truly answers the prayers of the saints! Now we are more convinced of its power. Our Heavenly Father is the fountain of prophetic prayers because the desire of His heart is to respond to our intercession for our blessing. What you have read are the testimonies of what He has done and wishes to do in your community and in your nation. He did not make us "kings" and "priests" in vain, but for the purpose of fulfilling His will in the earth.

To take whole nations and saturate them with the Gospel of Jesus Christ is, without a doubt, an ambitious project, the product of a dream. Nevertheless, this vision is rooted in the heart of the Son of God, for He said, "Go ye therefore, and teach all nations, baptizing them in the name of the Father, and of the Son, and of the Holy Ghost, teaching them to observe all things whatsoever I have commanded you and, lo, I am with you always, even unto the end of the age" (Matt. 28:19-20).

Even though the Great Commission is an astounding task, this verse explicitly teaches that, in addition to the *vision*, God provides the supernatural *provision*. Now we have before us a road upon which we can march boldly into the future in order to see our communities and nations move toward transformation. This road is paved with the stones of spiritual mapping, spiritual warfare, evangelism, discipleship through assimilation of new believers, and Christian education.

We are very grateful to each one of the authors, and we pray that God uses this book to awaken in you a hope to see your country transformed.

But we must remember that strategies to see our nations transformed by Christ's power are not sufficient in themselves to make the difference. Those who implement and execute them by God's leading and power will be the ones who see transformation.

May we each be numbered among those who hear, "Well done, good and faithful servant" (Matt. 25:21).

Notes

Chapter 1

1 Harold Caballeros, "Defeating the Enemy with the Help of Spiritual Mapping," Breaking Strongholds in Your City, Ed. C. Peter Wagner, Regal Books, 1993, Ventura, CA, p. 123.

2 George Otis, Jr., Spiritual Mapping Research Questions, Lynnwood, WA, The Sentinel Group, 1997.

3 A.T. Pierson, The Acts of The Apostles, New York: The Baker and Taylor Company, 1894, p. 352

Chapter 7

4 Robert Linthicum, City of God, City of Satan (Spanish edition), Editora Misión, p.87

Chapter 8

5 George Otis, Jr., "An Overview of Spiritual Mapping," Breaking Strongholds in Your City, Ed. C. Peter Wagner (Ventura, CA: Regal Books, 1993), P. 42.

6 F.F. Bruce, The Book of Acts (Grand Rapids: William B. Eerdmans Publishing Company, 1954; revised edition, 1988), p. 366.

7 Clinton E. Arnold, Ephesians: Power and Magic (Grand Rapids: Baker Book House, 1992), p. 1.

8 F.F. Bruce, Paul: Apostle of the Heart Set Free (Grand Rapids: William B. Eerdmans Publishing Company, 1977), p. 295.

9 Bruce M. Metzger, "St. Paul and the Magicians." Princeton Seminary Bulletin 38 (June 1944): 27.

10 Bruce, Paul: Apostle of the Heart Set Free, p. 291.

11 Paul Trebilco, "Asia,," The Book of Acts in Its Graeco-Roman Setting, ed. David W.J. Gill and Conrad Gempf (Grand Rapids: William B. Eerdmans Publishing Company, 1944), p. 317-318.

12 Bruce, The Book of Acts, p. 375.

13 Arnold, Ephesians, p. 21.

14 Mario Roberto Morales, "La Quiebra de Maximon," Cronica Semanal (June 20-24, 1994): 17.

Chapter 9

15 Wilfred Owen, The War Poems, ed. Jon Stallworthy (Chatto & Windus Ltd., 1994), p. 61.

Chapter 11

16 Daisy Osborn went home to be with the Lord on May 27, 1995, after 53 years of powerful ministry with her husband into 73 nations.

Chapter 13

17 Oswald J. Smith, Building a Better World (London, England: Marshall, Morgan Scott, n.d.), p. 50.

Chapter 16

18 God's practice of dealing distinctly with different cities is seen in the unique messages He spoke to the seven churches featured in Revelation chapters 2-3.

19 See Genesis 32:26, I Chronicles 16:11, Daniel 6:10, Luke 11:5-10, Hebrews 11:6, James 5:16.

20 In the early 1990s, a group of Japanese intercessors rented six railroad coaches, which they dubbed the "Glory Train", and rode the mobile prayer platform through all of Japan's prefectures.

21 Witchcraft is widespread in Pakistan. Initiates learn to control their emotions particularly fear-during the course of intense encounters with demonic powers. During the final initiatory stage the demons appear in a variety of terrifying forms. If fear gets the best of the initiate, the demon(s) will kill him. If the initiate controls his fear, the demon(s) will be his to "command". The only requirement is that the initiate "entertain" the demon(s) every Thursday night. This entertainment takes the form of a ritual, known as chowky, that involves dancing and/or violent head and neck shaking (almost like seizures). Many witches die when they get older and are no longer able to fulfill their Thursday evening vows.

22 Robert Bakke, "Prayer: God's Catalyst for Revival," Pray!, Premier Issue, 1997, p. 16. Mr. Bakke directs the National Prayer Advance for the Evangelical Free Church in America.

23 Harold Caballeros, "Defeating the Enemy with the Help of Spiritual Mapping," in C. Peter Wagner, Breaking Strongholds In Your City (Ventura, CA: Regal, 1993), p. 144.

24 As I noted in my recent book The Twilight Labyrinth (Grand Rapids: Chosen, 1997), pp. 281-282:

In asking intercessors to petition God for an "open door," Paul is acknowledging three important truths: 1) Unsaved people are bound in a prison of deception; 2) God must breach this stronghold if the Gospel is to enter; and 3) Prayer is an important means of persuading God to do this.

If we want to liberate enchanted minds so they can understand and respond to the Gospel-we must first neutralize the blinding influence of demonic strongmen. Jesus talks about this process in Mark 3:27 when he says, "No one can enter a strong man's house (the human mind) and carry off his possessions unless he first ties up the strong man. Then he can rob his house" (emphasis added).

We are not asking God to "make" people Christians, or to expel demonic powers that have become objects of worship. Such requests violate man's free will and God will not honor them. What we are appealing for is a level playing field, a temporary lifting of the spiritual blindness that prevents men from processing truth (the Gospel) at a heart level.
25 Ibid., p. 300.
26 Ibid., p. 301.

Chapter 18

27 This includes many disparate tendencies such as the worship of nature, a fascination with the esoteric leading to many new and ancient forms of occultism: pagan demon worship, extraterrestrial encounters, fantasy "games" and "virtual reality" experiences, traditional witchcraft and a revival of ancient beliefs and rituals.
28 Its spokesmen often lump together committed Christians with religious fanatics under the label of "religious fundamentalists." According to them, we would "force" our views upon the rest of the people and are ultimately dangerous to liberty, unity and peace.
29 The phenomenon is sufficiently documented to merit an international gathering in Washington, D.C., in 1998; U.S. foreign policy is taking notice of the trend.
30 Dan 12:4 may refer to this fact.
31 An immodest and unnecessary insistence on geocentricism brought much embarrassment to the medieval Church. It was not upon the planet, but upon its steward, that God had centered His creation. By insisting upon a biblical "truth" which Galileo's calculations demolished, the Church lost much authority. Something similar might have occurred when Biblical dating was abandoned by much of the Church, toward the end of the 19th Century. Making a major issue of a minor one (such as fixing our eternal faith upon a contingent reading of "solar" rather than "epochal" days in the account of Creation) could lead the church to promote plausibility as revelation. The church should teach truth, eternal, unchanging, universal. Facts should be explained by a lesser authority. To do otherwise causes weak Christians to lose their way. Also, if the evidence later disproves the fact which had been declared a "truth," the Church has lost the moral authority to speak on other scientific issues. May God spare us from falling into that error in the brave new world of cloning and human genetic engineering.
32 Write to P.O. Box 65078, Chesapeake, Virginia 23467-5078.
33 Special relationships as symbols of moral realities: Generally speaking, in the Bible, "up" can mean more important, powerful, greater and "down" can mean baser, lower. Heights are symbols of authority. This is why the city of a

great King, mount Zion, is located "on the sides of the north."
The symbolic and moral meaning of words can combine. Thus "throne" denotes authority and "above" means higher authority. The classical passage illustrating this is when Satan's ambition is exposed; in just two verses he makes eleven references to things above: "I will ASCEND into HEAVEN, I will EXALT my throne ABOVE the STARS of God: I will sit also upon the MOUNT of the congregation, in the sides of the north: I will ASCEND ABOVE the HEIGHTS of the CLOUDS: I will be like the most HIGH."
God answers with nine images of things below: "Yet thou salt be brought DOWN to HELL, to the sides of the PIT.... But thou art cast out of thy GRAVE like an abominable branch,... that go DOWN to the stones of the PIT; as a carcass TRODDEN UNDER FEET" (Isa. 14:11-19).
Other related words are:
"Mountains, heights" which denote places of influence. It is useful to remember that in military tactics, whoever controls the heights controls the valleys (see our discussion of the Battle at Rephidim, below). "High places" in biblical terms refer specifically to places where the deity is invoked and sacrifices offered. Another very clear passage on this contrast is Isaiah Chapter 2, and many shorter texts, such as Ps. 48:2. It is very important that only God be honored from such places.
"Thrones, powers, dominions, principalities," also denote authorities.
The specifically political significance of mountains illustrated by the third temptation of Jesus, in which Satan takes him to a "high mountain" from which he shows him "all of the kingdoms of this world, and their pomp" (Luke 4:5). It is corroborated by the references to the last days in which the "mount of the Lord "will be set higher than every other mount, describing the final rulership of the Lord Jesus Christ on the earth.
34 Some paid with their life their faithful testimony: Abel, Heb 11:4, and many others Heb. 11:35-38. Some saw God's victory over their enemies in their lifetime, like Enoch, Noah, Jacob, Joseph, Moses and many prophets and kings, Heb. 11:5,7 and 21-35. And others died in hope, not seeing their faith fulfilled, such as Abraham, and -in a completed sense- all believers till today, Heb. 11.

For more information on teaching and ministry resources
from El Shaddai Ministries
Or
for the address of any of our contributors,
Please contact El Shaddai Church in Guatemala at:
E-mail: shaddai@ns.guate.net
Phone: (country code 502) 337-4777
Fax: (country code 502) 337-0316

Visit our website at: www.elshaddai.net